CHICAGO STUDIES IN AMERICAN POLITICS

A series edited by Benjamin I. Page, Susan Herbst, Lawrence R. Jacobs, and James Druckman

Also in the series:

In Time of War: Understanding American Public Opinion from World War II to Iraq
by Adam J. Berinisky

Us against Them: Ethnocentric Foundations of American Opinion
by Donald R. Kinder and Cindy D. Kam

The Partisan Sort: How Liberals Became Democrats and Conservatives Became Republicans
by Matthew Levendusky

Democracy at Risk: How Terrorist Threats Affect the Public
by Jennifer L. Merolla and Elizabeth J. Zechmeister

Agendas and Instability in American Politics, Second Edition
by Frank R. Baumgartner and Bryan D. Jones

The Private Abuse of the Public Interest
by Lawrence D. Brown and Lawrence R. Jacobs

The Party Decides: Presidential Nominations Before and After Reform
by Marty Cohen, David Karol, Hans Noel, and John Zaller

Same Sex, Different Politics: Success and Failure in the Struggles over Gay Rights
by Gary Mucciaroni

FILIBUSTERING

A Political History of Obstruction in the House and Senate

GREGORY KOGER

THE UNIVERSITY OF CHICAGO PRESS   Chicago and London

GREGORY KOGER is assistant professor in the Department of Political Science at the University of Miami.

The University of Chicago Press, Chicago 60637
The University of Chicago Press, Ltd., London
© 2010 by The University of Chicago
All rights reserved. Published 2010
Printed in the United States of America

19 18 17 16 15 14 13 12 11 10   1 2 3 4 5
ISBN-13: 978-0-226-44964-7 (cloth)
ISBN-13: 978-0-226-44965-4 (paper)
ISBN-10: 0-226-44964-5 (cloth)
ISBN-10: 0-226-44965-3 (paper)

Library of Congress Cataloging-in-Publication Data
Koger, Gregory.
    Filibustering : a political history of obstruction in the House and Senate /
Gregory Koger.
        p.   cm.
    Includes bibliographical references and index.
    ISBN-13: 978-0-226-44964-7 (cloth: alk. paper)
    ISBN-13: 978-0-226-44965-4 (pbk: alk. paper)
    ISBN-10: 0-226-44964-5 (cloth: alk. paper)
    ISBN-10: 0-226-44965-3 (pbk.: alk. paper)
        1. Filibusters (Political science)—United States—History.   2. United States. Congress—
Rules and practice—History.   3. United States. Congress—History.   I. Title.
    JK1041.K64   2010
    328.73'0775—dc22   2009041748

Contents

Illustrations

FIGURES

TABLES

Preface

I beg every member of this body who wants to throw himself into the arms of Morpheus to go home at once. I mean by the "arms of Morpheus" that whoever wants to go to sleep should go to sleep. . . . I will be here 24 hours from now getting through with this conversation on this bill. Do not fool yourselves. I will be here a long time.

Huey Long (D-LA), speaking in Congress in June 1935

In some pursuits, we measure our passion with time. This book is made of the stuff it describes: midnight hours stolen from slumber, effort made easier with teamwork, and the creative use of available options.

Six years ago, I set out to write a comprehensive book about filibustering that provides a general overview of how legislators obstruct (and respond to obstruction!), measures filibustering in both chambers of Congress over time, and explains patterns of filibustering in both chambers. Such a book would, I hoped, provide the basis for more comparative studies of obstruction and a deeper understanding of how filibustering influences congressional lawmaking, parties, committees, and representation. I have enjoyed my time with this project and the characters who fill its pages.

This book originated with research I did for Barbara Sinclair and Scott James. For Barbara, I coded the progress of major legislation over the last fifty years and learned about the subtle and significant effects of modern filibustering. For Scott, I began reading the classic institutional works on Congress, which described the tactics of historic filibustering and told tales of dramatic filibusters and reforms in the U.S. House. After writing a dissertation about the evolution of congressional rules, I began to write this book as a *prequel* to my work on institutional choice. In the early stages, I benefited immeasurably from collaboration with Kathleen Bawn, who worked with me to develop general models of intensity and filibustering.

Along the way, I have learned from the suggestions of colleagues. Charles Stewart, Douglas Dion, Jason Roberts, Justin Fox, Sarah Binder, and Gerald Gamm discussed conference papers that went into this book. Seminar audiences at Texas Tech, Syracuse, South Carolina, and Georgetown provided helpful suggestions; I am especially grateful to the Foley Center at Washington State for inviting me for an early presentation of this work and to my colleagues at the University of Miami for comments at a departmental colloquium. Live elegantly, my friends.

In the final stages, Barbara Sinclair, Fang-yi Chiou, and two anonymous reviewers read full-length drafts and provided excellent suggestions. Hans Noel, Larry Evans, Charles Gregory, Ben Bishin, Jamie Carson, Jennifer Victor, Seth Masket, Emily Orchard Wanless, and Michael Lynch also read portions of the manuscript, and I thank them. I also thank Ben Page, John Tryneski, and Rodney Powell, who have been supportive and patient with this first-time author.

This project has been sustained by research grants from the University of Montana and an American Political Science Association Small Research Grant. I thank Tim Sweeten, Emily Orchard Wanless, Charles Gregory, and especially Tessa Zolnikov for research assistance, and I thank the staff of the K. Ross Toole Archives at the University of Montana for their assistance with the papers of Mike Mansfield.

Of course, none of this would be possible without the parents who invested time and treasure in me. Mom and Dad, thanks for showing me the world and welcoming me back home. Nor would it be possible without the ladies whose time means everything to me. Brooke, Chase, and Camryn, from Los Angeles to Missoula to Miami, home has been wherever you are. This book is for you.

I
Foundations

CHAPTER 1

Introduction

Over the last fifty years, there has been a quiet revolution in American politics. A major hurdle has been added to the legislative process: the ability of senators to block bills and nominations unless 60 percent of the Senate votes to override a "filibuster." Unlike the president's legislative veto, which is written into the Constitution, the "right" to filibuster in the Senate is based on tenuous precedents and informal practices. At no point did senators consciously choose to remake their chamber or transform American politics. It just happened, and it happened so quietly we barely noticed.

The rules of the Senate allow senators to end a filibuster by invoking *cloture*. As currently written, this rule limits debate on a bill or nomination to thirty hours if—and this is the critical point—*three-fifths* of the Senate vote to impose the limit. Now more than ever, senators use this rule frequently as their only antidote against a rash of anyone against anything. During the 110th Congress (2007–8), the Senate voted 111 times (16.9 percent of all roll call votes) on the question of whether cloture should be imposed. Yet, the more senators use this rule and refine it to make it more effective, the more they filibuster. This book argues that this is no coincidence: filibustering has not increased *despite* senators' increased use, and improvement, of the cloture rule; it has increased *because* of it. To unravel this paradox, we need a clear understanding of the "obstruction game"—the tactics and strategy of filibustering. We also need to trace the history of filibustering in Congress; the present is confusing because we do not really understand the past.

A TALE OF TWO SENATES . . . AND A HOUSE

One reason it was difficult to notice the transformation of the Senate is that filibustering has become an invisible act. The *American Heritage Dictionary* (4th ed., 2000) defines *filibuster* as "the use of obstructionist tactics, especially prolonged speechmaking, for the purpose of delaying legislative action."[1] Modern senators, however, do not make long speeches to prevent a vote. Nor do they use other typical forms of filibustering, like forcing dozens of unnecessary roll call votes or refusing to participate in floor votes. Instead, a typical "filibuster" occurs when a senator refuses to agree to a time to hold a vote on a measure and, implicitly, threatens to drag out the debate indefinitely.

This new veto empowers Senate minorities to frustrate majorities. Despite their 58–41 majority at the beginning of the 111th Congress (2009–10), Senate Democrats were compelled to trim their first major bill, a "stimulus" package of spending and tax cuts, from $940 to about $780 billion ($787 billion in the final law) to gain the votes of a centrist bloc of moderate Democrats and three Republicans—Susan Collins and Olympia Snowe of Maine and Arlen Specter of Pennsylvania—a price of $35 billion in cuts per Republican vote. Three weeks later, Democratic leaders had to stall an omnibus spending bill because they were one vote shy of the sixty votes they needed. Of course, Senate Democrats could have had that extra vote if Al Franken, the Democratic candidate in the 2008 Minnesota Senate race, had become a senator after he was certified as the winner of the election on January 5. However, they dared not do so because Republicans threatened to filibuster if an attempt was made to seat Franken before his opponent, Norm Coleman, exhausted his court challenges (see Schatz 2009; and Raju 2009).

Filibustering has not always been so easy, nor has the majority always been so passive. A century earlier, in the midst of a financial crisis, a small band of senators led by Robert La Follette (R-WI) struggled to block a banking bill they considered a gift to the financial elite. On May 29, 1908, La Follette prepared to occupy the floor of the Senate until dawn. He covered his desk with books to read aloud when imagination failed him. Whenever attendance was low, he requested that a majority of the Senate be rounded up to hear him speak. His filibuster lasted for eighteen hours; when he passed on the task of holding the floor to a coconspirator the next morning, his voice was still strong, but his feet were sore from standing. However, the bill passed hours later, hastened by some impromptu restrictions on filibustering and trickery by Senate majority leader Nelson Aldrich (R-RI).[2] While La Follette lost this legislative battle, he won a larger political victory. His ostentatious filibuster—the longest on record until the 1950s—lingered in public memory for decades and solidified his credentials as a Progressive rebel against the Republican establishment.

Over the last century, there has been a dramatic evolution in *how* legislators filibuster. Classic filibusters were contests of endurance, not votes. They were dramatic and unscripted marathons. *And they were exceedingly rare.* Modern filibusters are so common that the sixty-vote threshold for cloture is the de facto requirement to pass most major legislation and threats to filibuster permeate the day-to-day operations of the Senate. The institutionalization of this "sixty-vote Senate" constitutes a historic development in the legislative process.

Why, when, and how did the classic Senate of La Follette's day become the staid Senate of today? The central claim of this book is that classic filibustering was a *bargaining game* and that, consistent with theoretical analyses of bargaining, the team that was more patient tended to win (Bawn and Koger 2008; Rubinstein 1982). Obstructionists had to make effort to stall the Senate, while the majority had to be willing to wait for them to make a mistake or become exhausted. In the early twentieth century, majorities were generally pretty patient unless some deadline loomed, so filibusters were fairly rare. As the workload of the Senate increased and opportunities to travel expanded, senators became too impatient to wait out a filibuster. The turning point was the 1960s, when they began using a previously dormant cloture rule to quell obstruction on major bills. In doing so, they reduced the incentives against filibustering since anyone could threaten to filibuster any proposal without fearing that he or she would have to hold forth on the Senate floor for hours. The sixty-vote Senate is the product of impatience.

This cycle of decreasing costs and exploding obstruction has occurred before in congressional history. During the nineteenth century, members of the U.S. House of Representatives used a variety of parliamentary tactics to slow legislation and, eventually, completely paralyze the lawmaking process. Franklin Burdette writes in his classic book on filibustering: "Tactics patently obstructive . . . were characteristic of the House long before they became common in the Senate" (1940, 14). Unlike the modern Senate, however, the members of the House responded to this gridlock with drastic reforms to ensure that the majority can work its will (Binder 1997; Dion 1997; Schickler 2001), and these reforms dramatically increased the ability of House majorities to pass legislation (Cox and McCubbins 2005).

The U.S. House offers an interesting comparison with the Senate. The two chambers were born from the same Constitution and nurtured in the same political environment. By studying such similar cases, we can better understand how the institutional features of a legislature—such as chamber size—promote or discourage filibustering. No previous study of filibustering has covered the entire scope of congressional history. This bicameral approach provides a fuller view of filibustering in congressional history and helps us think in general terms about legislative obstruction wherever we see it. After all, the U.S. Congress is not the only legislature that tolerates filibustering; while searching for news articles on the U.S. Senate, I found references to obstruction in twenty state legislatures, nineteen foreign legislative bodies, and the United Nations. Hence, the broader purpose of this book is to develop a general framework for studying obstruction and apply that framework to the puzzling history of the U.S. Congress.

This project is vital to our understanding of the Senate, the lawmaking process, and legislative parties. Filibustering is the defining activity of the contemporary Senate, as a senior leadership aide explained: "Obstructionism is woven into the fabric of things. The [party] leadership deals with it on a day-to-day, even a minute-to-minute basis. . . . [Y]ou can't underestimate the importance of it. There are offshoots of obstructionism every day" (quoted in Evans and Lipinski 2005, 228). Filibustering touches most major legislation in today's Senate, and, historically, filibusters have been at the center of some of America's most important decisions. Filibustering is also critical to the study of when Congress is more likely to pass important laws (e.g., Binder 2003; Chiou and Rothenberg 2003, 2006; Clinton and Lapinski 2006; Krehbiel 1998; Mayhew 1991), including research utilizing the pivotal politics model discussed below. For this body of research, the key findings are that there was ample filibustering in the historic House and, especially, that the influence of Senate filibustering is contingent on whether Senate majorities have enough time to outlast obstruction. In comparison, the existence of a formal cloture rule and the threshold for imposing cloture have relatively little effect.

Filibustering is an interesting counterweight to the polarization of congressional parties, another topic of popular and scholarly interest (e.g., Lebo, McGlynn, and Koger 2007; McCarty, Poole, and Rosenthal 2006; and Theriault 2008). Curiously, the rise in congressional partisanship since 1970 has coincided with a surge in Senate filibustering, with the result that our everstronger parties in Congress face ever-increasing hurdles to their legislative goals. Historical studies of congressional parties suggest that they have long possessed "negative agenda power," that is, the ability to keep some proposals from reaching the chamber floor (Campbell, Cox, and McCubbins 2002; Cox and McCubbins 2005; Gailmard and Jenkins 2007). We shall see, however, that legislative minorities with the power to block legislation may use that power for "positive" ends by bargaining to push issues *onto* the chamber floor.[3]

RESEARCH ON FILIBUSTERING, PAST AND PRESENT

Despite the substantive and theoretical importance of filibustering, political scientists have generally avoided the topic. It is telling that a recent major work on filibustering, Sarah Binder and Steve Smith's *Politics or Principle?* (1997)—the first book on obstruction since Burdette (1940)—was organized as a refutation of myths about filibustering because myths flourished in the absence of scholarly research.[4] Binder and Smith point out that filibustering in the Senate was neither intended by the authors of the Constitution nor common in the nineteenth-century Senate. Historically, they claim, legislators have obstructed for partisan and parochial ends as well as on important matters of principle, while voting on cloture and cloture reform is based on political and policy interests. Thus, filibustering is a form of ordinary politics and can be studied using the techniques of contemporary political science.

And filibustering is a worthy topic for study. It has increased dramatically over the last fifty years (Beth 1994; Binder and Smith 1997; Oppenheimer 1985; Sinclair 1989) to the extent that we now have a sixty-vote Senate (Sinclair 2002) because cloture is often necessary for the passage of a major bill. Since the contemporary Senate is polarized along partisan lines (Theriault 2008), modern filibustering is often a partisan contest, with a united minority party blocking majority party proposals for some sort of *political* gain as well as policy payoff (Binder and Smith 1997; Evans and Lipinski 2005; Evans and Oleszek 2001; Sinclair 2006). The emergence of this filibuster-saturated environment motivates research on how it works and why it developed.

The Pivotal Politics Model

In a major work, *Pivotal Politics* (1998), Keith Krehbiel incorporates the Senate filibuster into a simple model of the legislative process. In this model, the Senate filibuster is one of the fundamental "pivots" in American politics on par with the presidential veto: no policy change occurs unless a legislative coalition can override a filibuster and circumvent a veto. The pivot model highlights the importance of the cloture threshold for shutting off a filibuster, explains how filibustering reduces the significance of divided versus united party control of Congress and the presidency, and has inspired others to apply and amend the pivot approach (e.g., Alter and McGranahan 2000; Brady and Volden 2006; Chiou and Rothenberg 2003, 2006).[5]

Although the pivot model was developed to explain the lawmaking process of the 1990s (Krehbiel 1998, xiii), scholars have applied this framework to the post–World War II era (Chiou and Rothenberg 2003; Krehbiel 1998), the period 1921–94 (Krehbiel 1998, chap. 5), and the period 1881–2000 (Chiou and Rothenberg 2006). With the exception of Chiou and Rothenberg (2006), these analyses do not account for variation in the "price" of obstruction and, hence, the willingness of senators to take advantage of their right to filibuster. Indeed, Krehbiel (1998, 96) is "agnostic" about whether filibustering has increased over time.[6]

However, we cannot understand filibustering without a clear account of how the Senate became a sixty-vote chamber. Subsequent research finds that, before Rule 22 was enacted in 1917, simple majorities in the Senate were often able to pass legislation (Chiou and Rothenberg 2006; Wawro and Schickler 2004, 2006), and even in the 1930s it seemed that senators expected the majority to win (Mayhew 2003). As a result, we need to look beyond the formal rules of the Senate to understand the true impact of filibustering and how that impact has changed over time.

The Emergence of the Sixty-Vote Senate

Political scientists have proposed several explanations for the proliferation of Senate filibustering. Bruce Oppenheimer (1985) began the conversation by attributing the increase in filibustering to the rising legislative workload. As the role of the federal government in American society increased over the course of the twentieth century, the workload of the Senate swelled, the time of the Senate became more valuable, and threats to waste the Senate's time by filibustering became more credible and frequent. Like subsequent scholars, Oppenheimer faced the challenge of measuring the crucial elements of this story: the value of time and the frequency of filibustering. He measures time constraints in the Senate with pages of the *Congressional Record* (1931–56) and the length of sessions (1950s–70s). He uses the number of cloture votes to measure filibustering but also notes that they are not an accurate indicator of obstruction since senators did not always apply the cloture process to filibusters.

Several subsequent sources endorse Oppenheimer's account (Binder and Smith 1997; Koger 2002; Sinclair 1989)—and for good reason. However, that account leaves two tasks for future researchers: developing a more precise measure of filibustering and devising a more specific measure of the value of legislators' time. The lack of such measures has made it difficult to integrate Oppenheimer's "time constraints" approach into subsequent research. Researchers whose work is based on the pivot model, for example, have generally ignored Oppenheimer and his work's implications for their theories and empirical analyses.

A second explanation for the recent boom in Senate filibustering is that Congress is becoming more *polarized*. Binder, Lawrence, and Smith (2002) analyze the number of filibusters—as cataloged by Beth (1994) and extended by the authors—from 1917 to 1996 and find that, among other factors, majority party strength and institutional innovations—but not external workload—are correlated with patterns of obstruction. A nagging concern, however, is that Richard Beth (1995) stresses that the list he prepared for the Congressional Research Service is based on varying and inconsistent standards for identifying a filibuster; hence, it should not be used as a reliable measure of Senate obstruction. Finally, Mixon, Gibson, and Upadhyaya (2003) study the number of cloture votes from 1959 to 1998 and conclude that the 1986 decision to broadcast Senate proceedings on cable television significantly increased the incentive for senators to filibuster for position-taking purposes. Of these studies, only Binder, Lawrence, and Smith (2002) test multiple explanations to determine which one provides the best fit to the pattern we observe. Furthermore, each uses data from a limited span of the twentieth-century Senate; a longer span and a comparison chamber would increase our ability to make general conclusions about the Senate and legislative obstruction.

Most recently, Wawro and Schickler (2006) focus on the causes and consequences of the adoption of the Senate cloture rule in 1917. They analyze final-passage margins on major legislation and the ability of the Senate to pass appropriations bills on time as indirect indicators of the influence of filibustering before and after the 1917 rule was adopted.[7] They find that narrow majorities were often successful at passing legislation before 1917 but that bill passage coalition sizes during short sessions increased after 1917 while their variance decreased. Furthermore, the cloture rule may have made it easier for the Senate to pass appropriations bills. However, this analysis—which ends in the 1940s—does not answer our motivating question: Why did filibustering increase over the course of the twentieth century?

This book extends Wawro and Schickler's analysis of the 1917 rule in two ways. First, it measures the effects of the 1917 rule on obstruction per se. Second, it tests the influence of variables that Wawro and Schickler consider *theoretically* important but that were not included in their empirical analyses of coalition sizes: informal norms, threats of cloture reform, and the relative costs of obstruction. Once these factors are included as explanations for increasing obstruction and coalition size, we observe that the adoption of a formal cloture rule in 1917 had no immediate effect on lawmaking in the Senate.

In sum, we must explain why the Senate is increasingly gridlocked by obstruction. No previous study has measured and explained filibustering over the entire history of the U.S. Congress. Most recent pivot research on the Senate filibuster is ahistorical and neither explains the rise of Senate filibustering nor controls for historical variation in the effect of obstruction on the lawmaking system. Other studies offer contradictory explanations for the escalation of Senate filibustering, highlighting the challenge of systematically measuring filibustering and the price of time.

A THEORY OF OBSTRUCTION

While it has proved difficult to measure filibustering and determine why we observe increasing Senate obstruction, previous research provides the building blocks for a theory of obstruction (esp. Luce 1922; Oppenheimer 1985; and Wawro and Schickler 2006). At some point in the past, filibustering was a costly tactic, one that senators were reluctant to employ unless they thought they could outlast the majority. The majority was more likely to concede as the Senate's workload increased or as deadlines (e.g., the end of a Congress) approached. This form of competition eventually gave way to the use of cloture as a response to obstruction; yet, even as the Senate modified its cloture rule to make it easier to shut off debate, the number of Senate filibusters increased steadily.

In chapter 2, I weave these claims into a general theory of obstruction that applies to the range of congressional history and, potentially, other legislatures as well. In this model, filibustering is a strategic game between teams of legislators in which legislators receive both policy and position-taking payoffs, incur penalties for wasting time, and pay special costs for active filibustering.

One insight from this theory is that the majority faction's choice of anti-filibuster tactics has a significant influence on whether minorities obstruct. If the minority expects that the majority will attempt to wait out a filibuster, the would-be obstructionists must calculate whether the expected rewards are worth the price. If, on the other hand, the minority expects the majority to concede or to attempt cloture, the price for obstruction is much lower, and filibustering is more likely.

This theory redirects our attention from the formal rules for limiting debate to factors that influence the value of time. When the price of waging a filibuster is extremely high, we expect to see few filibusters. When the majority cannot afford to wait out a filibuster (and, hence, the price of filibustering is low), the majority will shelve bills in anticipation of a filibuster or, if they do schedule such bills, use procedural solutions (e.g., the Senate's cloture process) rather than attrition. At the same time, the model suggests that partisanship and institutional changes are also important factors, and I test these as well.

A third unconventional feature of this theory is the role of position taking as an incentive to filibuster or to provoke a filibuster. While research on Congress has long noted legislators' incentives to posture for external audiences (Arnold 1990; Mayhew 1974), most contemporary legislative models (e.g., Krehbiel 1998) assume that legislators' sole functional goal is to achieve policy outcomes that correspond as much as possible to their notions of good policy. My theory helps explain why legislators might engage in filibusters they expect to lose and why legislative majorities bring bills to the chamber floor that they expect to fail; they are playing to voters, donors, and interest groups who reward the effort.

Fourth, one of the rules of the game is that the majority can change the rules of the game.[8] This "nuclear" option may deter legislators from engaging in a filibuster that they would otherwise win. In 2005, the Republicans may have successfully used this strategy to convince the Democrats to back down on filibusters against judicial nominees (see chapter 8), and there have been a few other cases of deterrence by reform, cases noted in chapter 8.

However, this book does *not* attempt to explain when and why legislators restrict obstruction (on this topic, see, e.g., Binder 1997; Dion 1997; and Schickler 2001). While the effects of these reforms are directly relevant, the politics of reform are too interesting and important to force into an already-thick book. Before we can understand the evolution of these rules, we should first understand what filibustering is, how it works, and why it varies.

MEASURING OBSTRUCTION AND TESTING THEORIES

One obstacle to research on congressional filibustering is the lack of accurate and consistent measures of obstruction. The best previous list—Beth (1994)— has, as we have seen, been severely criticized for its varying and erratic standards for identifying a filibuster (Beth 1995). Furthermore, recent research on filibustering stresses that overt filibustering is just the tip of the iceberg; covert threats to filibuster have a significant effect on legislative outcomes as well (Evans and Lipinski 2005; Krehbiel 1998; Oppenheimer 1985). Ideally, one would find some way to measure these threats—or at least their effects—as well. A good measure will also be sensitive to the varying tactics used to filibuster over the course of congressional history. For the first century of that history, members of the House and Senate often filibustered using *dilatory motions* and *disappearing quorums*, so our measures should reflect this variation.

I use two different methods to measure filibustering, each tailored to a specific time period. For the historic Congress (1789–1901), I scan the records of both the House and the Senate for votes apparently held simply to waste time and for votes on which it appears one party may be trying to "break" a quorum by refusing to vote. For the modern Senate (1901–2004), I switch to an approach based on secondary sources. I use a data set of over six thousand *New York Times* articles and over twelve hundred articles from *Time* magazine and *Congressional Quarterly* publications to identify both overt filibusters and threatened obstruction in the Senate. This switch in measurement strategy is motivated by the evolution of senators' filibustering tactics and the availability of media accounts for the twentieth century. The use of dilatory motions and disappearing quorums to obstruct died off in the early twentieth century and was replaced by lengthy speeches as the dominant form of obstruction. Instead, I rely on reporters covering the Senate to help me identify filibustering. Together, these measurement schemes provide a rich and unprecedented analysis of filibustering across the span of congressional history. We learn who filibustered, when legislators filibustered, and how their obstruction affected the legislative process.

Once we know how much filibustering has occurred, we can understand why it happens, especially the emergence of the sixty-vote Senate. I compare plausible explanations using new measures of the demand for legislative output and the opportunity cost of congressional work, and I test for the influence of multiple rules changes, partisan polarization, Senate norms, and the threat of cloture reform. This approach enables me to evaluate the relative importance of each possible cause of filibustering.

This book utilizes a blend of methodological approaches. On the one hand, this is a conventional piece of modern social science research with an explicit theory, hypotheses, data, methods, and results. However, I also include historical case studies to convey the nuances of real filibusters and describe critical events in congressional history, and I utilize archival research that provides fresh insight into the emergence of the sixty-vote Senate.

OUTLINE OF THE BOOK

Chapter 2 provides an introduction to filibustering and the foundation for the rest of the book. It describes the tactics of an obstruction game and explains how filibustering is actually a series of choices: scheduling bills, deciding to obstruct, and the response of the majority. It then develops the claims that I test in the rest of the book and that can be tested in a variety of legislatures.

The three chapters in part II apply this theory to filibustering in the House and Senate from 1789 to 1901. In chapter 3, I illustrate the key patterns of this era: filibustering was more common in the House than in the Senate and increased in both chambers over time. Chapter 4 identifies the issues that provoked obstruction and describes the effects of filibusters on legislative outcomes; interestingly, budgetary legislation and civil rights legislation were common topics for filibusters, as were rules changes and organizational choices in the House. Chapter 5 explains why we observe these historical patterns: filibustering increases as chamber time became increasingly valuable and as minority party unity increases. Filibustering decreases in the House after the majority adopted an effective closure rule in 1894.

Part III explains the evolution of filibustering in the twentieth-century Senate. Chapter 6 identifies filibusters using articles from the *New York Times*, the *Congressional Quarterly*, and *Time* magazine and measures the effects of filibusters. As expected, I find a pattern of increasing filibustering over time; I also find a surge of filibustering *after* the adoption of the Senate's cloture rule in 1917, especially during the last three months of each Congress. Filibusters have often led to the defeat or revision of legislation, but many filibusters are waged to force other issues onto the chamber floor, while others seem to be waged to garner publicity and public acclaim. Chapter 6 also finds a puzzling increase in the size of winning coalitions after 1960, just as senators begin strengthening their cloture rule.

Chapter 7 explains why we observe these phenomena—increasing obstruction, larger coalition sizes, and the emergence of cloture as the primary response to filibustering. I estimate the effects of time scarcity, partisanship, and institutional changes on Senate filibustering, and I find that the primary cause of the filibustering boom is that senators increasingly value their time too much to waste it on prolonged filibuster battles. Furthermore, I find a significant increase in filibustering during short sessions after the adoption of the 1917 cloture rule, a general increase in filibustering after the 1975 amendment to the Senate's cloture rule, and otherwise little relation between cloture reform and filibustering.

Chapter 8 traces the game of filibustering in the twentieth-century Senate. In particular, when and why did senators switch from waiting out filibusters to trying to invoke cloture? Using a combination of news articles, archival records, and quantitative measures, I find a clear shift in tactics during the 1960s. Senate majority leader Mike Mansfield (D-MT) persuaded other senators that attrition was no longer a viable strategy and that cloture was a collegial alternative to rolling in the cots. Behind the scenes, senators gradually institutionalized the unchallenged ability of every senator to filibuster. They developed standard routines for threatening obstruction, resolving policy disagreements, and negotiating the floor agenda. Chapter 8 concludes with an account of a recent challenge to the sixty-vote Senate: the threat by the Republicans to suppress filibustering against judicial nominees. This nuclear option contest neatly illustrates the continuing debate over congressional obstruction.

Finally, the afterword applies the insights of this text to future debates over Senate rules. After surveying arguments for and against obstruction, I give advice on reforming the Senate. Since the primary goal of this book is to inform rather than advocate, I do not recommend any specific institutional change. Using the theory and evidence presented in the text, however, I do help would-be reformers evaluate which reform options will best advance their goals. A key conclusion of this chapter is that senators who seek to reform but not eliminate obstruction should consider making it more difficult to wage a filibuster and easier to wait out a filibuster, thus restoring the classic balance of power in the Senate.

This book traverses congressional history with general measures and keen details. The central thesis connecting these pieces is that obstruction varies with the price legislators must pay to filibuster. Rules, issues, and political alignments are also part of the story, but the critical (and underrated) factor is the patience of the majority compared to the resolve of the obstructionists. This book pays attention to the *tactics* of filibustering so that we understand why the price of obstruction varies and how to measure it. By the same token, this is also a book about intensity, as victory in a filibuster often goes to the legislators who fight with greater passion. In large and small ways, American politics has been shaped by legislators who care deeply about its future and use extraordinary measures to work their will.

A Theory of Obstruction

Obstruction as it is practiced in the United States Senate is often, indeed characteristically, complex in motives, in techniques, and in participating personnel. There is a popular tendency to think of filibustering simply as an attempt to defeat measures by long speeches and by other means of delay. That this conception is both inadequate and inaccurate needs little demonstration after a survey of the long history of Senate filibusters.

Franklin L. Burdette, Filibustering in the Senate

I begin the story by describing the tactics of filibustering, and then I present a theory of filibustering. There are two benefits to a general theory of filibustering strategy. First, there is tremendous value in seeing filibusters stripped to their essence. Many experts can describe modern Senate obstruction; a few can describe filibusters in previous eras, state legislatures, or overseas; but a good theory helps us identify the recurring elements across these contexts. A general theory is especially important given the scope of this project. The tactics of filibustering vary greatly across congressional history, so we need a clear framework to tie the threads of this project together.

Second, a general model of obstruction highlights the strategic interaction of a filibuster contest. Recent work on obstruction portrays it as a simple veto game: a proposal appears on the chamber's agenda, and a pivotal actor decides whether to let it pass (Alter and McGranahan 2000; Brady and Volden 2006; Chiou and Rothenberg 2003, 2006; Krehbiel 1998). These pivot models do not, however, predict if and when filibusters will occur. Since the cloture rule determines the threshold for whether a filibuster succeeds or fails, it is immaterial whether the result is achieved via cloture vote, compromise, or keeping a bill off the Senate agenda. Furthermore, the pivot model is based on strong simplifying assumptions: (*a*) legislators are solely motivated by policy outcomes, (*b*) they consider policy issues one at a time, and (*c*) there is no special cost attached to obstructing. In practice, legislators care about getting elected per se, they link issues together, and they are likely to find filibustering physical challenging. Finally, the pivot approach cannot explain the transformation of filibustering from a rare, spectacular revolt against the regular order in the textbook Senate to an institutionalized minority veto in the contemporary Senate. The pivot model helps us understand the contemporary Senate, but not how the Senate reached this condition.

This chapter highlights four features of filibustering minimized by pivot models: agenda setting, costly effort, endogeneity, and strategic responses. Legislative majorities—usually the majority party—have the power to decide whether to make a proposal and what kind of proposal to make. An opposing minority then decides whether its members are willing to pay the costs of holding the floor day and night and to explain their behavior to their constituents. The model also includes a menu of response options for the majority. For most of congressional history, the dominant response was attrition—waiting until the minority exhausted itself. The procedural responses of the previous question (PQ) and cloture (House and Senate, respectively) represented a second option. The former was used, but ineffective, during the decades before the 1890s; the latter was neither used nor effective until the 1960s. A third response is reform: changing the rules of the game to make filibustering more difficult or closure more effective. This model incorporates three distinct responses to highlight the importance of the majority's response to obstruction.

This theory provides several nonobvious insights. First, filibustering may be deterred by costs in the form of negative public opinion or the physical effort of a war of attrition. Second, political rewards for effort rather than outcomes can induce filibustering and agenda setting that would otherwise be futile. Finally, obstruction has indirect consequences: the mere threat of obstruction may deter the majority from proposing legislation or motivate it to moderate its legislative proposals.

I begin with a discussion of the tactics of filibustering and responding to a filibuster. Just as scholars of international relations are drawn to the study of military technology as an explanation for patterns of war and peace, we must understand how legislators go about obstructing business and how majorities respond to a filibuster.

THE TACTICS OF FILIBUSTERING

I define *filibustering* as "legislative behavior (or a threat of such behavior) intended to delay a collective decision for strategic gain." Obstruction often consists of the unusual use of ordinary privileges. It is perfectly normal for a legislator to give a speech on the chamber floor, offer amendments, move to adjourn when the hour is late, or miss an occasional vote, yet each of these activities can be obstructive in large doses.

Prolonged Speaking

First, legislators can make *prolonged speeches* to consume time. This is the easiest tactic to understand: an obstructionist can delay votes as long as he and his allies keep talking. The longest congressional speech on record is Strom Thurmond's twenty-four-hour opposition to the 1957 civil rights bill (Caro 2002).[1] Although Thurmond claimed at the end of his marathon, "I feel so good that I believe I could speak quite a long time" (*Congressional Record* 103, pt. 12 [August 28, 1957]: 16456), twenty-four hours seems beyond the maximum speaking time for a typical legislator.

Parliamentary rules influence the effectiveness of prolonged speaking. A legislature may impose a maximum time limit on speeches, cap the number of speeches a legislator can give on each issue, or insist that all speeches be germane, that is, relevant to the issue under discussion. The Senate has never had a formal limit on speech length; the House had no limit until 1841, when members adopted a one-hour maximum.[2] Senate precedents dating back to 1872 give senators the right to talk about any topic within the limits of decorum, while, in the House, "it has always been held, and usually quite strictly, that . . . the Member must confine himself to the subject under debate" (Hinds 1907, 5:49).[3] Furthermore, the rules of both chambers require speakers to stand at their desks while they speak—no sitting, no walking, no bathroom breaks—intensifying the strain of a prolonged speech.[4]

Dilatory Motions

By itself, prolonged speaking is an exhausting tactic. Obstructionists often supplement speeches with parliamentary motions intended to waste time. These include motions to adjourn (quit for the day), to recess, and to vote on disputes over parliamentary procedure. A single member obstructs by making a dilatory motion, requesting a roll call vote, and gaining the support of one-fifth of the members present in the chamber.[5] Thus, a single member cannot succeed alone, but a relatively small faction can delay action indefinitely.

Dilatory motions are effective because, in both chambers, votes are taken in order of their priority rather than the order in which legislators request them. While priority rankings vary by chamber and over time, the current Senate Rule 22 lays out a fairly typical hierarchy: (1) to adjourn, (2) to adjourn to a date certain, (3) to recess, (4) to go to executive session (Senate only), (5) to lay a question on the table, (6) to postpone indefinitely, (7) to commit (to a committee), (8) to amend. In the House, the PQ motion has always occupied a medium rank below adjournment, setting a time for adjournment, and (for much of the nineteenth century) recessing. Thus, legislators can stall amendments, final passage of a bill, and even PQ motions by repeating these high-priority motions. Since each vote lasts from five to forty-five minutes (depending on chamber size and voting process), a few dilatory motions can stall a chamber for hours.

We should note that the House and the Senate can make decisions without roll call votes. The simplest method of voting is a *voice vote*: the presiding officer invites those in favor of a proposal to say *aye*, those opposed to say *nay*, and then announces which side seems to have the most support. A second option is a *standing vote*, in which the ayes and nays take turns standing. In the U.S. House, a third option was a *teller vote*: two or four members were appointed to count votes, and members voted by walking between one of two pairs of counters, one signaling aye, the other nay. Thus, when members asked for a roll call vote, either they had tried other voting methods and knew the outcome in advance, or they were consciously choosing a slow and public means of counting votes.

Disappearing Quorums

Article 1 of the U.S. Constitution states: "A majority of each [chamber] shall constitute a quorum to do business." If less than a majority of a legislature is present, no formal decisions can be made except whether to adjourn or to compel the attendance of missing members. What if members are present but refuse to participate? For decades, the House and Senate did not count nonvoting members toward a quorum since the power to declare members present could be abused.[6] If some members were absent owing to illness or campaigning, a minority of a chamber could block action by refusing to participate.

Consider a historical example. On the final day of the Forty-seventh Congress (1881–83), the House Republicans brought up a contested election between Samuel Lee (R) and John Richardson (D) of South Carolina to decide which candidate was the rightful winner. Few issues excited partisan loyalties like these disputed cases, but the roll call record makes it appear that several votes were near unanimous. Why? The Democrats refused to vote. As figure 2.1 shows, Democratic participation varied wildly during the night and morning of March 3–4, 1883. Nine of the last ten votes of the Forty-seventh Congress were disappearing quorums. Richardson kept his seat because the Republicans could not prove that at least half the membership was in the chamber.

This tactic is also used in state legislatures. In 2003, Democratic minorities in the Texas House and Senate filibustered to block a Republican redistricting plan that would swing several U.S. House districts from Democratic to Republican. Texas Democrats even fled the state to avoid being forced to attend by state authorities. In the end, the Senate Democrats returned only when the Republicans imposed escalating fines for absences.[7]

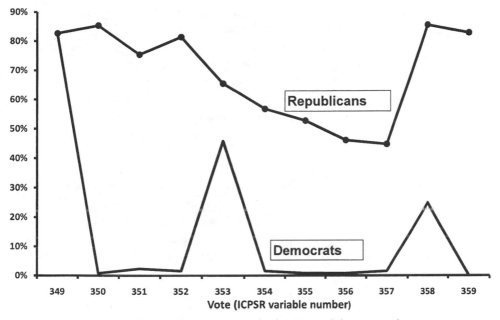

Figure 2.1. Vote participation by party, *Lee v. Richardson* contested election, March 3, 1883.
Note: The *x*-axis refers to variables assigned to each vote by the Inter-University Consortium.

RESPONSES TO OBSTRUCTION

What can legislative majorities do when faced with a filibuster? Scholars and journalists often focus on the availability—or lack thereof—of explicit mechanisms within chamber rules for limiting debate and dilatory behavior. This focus on formal rules, such as the PQ motion in the House of Representatives, is understandable but misguided. As demonstrated in chapter 3, seemingly powerful formal rules are not necessarily effective against all modes of obstruction. Nor are legislative majorities powerless to stop a filibuster without a formal rule in place, since attrition was a viable response to a filibuster for much of congressional history.

Formal Rules

The Previous Question

Since 1811, House members have been able to end debate on a question by moving the previous question. A simple majority is required to approve a PQ motion. The rules of the Senate have not mentioned a PQ motion since 1806. As we shall see, the fact that the House had a PQ motion did not, by itself, prevent filibustering. Nor did the lack of a PQ motion mean that senators had no viable response to obstruction.

The PQ has not always been used to cut off debate. It originated in the British Parliament (Alexander 1916, 180–81; Luce 1922, 270–71). Its primary use in Parliament, the Continental Congress, and the first decade of the U.S. Congress was to avoid awkward discussions and put off unpleasant decisions (Cooper 1962; Binder 1997, 49–50). In Congress's early years, discussion on the main issue continued if the PQ motion was approved; if the motion failed, the decision was put off to another day. Debate was allowed on PQ motions in the House until 1805, so, rather than ending debate, a PQ motion was vulnerable to a separate filibuster. This phase ended in February 1811, when a House majority reinterpreted the rule so that debate ended if the PQ was approved. While the PQ seems to empower a majority to cut off debate and vote on a proposal, in practice obstructionists could still use dilatory motions or disappearing quorums to filibuster.

Suspension of the Rules

Another way to circumvent obstruction is to "suspend," or ignore, the standing rules. Ordinary rights to speak, amend, or make motions may be suspended to accelerate the passage of a bill, and ordinary agenda-setting procedures may be suspended to ensure the swift consideration of an important bill. The standing rules of both the House and the Senate allow motions to suspend the rules. Initially, a simple majority could suspend the rules in both chambers. In 1822, the House amended its rules so that a two-thirds supermajority was required.[8] The Senate never amended its rules to require a supermajority, but, in 1915, it established a still-observed precedent that a two-thirds majority is necessary (Koger 2007). Suspension motions are not commonly used in the Senate to limit obstruction.

Cloture

A Senate rule that *is* often invoked to limit obstruction is Rule 22, the cloture rule.[9] The Senate cloture rule was first adopted in 1917 (see Koger 2007; Wawro and Schickler 2006, 2007) and has been amended several times since. Several features of the cloture rule have been constant from 1917 to the present:

- Sixteen signatures are required to file a cloture petition with the Senate.
- Two days after a petition is filed, the Senate interrupts all business to vote on the petition.
- If a sufficient supermajority of the Senate agrees, each senator is limited to a single hour of debate time on the pending measure; since 1975, overall debate time has been capped as well.

Table 2.1. Senate Cloture Rule Provisions, 1917–Present

Year Adopted	Applies To	Threshold for Bills	Threshold for Amendments to Rules	Overall Debate Limit
1917	A "measure"	⅔ of voting senators	⅔ of voting senators	
1949	Any measure, motion, or other pending issue	⅔ of *all* senators, voting or absent	None; cloture is not possible	
1959	Same	⅔ of voting senators	⅔ of voting senators	
1975	Same	⅗ of *all* senators	⅔ of voting senators	
1976	Same	⅗ of *all* senators	⅔ of voting senators	
1979	Same	⅗ of *all* senators	⅔ of voting senators	100 hours[a]
1986	Same	⅗ of *all* senators	⅔ of voting senators	30 hours[a]

[a] Each senator is entitled to ten minutes for speaking if the overall limit is reached. Senators can yield their time to floor managers or party leaders, but no manager or leader can gain more than two hours this way. One nondebatable motion per day to increase the time limit is permitted; three-fifths of all senators must support the motion for it to succeed.

· Once time has elapsed, a vote is held on the pending measure and all amendments under consideration.

The threshold requirement for invoking cloture, the issues that cloture can and cannot be used for, special requirements for cloture on rules changes, and the per senator and entire Senate limits on deliberation after cloture is invoked have varied over time. Table 2.1 summarizes the evolution of the cloture rule on these issues.

Over time, senators have strengthened the cloture rule so that its threshold is lower, its limits on debate tighter, and its scope broader. A number of provisions in the current rule ensure that senators cannot filibuster after cloture is invoked. The 1979 reform imposed an overall cap of one hundred hours on debate after the Senate approves a cloture petition, and, in 1986, this cap was lowered to thirty hours. The 1979 reform also made it more difficult to filibuster after a successful cloture vote by calling up dozens of amendments for votes. No senator may call up more than two amendments unless every other senator has had a chance to do the same, so a single senator cannot dominate the postcloture debate.[10]

Unanimous Consent Agreement

Like suspension motions, both chambers often curtail debate and filibustering by agreeing unanimously to do so. Any member can defeat a request for unanimous consent by objecting. This process is more common in the

Senate, and Senate rules formally regulate the adoption and amendment of unanimous consent agreements (UCAs) (Smith 1989; Smith and Flathman 1989). Obviously, this procedure can limit obstruction only in cases where a UCA is adopted before a senator realizes that he or she would like to filibuster; otherwise, anyone can object to the UCA and preserve the right to filibuster. UCAs are, thus, not an effective constraint on filibustering.

Ruling Legislators Out of Order

Since 1787, both chambers have permitted the presiding officer to determine that legislators are violating chamber rules (Beeman 1968). In the Senate, any senator may recommend that another senator be ruled out of order. Once the presiding officer deems a legislator out of order, he or she must sit down and cannot speak again without the permission of the chamber. A legislator may appeal a decision that he or she is out of order, and these appeals are decided by majority vote. This tactic can provide majority closure against a limited number of members. In June 1948, a filibuster by Senator Taylor (D-ID) against a bill extending the military draft was cut short when Taylor read aloud a telegram praising him as the "one honest Senator who respects his duty to represent the desires and interests of the people instead of the special interests of enemies of peace." Since by implication the telegram insulted all other senators, he was ruled out of order, the filibuster ceased, and the bill passed ("Filibuster Killed" 1948).

Attrition

When legislative majorities do not have an effective rule for limiting debate or available options are too unpopular to use, the primary alternative is to wait until obstructionists are exhausted or prohibited from making another speech. In this case, filibusters are *wars of attrition* in which both sides compete to see which will outlast the other; the team that lasts longer wins. Each side must decide how much time it is willing to commit to a filibuster, and time is expensive. For obstructionists, the primary cost is the effort required to speak or otherwise dominate floor proceedings. For majorities, time is expensive to the extent that (*a*) they must remain in and near the chamber to ensure the presence of a quorum and (*b*) there are *opportunity costs* for the chamber time used, that is, the forgone uses of the same time for legislators as individuals and for the chamber collectively. Majority members might rather be sleeping at home or debating and passing other bills that they value as much or more.

There is a voluminous theoretical literature on bargaining situations.[11] A critical insight that applies to filibusters is that, if the two sides have asymmetrical costs for waiting, the team that is more patient will win (Rubinstein

1982). For the sake of position-taking benefits, an opposition that cannot win will still filibuster, and majorities will still bring up legislation that cannot pass (Bawn and Koger 2008), but the outcome depends on the relative patience of the two teams.

There are several tactics that majorities use to expedite this strategy. First, bill supporters can refrain from speaking so that the filibustering minority must take responsibility for occupying the floor. Second, majorities can strictly enforce the requirements that speakers stand at their desks—no sitting, no walking. Third, majorities can lengthen the number of hours of debate per day or even stay in session all day and all night. This accelerates the physical exhaustion of the filibusterers. Fourth, majorities can continue a legislative day for several calendar days or weeks so that the obstructionists eventually use up their allotted speeches on a topic. Fifth, if attendance is low, each chamber can demand the presence of absent members and punish members who have been absent.

Parliamentary Innovation

The final category of responses to obstruction is, broadly, changing the rules or precedents of the chamber so that filibustering is more difficult or closure more effective. This can be a difficult and costly strategy to implement. If a legislative minority is able to obstruct under existing rules, any proposal to formally amend those rules is subject to a filibuster (Binder 1997; Binder and Smith 1997). In earlier work (Koger 2002, 2008), I explain how a simple majority of the House or Senate can restrict obstruction if a majority is willing to use extraordinary parliamentary tactics. Congressional majorities often achieve reforms by setting or revising parliamentary precedents rather than formally changing chamber rules. Just as the Supreme Court has ample latitude to interpret the meaning of the U.S. Constitution, each chamber is the final arbiter of the meaning of its rules by simple majority vote.[12] This approach enables majorities to circumvent the chicken-or-egg problem of filibusters against rules changes. As discussed in chapter 3, a clear example of antifilibuster precedents is Speaker Reed's rulings in January 1890.

There are several ways in which a creative and determined Senate majority could radically restrict filibustering. For example, a senator could move the PQ, then a majority override the objection that the Senate rules do not permit a PQ motion. Or a majority could convert the motion to suspend the rules into an effective closure process by making this motion "nondebatable" and reversing the 1915 precedent requiring a two-thirds supermajority to suspend the rules (see Koger 2007). Or, after a Senate majority loses a cloture vote, a member of the majority could raise a point of order that a simple majority can invoke cloture.[13] The intriguing aspect of this approach is that the senator making the point of order can raise a second point of order that no debate is permitted on a point of order once cloture has been invoked![14]

One implication of this is that we need a satisfying explanation for the persistence of filibustering in the Senate but not the House (see Koger 2002). Another is that it is possible for senators to deter a minority from filibustering by making a credible *threat* to restrict the right to filibuster. Senators may then refrain from filibustering against one bill so that they can retain the right to filibuster against other bills (Koger 2004).

The costs of nonconsensual reform can be immense. Members of the majority would be restricting their own right to filibuster in the future. The majority may face public criticism for extreme breaches of Senate tradition.[15] After the reform is imposed, members of the losing side may retaliate by refusing to cooperate in myriad ways; the "losers" might even possess institutional positions that enable them to punish the "winners," for example, by depriving them of desirable committee positions.

A THEORY OF OBSTRUCTION

Now that we have surveyed the multiple forms of obstruction and the ways that legislators respond to filibustering, we can develop a model of filibustering that illuminates the indirect effects of obstruction and helps us understand why legislators would choose *not* to filibuster.[16]

For simplicity, let us think of a filibuster as a contest between two teams of legislators, Pro and Con.[17] I assume that Pro comprises a chamber majority and that Con is a minority coalition. The Pro coalition would like to pass a proposal moving a particular policy toward its notion of good (and politically rewarding) public policy; the Con team is opposed to any change Pro might make on that issue.

What are they fighting for? I assume that legislators' positions on the policies that Congress enacts depends on some combination of concern for the public welfare and concern for their political careers. In addition, legislators may be rewarded or punished for the positions they take and the efforts they make. After all, they are elected individually, and citizens hold them responsible for their individual actions as well as Congress's collective achievements. Specifically, presidents, party leaders, interest groups, donors, and voters often evaluate them on the basis of their individual choices in addition to (or instead of!) their policy achievements. Finally, legislators suffer from limits on their time and energy, and these constraints vary with legislative context. Thus, they must decide how to allocate their time and effort, and devoting time and effort to one issue means paying opportunity costs, that is, delaying—and possibly ignoring—action on other issues (Hall and Deardorff 2006).

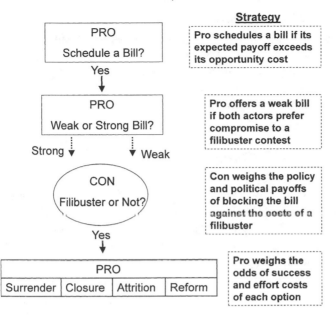

Figure 2.2. A model of obstruction.

We can think of filibustering as a four-step game, depicted in figure 2.2. In the first two steps, Pro decides whether to make a proposal (defined broadly; see below) and whether to make a "weak" or "strong" offer. Pro prefers a strong proposal but may settle for less to avoid a filibuster fight. Next, Con decides whether to filibuster. A key factor in Con's decision, however, is Pro's likely strategy in the last stage; Con is more likely to filibuster if Pro is unlikely to force a mutually costly war of attrition or revise the rules. Finally, Pro responds by surrendering, attempting closure, attempting attrition, or revising the rules of the game. *Closure* is a generic term for attempting to shut off debate using an existing parliamentary rule. *Attrition* is an effort to outlast Con in a contest of stamina. *Reform* is manipulating the rules of the chamber.

By *proposal* I mean a bill, resolution, treaty, or nomination. For treaties and nominations, obviously, the agenda setter is the president, but, otherwise, the logic is the same; the president decides whether to make a proposal (a minor consideration for nominations but a major one for treaties) and what kind of proposal to make. In the case of Supreme Court nominations, for example, presidents typically choose from a pool of candidates who vary in their acceptability to the Senate. The next three sections proceed stage by stage, explaining strategic choices, and deriving general predictions.

While this theory is designed to explain the fate of individual proposals, my research question is systemic (obstruction in the House and Senate over time), and my data are aggregated by year or congressional session. The theory predicts actions when parameters reach unobserved thresholds for each case, while my data measure (as well as is possible) overall change in these variables over time and across chambers. So, when I state hypotheses below, they are expressed in relative terms: as X changes, we expect more or less of Y. Implicitly, this means that, as X changes, we should observe more (or fewer) cases that meet the necessary conditions for a filibuster to happen, which we observe in the aggregate as more or less Y.

RESPONDING TO A FILIBUSTER

Curiously, the best place to begin is at the end of the story. Using the logic of backward induction, we first analyze Pro's response to a filibuster, and then we can discuss how Con's strategy depends on Pro's strategy. While the choice between reform, attrition, and closure is simple in theory, it is crucial for this book. A key institutional variable in congressional history is the availability and effectiveness of the closure option. The House lacked an effective closure rule before the 1890s. The Senate had no closure option before 1917, and, for much of the twentieth century, the combination of a supermajority threshold and clever anticloture tactics combined to ensure that closure was an uncertain option. The transition from attrition to closure as the dominant response to obstruction, furthermore, marked the emergence of the supermajority Senate.

At the last stage, Pro simply takes the path that offers the most reward at the lowest price. If closure and attrition are forlorn options and reform is impractical, Pro might just surrender; if it surrenders, it loses the investment it has already made in the bill and reaps no gain. For this reason (as discussed below), I expect Pro to avoid proposals it will eventually surrender at the agenda-setting stage, and I focus on Pro's remaining options.

Pro considers two factors when choosing between closure, attrition, and reform: likelihood of success and relative exchange costs. For closure, the Pro coalition must consider whether it can muster enough votes to win. For attrition, it must estimate how long the Con team can conduct an active filibuster, how long the members of the Pro team will be willing to endure the human costs of an active filibuster (e.g., remaining in or near the chamber all day and all night), and how long it is willing to put off other legislation waiting for the attention of the chamber. As Pro becomes increasingly certain that its members can outlast Con, the likelihood of success by attrition increases. The probability of winning with each tactic varies over the course of a Congress, so senators' preferred responses may vary within a two-year Congress as well. Over time, the overall success rates and costs of each tactic may vary as well.

Pro's decision to reform the rules also hinges on the costs of reform and likelihood of success, which are closely linked. For both teams, the costs of reform include the diminished opportunity to obstruct in the future. Further-more, members of the Pro team may be insincere and prefer to allow the Con team to block proposals they privately oppose, or they may support Con's abil-ity to block strong proposals in favor of weak offers. Thus, some Pro members are willing to vote for a proposal but not willing to reform chamber rules to ensure the passage of that proposal. Furthermore, legislators who have their rights diminished in midfight may be especially bitter and retaliate with their remaining powers—hence the Democrats' threat of a "nuclear" counterstrike in 2003 (see chapter 8). This behavior increases the costs of a reform strategy.

Additionally, there is a public dimension to Pro's choice of tactics. In the past, legislative majorities have feared that using a closure approach will tar-nish their image. For years after the 1811 transformation of the PQ, House members were reluctant to use it because of its connotation that the majority is suppressing open debate in the legislature (Binder 1997). For decades after the adoption of the Senate cloture rule in 1917, senators remained proud of the chamber's tradition of "free speech" and were reluctant to invoke the rule. Attrition, however, can also imply political costs or benefits. As discussed in chapter 7, one of the reasons that Mike Mansfield resisted attrition as a strat-egy in the 1960s was that he felt press coverage of all-night filibusters harmed the public reputation of the Senate. At the same time, we observe a number of cases in which a majority brings up doomed legislation just to make it clear that they supported the bill. Third, reforming chamber rules can have pro-found political implications. On the one hand, while the general public typi-cally is indifferent or opposed to filibustering, changing the rules in midgame can also offend citizens' sense of fair play. In 1890, for example, Democrats used the House Republicans' procedural innovations as part of a very success-ful campaign message. However, there may be political benefits for reform as well; from the 1940s to the 1970s, an evolving coalition of interest groups pro-moted congressional reform, including liberalizing the Senate's cloture rule (Zelizer 2004). Support for reform became one of the criteria for these groups' support, providing an electoral incentive for institutional change.

There are several moving parts in this story—multiple strategies, com-plex preferences, and change over time—but these ideas are easily depicted. Figure 2.3 illustrates hypothetical payoffs for different strategies to advance a hypothetical bill at different points during a session of Congress. The utility of using a given strategy is shown on the vertical axis, while the time point within a session is shown on the horizontal axis.

In panel *a*, attrition (A) is the most rewarding strategy for most of the session, then closure (C), then reform (R). Surrender (S) is implicitly the zero baseline. We can write this:

$$A > C > R > S.$$

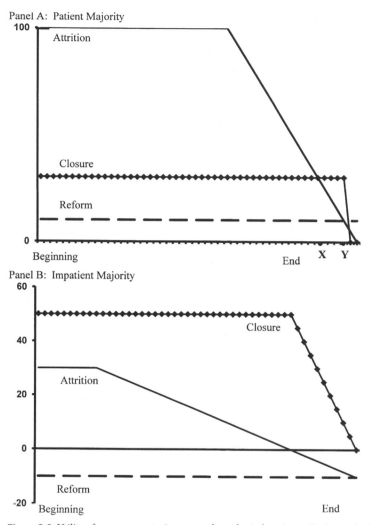

Figure 2.3. Utility of response strategies across a hypothetical session. *a*, Patient majority panel. *b*, Impatient majority.

Then, as the backlog of bills awaiting floor time grows and the number of days left in the session dwindle, attrition becomes a less attractive option, so closure (which had been less rewarding on this bill because it is less likely to succeed or more costly to use) becomes the best response after the time point labeled X. However, as the end of the session draws close, closure becomes a worthless strategy because a cloture vote take place on the second day after a petition is filed. Formally, this requirement means that the only way to invoke cloture in the last two days of a session is to anticipate the filibuster ahead of time. In practice, the two-day lag makes Rule 22 less and less effective at the end of a fixed session because a determined (and obnoxious!) senator could potentially force the filing of cloture petitions at multiple points in a proposal's progress; he or she could also take other proposals hostage or filibuster against buffer bills to multiply the number of cloture petitions and votes required to legislate during the busiest time of the session ("Bar on Filibusters" 1935, 1). In the final days, reform is the only strategy left. In figure 2.3*a*, the majority would rather reform than lose, so we would expect to see either no filibusters or swiftly imposed limits on filibustering.

A different configuration of response payoffs is shown in panel *b*. Here, cloture is the best option for the entire session but decreasingly effective toward the end. Attrition is possible early on, but, eventually, the costs of attempting attrition outweigh any benefit. Notably, reform is such a costly option that bill supporters would rather surrender completely than change the rules of the chamber. While figure 2.3 is obviously stylized, it foreshadows the story of this book: attrition used to be a better response option than closure or (usually) reform, but, eventually, closure became a more feasible option for frustrated majorities.

This discussion provides two testable claims (focusing here on the choice between attrition and closure):[18]

HYPOTHESIS 1: Pro is more likely to prefer attrition to closure to the extent that attrition offers a higher probability of success.

HYPOTHESIS 2: Pro is less likely to prefer attrition to closure to the extent that attrition requires greater physical effort, opportunity costs, and political harm than closure.

THE DECISION TO FILIBUSTER

When do legislators filibuster? Legislators' calculations are based on the policy and position-taking payoffs of filibustering and on the majority's likely response to a filibuster.

First, let us consider position taking. For most of congressional history, filibustering has been a public act that anyone outside Congress could observe and reward or punish. These external rewards may induce filibustering; legislators may obstruct solely for public consumption or for the combination of policy benefits and position-taking rewards (see Bawn and Koger 2008). By the same token, external payoffs can be negative, with the result that the minority may choose not to filibuster a bill it opposes.

Second, Con's decision to filibuster depends on Pro's anticipated response:

- Surrender: If Pro will surrender in the face of a filibuster, then Con will filibuster a bill if the net policy and political benefits of blocking it are positive.

- Closure: If Pro will attempt closure and has some chance of success, then the policy incentives to filibuster are diminished. This matters only if Con's policy preferences and position taking preferences are in conflict. If Con opposes the bill but there are political costs to filibustering, then it will filibuster only if the expected policy gains exceed the political costs.[19]
- Attrition: If Pro attempts to outlast Con, Con faces a complex choice. As above, the likelihood of winning the battle is important. However, there is a new component to the choice: the price of waging an active filibuster. Con must guess how long the battle will last and how much it will cost and weigh these costs against the expected policy gains and political payoffs.
- Reform: If Pro is willing to revise the rules of the game to ensure the passage of a proposal, then Con's prospects for winning a filibuster shrink to zero. Furthermore, to the extent that Con's ability to obstruct subsequent proposals is diminished, the policy costs of provoking anti-obstruction reforms can be severe. Unless there are extreme position-taking benefits to provoking such a confrontation, Con should be deterred by credible threats to diminish the right to filibuster.

In theory, we may assume that Con can perfectly predict Pro's response. In practice, Pro may attempt to signal its resolve before Con chooses a strategy. In December 1913, for example, Senate Democrats voted to extend the daily meeting hours of the Senate before Republicans decided whether to filibuster the next bill on the agenda—the Federal Reserve Act (Bawn and Koger 2008). The Democrats' action signaled that any filibuster would have to go on from morning to night, day after day. We might expect that Pro will always signal its intent to fight and win a war of attrition or to reform chamber rules since these threats would have the greatest deterrent effect. However, Con can, presumably, gauge these signals with some intelligence on the basis of Pro's recent behavior and the current legislative context. If Pro has not attempted attrition in years and has not won a war of attrition in decades, an attrition signal would not be very credible. If the Pro team includes members who are likely to filibuster on other issues (e.g., if it is a bipartisan coalition) or who appreciate the policy benefits of permitting obstruction, then Con may discount any of Pro's saber rattling as cheap talk.

This discussion yields several claims that prove useful in the chapters that follow. As above, I state them in "more or less" terms to predict the relations we should observe in aggregated data over time and space:

HYPOTHESIS 3: Con is more likely to filibuster as the external rewards for obstruction increase.

HYPOTHESIS 4: Con is more likely to filibuster as the policy rewards for blocking a bill increase.

HYPOTHESIS 5: If Pro is likely to attempt closure and there are political costs to filibustering, Con is more likely to filibuster as its likelihood of winning increases.

HYPOTHESIS 6: If Pro is likely to attempt attrition, Con is more likely to filibuster as (a) Con's probability of winning increases and (b) the costs of a war of attrition decrease.

HYPOTHESIS 7: Con is more likely to attempt obstruction as Pro responds with closure rather than attrition.

HYPOTHESIS 8: Con is less likely to obstruct when Pro makes a credible threat to reform chamber rules to ensure victory.

Hypotheses 3 and 4 assume that Pro's dominant response is surrender, attrition, or closure. Hypothesis 7 is an extension of hypothesis 6: since the effort required to filibuster shrinks to zero when Pro uses closure, only political and social costs can deter filibustering.

SETTING THE AGENDA WITH A MINORITY FILIBUSTER

Now we explore Pro's decisions whether to make a proposal and whether to offer a strong or a weak proposal. In practice, agenda setting in the House and Senate is a complex process based on cooperation and competition among party leaders, committees, and the membership of the entire chamber.[20] For simplicity, I treat these decisions as choices by the majority party or some other organized majority faction.

Scheduling a Proposal

The first choice is whether to make a proposal in a specific issue domain. Here, the opportunity cost of legislating is a key factor because legislatures typically have a limited amount of time in which to do their work. In the eighteenth and nineteenth centuries, legislators often hurried to finish their business so that they could return to their districts, their families, and their careers. The desire to return home was compounded by the inconvenience of summer in Washington, DC: thick and humid heat, mosquitoes, and long days of dull speeches in a sweltering chamber. By the twentieth century, these concerns were replaced by the sheer quantity of work to be done, especially after the New Deal and World War II dramatically increased the role of the federal government in American society. Legislators were torn between the need to visit their constituencies, do casework for constituents, govern the country with substantive legislation, and spend time with their families. Each additional day added to the length of a session detracts from other priorities. The scarcity of chamber time forces legislators to budget their time wisely.

The opportunity costs of developing and debating a proposal are the forgone uses of the same time. These costs increase for complex proposals and as time becomes scarcer. Some proposals (e.g., tariff revisions or appropriations) require more floor time than others for adequate deliberation. The opportunity cost of scheduling a proposal also varies with the availability of time and the other issues available for floor consideration. Time is especially scarce as Congress runs into deadlines, scheduled recesses, and the ends of sessions (Oppenheimer 1985; Yackee 2003). As the number of proposals awaiting floor consideration increases, the premium on floor time increases.

The expected gains from making a proposal must exceed the time and effort legislators invest in preparing it, organizing a coalition to support it, and taking the time of the chamber to debate and pass it. This implies a threshold test for every piece of legislation: in order to merit the time of its sponsors and the chamber, a bill must offer sufficient rewards to justify Pro's effort.

Filibustering can have a significant indirect influence on the agenda of a legislature. Pro discounts the expected benefits of a proposal when a filibuster will threaten its chances of passing. This means that it may decide not to schedule proposals that offer significant benefits if passed without a filibuster but insufficient reward if there is some risk that a filibuster could succeed. Pro also weighs the anticipated costs of fighting a war of attrition to defeat a filibuster. Owing to these additional costs and diminished expected rewards, it may refuse to develop and schedule proposals that Con will eventually filibuster.

It is difficult to prove why something does not happen. If we want to explain why the Senate did not consider civil rights legislation in the Sixty-eighth Congress (1923–25), for example, there are two perfectly plausible explanations: senators were deterred by the expectation that Southern members would filibuster any civil rights bill, or they just were not very interested in changing the racial status quo. How would one prove that the cause of inaction was deterrence and not indifference? How would one do so systematically across multiple issues for long spans of time?

Several scholars (Krehbiel 1998; Chiou and Rothenberg 2003; Wawro and Schickler 2004) use final-passage votes to indirectly measure such censoring. If controversial proposals are withheld from the floor or amended to end a filibuster, then one expects to see a supermajority of the legislature voting to approve them. Similarly, I expect that final-passage vote margins will vary with legislators' propensity to filibuster and the threshold for effective closure:

HYPOTHESIS 9: Final-passage margins will increase as the costs of filibustering decrease.

HYPOTHESIS 10: If majorities prefer closure as a response to filibustering, final-passage margins will vary with shifts in the threshold for closure.

Choosing a Proposal

Next, if Pro makes a proposal, what should it propose? We might imagine that the Pro team can make any proposal ranging from its ideal policy to the status quo. However, this choice can be narrowed down to two types of proposals: compromise or ideal. A compromise offer is moderated to win Con's support. An ideal proposal is the most preferred option if Pro does not try to compromise. Obviously, Pro prefers to impose its preferred policy rather than compromise, but it may prefer the certainty of adopting a compromise proposal to the risk and cost of a filibuster.

There are four possible scenarios at this stage. First, Con may be unlikely to filibuster any proposal, so Pro faces no risk or cost for making its ideal proposal. Second, Con may intend to filibuster any offer, so there is no room for compromise. This was the case with Southern senators and civil rights legislation for much of the mid-twentieth century. In this case, Pro might as well offer its ideal proposal and try to win.[21] Third, perhaps Con is open to compromise but Pro is unwilling to accept the terms of a compromise. This might be the case if Pro expects to win a filibuster contest, if the costs of winning are low, or if compromise requires a significant deviation from Pro's ideal proposal. Finally, Pro and Con may compromise if both prefer some policy change to a filibuster contest.

The primary insight we gain from this stage is that one of the effects of filibustering is indirect: under certain conditions, legislators propose moderate legislation to avoid filibusters that are costly to defeat or likely to succeed. Sometimes, this plays out in public: the House or Senate begins discussing a bill, members filibuster, a compromise is struck, and the bill passes. At other times, the compromise takes place ex ante, so we observe apparent unanimity. As above, we observe the effect of filibustering indirectly in the size of the coalition supporting proposals on final-passage votes.

EXPANDING THE MODEL

Of course, theories are abstractions that may not easily match the full range of observed behavior. One gap between theory and reality is the assumption that each contest is over the substantive content of a single-issue proposal. In practice, legislators often filibuster over the right to offer amendments to a bill or to bring up other issues. A second wrinkle is the practice of filibustering "buffer" bills. How can this theory accommodate such behavior?

Issues and Agendas

One of the more fragile parliamentary rights in Congress is the right to offer amendments. While many legislators profess a commitment to open deliberation and a hearing for all reasonable proposals, in practice the majority—especially when bound by the cords of party—may prevent the minority from offering amendments to bills.[22] They may do so to prevent killer amendments from cleaving their coalition or simply to avoid casting votes on controversial issues that could be used against them in the next campaign. This is an acute issue in the Senate, where the lack of a germaneness requirement permits senators to offer amendments on any "hot" issue they choose. In recent years, when the minority party senses that the majority party is promoting a bill for political purposes, it often responds by raising an alternative issue to compete for media attention and filibustering until the Senate allows a vote on its own "message" issue (Evans and Oleszek 2001).

We can accommodate this squabbling by expanding our notion of a proposal. In this view, a proposal is a set of policy positions on multiple dimensions, even if it is a substantive change on one dimension and no change on all other dimensions. Furthermore, Pro's proposal includes a set of procedures for considering the legislation. Thus, in the post–Civil War House, if the majority party brought up a bill to promote railroad expansion and promptly moved the PQ to shut off debate and amendments (but not obstruction!), the minority could object to the policy content of the bill *or* the manner in which the majority proposed to debate it *or* the fact that the majority was ignoring the pressing need for more rivers and harbors appropriations. This notion of a proposal is consistent with the theory, in which the initial take-it-or-leave-it proposal can just as easily be a multidimensional offer.

Compound Strategies

This model condenses filibustering into a single-shot game in which Pro makes a single proposal, Con makes a single decision, and Pro chooses a single response. In practice, a filibuster is often a multistage game in which the Pro team varies its proposal and strategies over time. In 1960, for example, senators supporting a civil rights bill first attempted attrition, then cloture, then proposed a compromise bill. How can we apply a static model to a dynamic process?

The easiest way is to think of each day as a separate iteration of the game. Pro wakes up each day and says, "Which proposal should I make? And how shall I respond to a filibuster?" And Con says, "Should I filibuster (again) today?" In many cases, we can ignore this day-to-day approach. It is most useful, however, when actors are learning about themselves and each other as they play. Legislators may be wrong about the determination level of their own team or the opposing team. They may also estimate the costs of filibustering incorrectly—it may be harder than it looks to wage a battle of attrition. This model does not incorporate this sort of uncertainty and updating, but, in practice, we observe shifting strategies during filibuster contests. For example, Pro may begin with a strong offer to test Con's resolve and, having gained some information, bargain in earnest to negotiate a compromise.

CONCLUSION

This chapter has described the tactics of filibustering and presented a theory of obstruction. This theory explains why we observe filibusters that are costly for both obstructionists and their opponents. There are three conditions for a filibuster to occur in equilibrium: (*a*) Pro makes a proposal that is unacceptable to Con, either because Pro is willing to chance a fight or because there is no proposal that Con will not filibuster; (*b*) Con prefers filibustering to acquiescing; (*c*) Pro prefers cloture, attrition, or reform to surrender. If both actors know the odds of winning, why are they both willing to fight instead of compromising ex ante? A key factor is the reward for position taking. It is possible for both sides to receive positive payoffs for taking strong stands and for these payoffs to outweigh any policy considerations or the costs of a war of attrition. Second, both teams may care deeply about an issue, with the result that, rather than compromise, they are willing to either win or lose entirely.

A second insight from this chapter is that filibustering has both direct and indirect effects on the legislative process. Obviously, minority filibusters have the direct effect of killing some legislation. Less obviously, legislators might propose a moderate bill to avoid a filibuster, or they might choose not to schedule bills because an anticipated filibuster either raises the costs or reduces the expected gains from scheduling a bill.

A third insight—and perhaps the most important one for understanding the evolution of House and Senate obstruction—is that tactics legislators use to *respond* to obstruction has a tremendous impact on whether opponents of a proposal attempt a filibuster. While the effects of closure rules vary with the nature of the rule, a switch from attrition to a supermajority closure rule would effectively lower the price of filibustering, leading to more obstruction.

The next step is to test this theory using the scope of congressional history as our laboratory. To do so, we must devise measures of obstruction and of the value of time (and, hence, the balance of power in wars of attrition) for the historical era (1789–1901) and the modern era (1901–present) and determine how well our theory predicts the rate of obstruction in the House and Senate.

II

The Historic Congress, 1789-1901

This part describes and explains filibustering in the historic Congress from its beginning in 1789 to the end of the Fifty-sixth Congress in 1901. There are several reasons that the historic era is an essential part of this study. First, politicians and pundits often make historical claims to validate their views on filibustering. Many of these claims are simply incorrect, half true, or baseless, so an accurate study will improve public debate on this topic. In particular, the fact that filibustering was more common in the U.S. House than the U.S. Senate shatters the notion that obstruction is somehow peculiar to the Senate or essential to its purpose in our constitutional system.

As scientists, we benefit from the comparison between the historic House and the historic Senate because we observe great variation in chamber size and parliamentary rules over time and across chambers. To political observers, the trajectory of the historic House is interesting as a parallel to the modern Senate: we observe a cycle of low obstruction, steadily mounting filibustering, institutional crisis, and drastic reforms to squelch obstruction. In part III, we observe that the Senate has gone through the first two steps of this narrative, and we grapple with the question of whether it will experience the same transformation.

In the next three chapters, we shall find that there was much more filibustering than previously known (chapter 3). This obstruction affected the course of congressional debates, especially during the antebellum period and the Gilded Age (chapter 4). While personalities and political controversies played a role in these clashes, the underlying pattern is that filibustering increased as the price for obstruction decreased, until the members of the House adopted drastic reforms to impose majority rule in the 1890s (chapter 5).

CHAPTER 3

The Escalation of Filibustering, 1789-1901

How much obstruction actually occurred in the historic Congress? When did it start? In which chamber did legislators filibuster more often? This chapter answers these questions with an unprecedented effort to measure obstruction during a period when the historical record is generally weak and inconsistent.

Careful measurement yields provocative insights. First, there was more obstruction in the House than the Senate from 1789 to 1901. This is apparent whether we look at the number of dilatory motions, disappearing quorums (DQs), or a combined measure of obstruction. The level of obstruction gradually increases in both chambers and peaks in the Senate in the 1870s and in the House in the 1880s. We observe filibustering by both the minority and the majority parties. I begin the historical review, however, with the Constitutional Convention of 1787.

FILIBUSTERING AND THE U.S. CONSTITUTION

No matter what you might hear from confused senators, the Constitution does not explicitly include a right to filibuster (Binder and Smith 1997). However, article 1 does codify legislative rights that could be used to obstruct. A review of the founders' attitudes toward supermajority rule and filibustering suggests that these provisions were not included to promote obstruction but that the founders anticipated that they would permit filibustering as a side effect.

Federalist No. 22, written by Alexander Hamilton, suggests that the authors of the Constitution were generally wary of supermajority limits:

If a pertinacious minority can control the opinion of a majority, respecting the best mode of conducting it, the majority in order that something may be done must conform to the view of the minority; and thus the sense of the smaller number will overrule that of the greater and give a tone to the national proceedings. Hence, tedious delays; continual negotiation and intrigue; contemptible compromises of the public good. And yet, in such a system it is even happy when such compromises can take place: for upon some occasions things will not admit of accommodation; and then the measures of government must be injuriously suspended, or fatally defeated.[1]

Does the Constitution nonetheless promote minority rule in Congress? By now, we know that two common forms of filibustering are refusing to vote and repeatedly calling for roll call votes, so the Constitution's provisions for a quorum and roll call votes were crucial to the ability to filibuster. During a discussion of the constitutionally mandated threshold for a quorum in both chambers (August 10, 1787), delegates to the convention linked the minimum number of legislators required to make a decision to potential filibustering by "secession," or quorum breaking. Madison's notes of the Constitutional Convention indicate that John Mercer of Maryland "was also for less than a majority [quorum requirement]. So great a number will put it in the power of a few, by seceding at a critical moment, to introduce convulsions, and endanger the government. Examples of secession have already happened in some of the states." To this George Mason of Virginia replied: "This is a valuable and necessary part of the plan." Madison's notes go on to indicate: "He [Mason] admitted that inconveniences might spring from the secession of a small number; but he had also known good produced by an apprehension of it. He had known a paper emission prevented by that cause in Virginia" (Madison 1908, 132–35).

Madison did not share Mason's support for obstruction. In Federalist No. 58, he wrote: "Lastly, [a higher quorum requirement] would facilitate and foster the baneful practice of secessions, a practice which has shown itself even in states where a majority only is required; a practice subversive of all the principles of order and regular government; a practice which leads more directly to public convulsions and the ruin of popular governments than any other which has yet been displayed among us." Clearly, Madison did not hope for the filibustering permitted by the quorum requirement. Instead, the majority quorum requirement in article 1 can be understood as a balance between the delegates' fear of mischief by small numbers of legislators and their concern that a high threshold would paralyze Congress at critical moments (Luce 1922, 31; see also Federalist No. 58). Similarly, the provision requiring that requests for roll call votes be seconded by one-fifth of those present represents a middle ground between allowing a single member to request a vote (which may lead to abuse) and not recording votes at all (Madison 1908, 136). Thus, the founders may have anticipated that an occasional episode of filibustering might do more good than harm, but the Federalist Papers suggest that they did not intend obstruction to systematically impede majority action on most classes of legislation.

Table 3.1. Key Dates for the 85th, 108th, 18th, and 71st Congresses

	85th Congress	108th Congress
Election date	Nov. 6, 1956	Nov. 5, 2002
First session	Jan. 3–Aug. 30, 1957	Jan. 7–Dec. 8, 2003
Second session	Jan. 7–Aug. 24, 1958	Jan. 20–Dec. 9, 2004
Election of next Congress	Nov. 4, 1958	Nov. 2, 2004

	18th Congress	71st Congress
Election date(s)	July 1, 1822–Aug. 14, 1823	Nov. 6, 1928
Special session	None	Apr. 15, 1929–Nov. 22, 1929
Long session	Dec. 1, 1823–May 27, 1824	Dec. 2, 1929–July 3, 1930
Election date(s) for the next Congress	July 7, 1824–Aug. 30, 1825	Nov. 4, 1930
Short session	Dec. 6, 1824–Mar. 3, 1825	Dec. 1, 1930–Mar. 3, 1931

Another constitutional provision that facilitated obstruction was the original congressional schedule of "long" and "short" sessions. The modern Congress uses a work schedule adopted in 1933 to eliminate obstruction-prone short sessions. Since 1933, each two-year Congress meets for two sessions beginning in January and continuing until the House and Senate adjourn sine die (i.e., indefinitely) or until January 3 of the following year comes around. The 85th and 108th congresses, shown in the top half of table 3.1, are typical examples for their decades.

Note that sessions of contemporary congresses tend to last longer and that the second session may continue after the next Congress has been elected. Meetings held after an election are known as "lame-duck" sessions since members who lost elections or retired are still able to cast votes even though voters can no longer hold them accountable. The modern schedule was instituted by the Twentieth Amendment to the Constitution, which was ratified in 1933. Among other provisions, the Twentieth Amendment specified that congressional terms begin on January 3 after the biennial November elections so that the beginnings of sessions now correspond with calendar years.

Before 1933, a typical Congress consisted of a long session lasting from December of odd-numbered years to the following summer, then a short session from December of even-numbered years to the following March. There might also be an "early" or "special" session if the president calls one. The Eighteenth and Seventy-first congresses illustrate this pattern (see the bottom half of table 3.1). Note that the president may choose not to call a special session. The president may also call only the Senate into special session to consider nominations or a treaty. Also note that, during the eighteenth and nineteenth centuries, elections were not all held on the same day.

A key feature of this historic schedule was the short session. Short sessions lasted about three months, but legislators were still obliged to write, pass, and enact a full year's worth of appropriations bills. In addition, they were also often working to pass major legislative items that had been debated but not enacted during the long session. Thus, short sessions often had a heavier workload than long sessions. Furthermore, the last day of the session was fixed and known ahead of time. This means that a legislator contemplating a filibuster had the advantage of knowing exactly how long he would have to last; the rest of the chamber could not outwait the obstructionist by extending the session. Consequently, the short session was considered a ripe time for filibustering.

Bills "survive" from session to session but not from Congress to Congress. Once a bill is introduced, it is available for consideration until it becomes law or until the end of the Congress. Any bill that is reported out of committee or passed by one chamber during the first session, for example, remains at the same legislative situation in the next session. However, if a bill does not become law by the end of one Congress, it must be reintroduced and begin anew in the next Congress. This may influence legislators' filibustering strategies: a filibuster waged during an early session may only delay a bill until a later session, while a filibuster during the final days of a Congress may delay the bill significantly and allow a different set of legislators to make a judgment on the issue. If an obstructionist expects that the next Congress will be dominated by members who share his or her views, then filibustering at the end of a Congress can be especially worthwhile.

MEASURING FILIBUSTERING IN THE HISTORIC CONGRESS

Richard Beth (1995) outlines two basic strategies for identifying filibusters. First, one can catalog filibusters mentioned by classic historical works on Congress. Binder (1997) and Schickler (2001) use this approach to identify key procedural choices, and one could consult the same canonical literature to identify filibusters in the historic Congress. As Beth points out, however, these classic books were not written to catalog every important incident of filibustering in the historic Congress; instead, they mention specific filibusters as examples with the understanding that other such cases exist.[2]

Beth's second measurement strategy—which I adopt here—is to directly identify behavior in the historical record that was *probably* intended to strategically delay the legislative process. This approach is imperfect; some acts classified as obstructive are doubtlessly benign, while some filibustering escapes measurement. The standards used in this chapter are intended to balance these risks, but residual uncertainty remains. All quantities presented below should be understood as estimates, and our confidence in those estimates increases with the level of aggregation.[3]

Prolonged Speaking

One well-known tactic is making *prolonged speeches* to consume time. This is the easiest tactic to understand: an obstructionist can delay votes as long as he and his allies can keep talking. Two factors make this tactic impossible to measure in the early Congress. First, not all long speeches were dilatory—legislators often spoke for hours without any obstructive intent. Second, we lack accurate records of congressional debates for the eighteenth and nineteenth centuries. Since 1873, the *Congressional Record* has kept more or less verbatim accounts of floor debates, but, prior to that time, the *Annals of Congress*, the *Register of Debates*, and the *Congressional Globe* provide only an informal record. These publications sometimes summarize or ignore floor debates arbitrarily or provide verbatim accounts of speeches that members *wish* they had made.

There is, however, an excellent reason not to worry that our inability to measure dilatory speaking taints our estimates of filibustering patterns: speaking is hard to do. A legislative faction intent on obstruction is likely to use tactics that are less taxing on their members, such as dilatory motions or DQs, or at least blend in such tactics with their speeches.[4] We turn now to these less taxing methods.

Identifying Dilatory Motions

A second form of filibustering is making parliamentary motions to waste time, for example, repeatedly proposing that a chamber adjourn for the day. There have been recent efforts to measure dilatory motions in one chamber or the other. Sarah Binder (1997) uses motions to adjourn as a measure of filibustering (labeled *partisan need*) in the historic House. Douglas Dion (1997) analyzes votes on points of order in the House from 1869 to 1891. Gregory Wawro and Eric Schickler (2004, 2006) count the number of Senate votes on *defeated* motions to adjourn, to recess, to table a bill, to postpone, or to switch from legislative business to executive session. The focus on failed motions almost certainly improves measurement of dilatory motions.

In an effort to measure obstruction precisely, I identified every roll call vote on procedural motions typically used to waste time: to adjourn, to recess, to set a time to reconvene after adjourning, to set a time to reconvene after recessing, and to move from legislative to executive business (Senate only).[5] Obstructionists used these motions because they took priority over votes on amendments, final passage of a bill, and (in the House) the

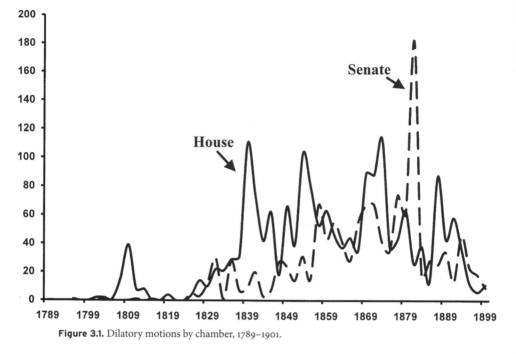

Figure 3.1. Dilatory motions by chamber, 1789–1901.

previous question motion to shut off debate. In the roll call records, they often occur in long sequences—adjourn, recess, set a time for adjourning, recess, adjourn—that suggest stubborn stalling. I identified a total of 2,339 such motions in the House from 1789 to 1901 and 1,983 such votes in the Senate. I then filtered out procedural motions that *passed* so that we can distinguish dilatory motions from efforts by the majority to dictate the schedule of the chamber. In the House, 494 of the suspected votes passed, leaving 1,845 dilatory motions. In the Senate, 713 suspected votes passed, leaving 1,270 dilatory motions.

Figure 3.1 presents the number of dilatory motions in each two-year period for the House and Senate. In the House, the use of dilatory motions peaks in the Twenty-sixth Congress (1839–41), the Thirty-third Congress (1853–55), and the Forty-third Congress (1873–75). The source of turbulence in the Twenty-sixth House was a struggle over control of the chamber and disagreements over economic policy, while almost all the dilatory motions in the Thirty-third House were targeted at a bill to organize the Kansas and Nebraska territories. Twenty years later, Democrats made repeated motions to stall consideration of a civil rights bill during the Forty-third House. The Senate time series is generally higher in the post-Reconstruction era, with a significant spike in the Forty-seventh Congress (1881–83) linked to a dispute over the control of the Senate chamber. The main pattern, however, is that there were more dilatory motions in the House than the Senate throughout most of the historic Congress era. This pattern would be even more pronounced if we weighted the number of dilatory votes by the size of the legislature since votes took longer to complete in the larger House.

Identifying Disappearing Quorums

A third filibustering tactic is the disappearing quorum, in which members refrain from voting in the hope that less than a majority of the chamber will participate in a roll call, rendering the outcome null and void. Consider a known case: In 1879, Senate Republicans filibustered against an army appropriations bill that would have limited troop deployments in the South (Burdette 1940; Haynes 1938; Kerr 1895). During a stretch of thirty-four votes on June 18 and 19, they used both dilatory motions and DQs with some effectiveness. On one June 18 vote to go into executive session, only three of thirty-three Republicans voted, while thirty of forty-two Democrats were present and voting. While it is impossible to infer intent with certainty from the roll call record, it seems unlikely that an overwhelming percentage of Republicans thought it was too nice a day to stay inside and work while most Democrats happened to find that vote worth attending.[6]

While the 1879 case is well documented, how can we systematically distinguish innocent shirking from defiant abstention? We are looking for an unusually high level of absenteeism in one major legislative faction compared to the other(s), so we must identify significant groups of legislators during each Congress and select a standard for seemingly strategic absenteeism. Of necessity, I focus my search on the participation rates of the two major parties at any given time—Federalists and Republicans, Democrats and Whigs, Democrats and Republicans.[7] For specific time periods and issues, one might meaningfully focus on specific party factions and/or cross-party coalitions, but parties are useful groupings if one is scanning the breadth of congressional history.

What is an "unusually high" level of abstention? I classified a vote as a DQ if more than half of one party voted, less than half of the other party voted, and the difference between these two proportions was statistically significant (using a t-test for the difference in proportions between two populations) at the .001 level.[8] While this method may miss some DQs (especially obstruction by a cross-party coalition) and falsely identify some absences as obstruction, it is generally effective at identifying DQs mentioned by descriptive histories.[9] Even if there is measurement error at the margins, this approach should identify the broad patterns of filibustering with some accuracy.

It is not necessary, by this standard, for the obstructing party to successfully deprive its opposition of a working quorum; *attempts* to obstruct

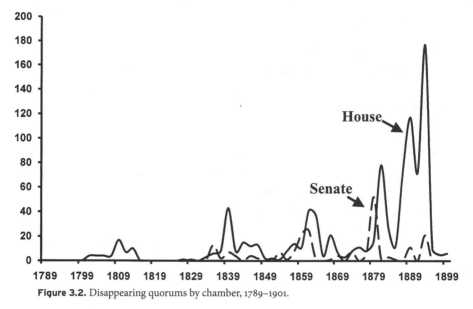

Figure 3.2. Disappearing quorums by chamber, 1789–1901.

are also significant. Below, I will distinguish between "successful" quorum breaking and "attempted" DQs, but both forms suggest that legislators who support a filibustered bill are under some pressure to remain in and around the chamber at all times.

Three patterns are worth noting. First, there were more DQs in the House (927) than in the Senate (209). Second, some DQs were due to majority party abstentions: there were 155 in the House and 28 in the Senate. Finally, less than half of all DQs (41.9 percent in the House, 36.4 percent in the Senate) successfully broke a quorum. These "unsuccessful" DQs are, nonetheless, significant because they raised the costs of fighting a filibuster by forcing bill supporters to stay in attendance on or near the chamber floor.

The use of DQs increased over time, as shown in figure 3.2. The temporal pattern and bicameral differences are clear. First, there were more DQs in the House than in the Senate. Senate DQs peaked in the Forty-sixth Congress, with 52, many of them against the 1879 army appropriations bill. The high point for the House, in contrast, was the Fifty-third Congress (1893–95), with 176 DQs during the struggle over the rules of the House described below. As in figure 3.1 above, there is also a great deal of variation over time to explain.

A key event for the use of DQs in the U.S. House was a precedent set in July 1832, when John Quincy Adams (Anti-Mason-MA) refused to vote on a censure resolution even though he was present and the House would not excuse him from voting. Despite the concern among some members that allowing members to not vote would invite chaos, the House voted 89–63

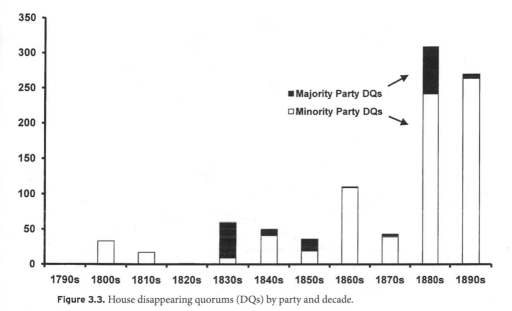

Figure 3.3. House disappearing quorums (DQs) by party and decade.

against punishing the former president.[10] Over the next ten years, strategic nonvoting increased dramatically in the House.

We can further distinguish between DQs by the majority and the minority parties. This is a relevant question for both models of obstruction (which may assume that one party or one pivot is most likely to filibuster) and theories of legislative parties that assume the majority party can keep measures it opposes off the chamber floor and, thus, would not need to filibuster (Cox and McCubbins 1993, 2005). Figures 3.3 and 3.4 illustrate the mix of majority and minority party DQs for the House and Senate, respectively. Clearly, the majority party occasionally filibustered proposals favored by the minority party. One example noted by historians (e.g., Alexander 1916) also shows up in the DQ data: an 1888 filibuster by (mostly Southern) House Democrats blocking a refund of direct taxes levied during the Civil War. Another surge in majority party DQs occurs during the Twenty-sixth Congress (1839–41), when the nominal majority party did not elect its own candidate for speaker and filibustered against (among other things) legislation to distribute revenue to the states (Adams 1969, 10:242).

We can further distinguish between DQs that break quorums (i.e., less than half the chamber votes) and those that do not. Figures 3.5 and 3.6 present these data separately for the House and the Senate. Note the significant difference in scale between the two chambers. There are two ways to view these figures. First, we can emphasize periods with a high rate of broken quorums, such as the House during the 1870s and 1880s and the Senate

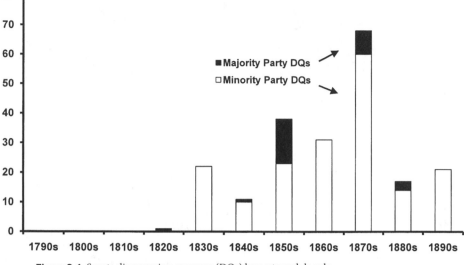

Figure 3.4. Senate disappearing quorums (DQs) by party and decade.

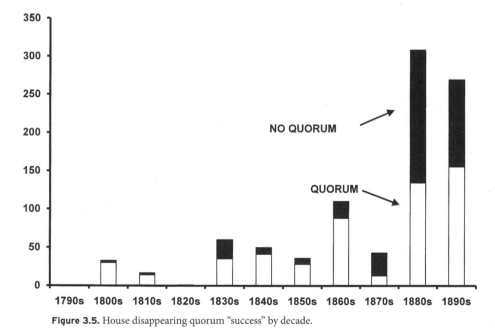

Figure 3.5. House disappearing quorum "success" by decade.

during the 1870s, 1880s, and 1890s. The increase in effective obstruction suggests that filibustering was rampant during the Gilded Age and probably had a significant impact on policy outcomes. When legislators refuse to vote but fail to break a quorum, that suggests that interparty differences were significant enough to motivate obstruction but that majorities were

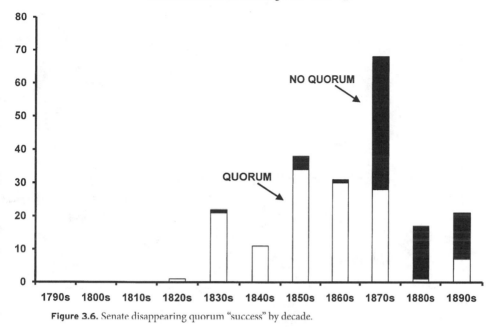

Figure 3.6. Senate disappearing quorum "success" by decade.

usually able to muster a quorum. Such is the case in the antebellum- and Civil War–era House and Senate.

A Combined Measure of Obstruction

The next step is to devise a single combined measure of obstruction. I use a point system: one point for a dilatory motion, one point for a DQ, one point for a DQ that breaks a quorum. The rationale for this approach is that dilatory motions and DQs are separate acts of filibustering, each of which harasses the majority. If a DQ is successful, that is worth additional weight because the chamber must cease to operate while it determines whether enough members are present and, if not, drags absent members back to their duties. Calculated this way, the House's obstruction score for 1789–1901 was 3,160, the Senate's 1,555.

Figure 3.7 displays the obstruction scores aggregated by chamber and Congress. The now-familiar patterns of rising obstruction over time and relatively higher levels of filibustering in the House recur when we combine dilatory motions and DQs into a single measure. The Senate has a higher obstruction score than the House in twelve of the first fifty-six congresses, while the House has a higher score in thirty-six of the first fifty-six congresses.

There is significant value to pooling our data on DQs and dilatory motions. In both chambers, legislators seemed to use these tactics as

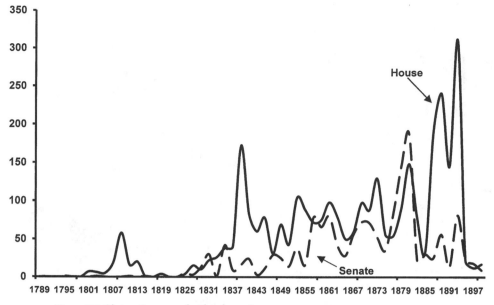

Figure 3.7. Obstruction scores by chamber, 1789–1901.

substitutes rather than complements. The correlation between the number of dilatory motions against filibustered bills (defined in chapter 4) and the number of DQs is a weak .165 in the House and .055 in the Senate. If we used only one measure, we would miss significant bursts of filibustering; the obstruction index offers a smoother, more-rounded portrait of historic filibustering.

Comparison of Measurement Schemes

One of the surprising findings of this section is that there was more obstruction in the House than in the Senate. Is this an artifact of measurement? Generally, how can we be sure that this chapter successfully measures filibustering?

First, consider how this scheme adds precision to our estimates of filibustering. Let us return to the June 1879 filibuster in the Senate. During the thirty-four-vote stretch on June 18 and 19, the Senate voted on fifteen dilatory motions, there were twenty-one DQs, and a quorum was present for only four of these votes. Table 3.2 separates these thirty-four votes by whether they were on dilatory motions, whether a quorum was present, and whether most of one party abstained while most of the other did not.

Table 3.2 suggests that we gain extra precision using a combined approach. Some no quorum votes are not attributable to a pattern of partisan

Table 3.2. Tactics Used during the 1879 Army Appropriations Filibuster

	Disappearing Quorum		No Disappearing Quorum	
	Quorum	No Quorum	Quorum	No Quorum
Dilatory motion	0	6	4	5
Not dilatory	0	15	0	4

Source: ICPSR 0004 (the congressional roll call voting records available from the Inter-University Consortium for Political and Social Research, available at http://www.icpsr.umich .edu), Forty-sixth Senate.

abstention, only some DQs occur on dilatory motions, and only some DQs result in a broken quorum. A variety of measurement strategies will identify a clear-cut filibuster, but, if we want to identify less obvious filibustering, we should strive for as much precision as the constraints of history allow.

Second, by almost any method of measurement that we choose, there was more filibustering in the House than in the Senate. Table 3.3 presents, for both chambers, the estimated level of filibustering using the measurement schemes of other authors. Each of these prior estimates was developed for a single chamber (as noted), so the extrapolation to a second chamber is not necessarily the intent of these authors; I display them for illustration.

Table 3.3. Comparison of Measurement Schemes

	House	Senate
Binder (House):		
Motions to adjourn	1,996	1,382
Dion (House):		
Votes on points of order	386	144
Votes without a quorum present	999	635
Wawro and Schickler (Senate):[a]		
Failed motion to adjourn	1,586	869
Failed motion to recess	67	35
Failed motions to go into executive session		258
Failed motion to postpone a bill:		
1789–1823	167	120
1823–1901	105	498
Total	1,925	1,780
New York Times:		
Filibuster mentions	137	90

Sources: Binder (1997); Dion (1997); and Wawro and Schickler (2006).

[a]Wawro and Schickler count only dilatory motions attributed to specific bills. The totals reported here included similar motions not attributed to a specific bill.

When I apply Binder's and Dion's strategies to the Senate, there is a surplus of filibustering in the House in the number of motions to adjourn, votes on points of order, and votes without a quorum present. Overall, Wawro and Schickler's scheme yields a surplus of House filibustering when applied to the lower chamber. This is true even if we use motions that were either unavailable (going to executive session) or severely constrained (the motion to postpone a bill) in the House. In 1822, the House revised its motion to postpone so that it could be offered only once at each stage in a bill's consideration. Afterward, it was little used in the House. However, senators continued to use the motion, sometimes for dilatory purposes. Wawro (2005), for example, describes an antebellum Senate filibuster in which senators alternated speeches, motions to adjourn, and motions to postpone in the classic pattern of a filibuster.

Despite this good example, I exclude motions to postpone because they were often used for benign agenda-setting purposes. In the nineteenth-century Senate, the agenda was nominally set by the order in which bills were reported from committees and placed on a list of bills known as the "calendar." Motions to postpone were used to switch from discussing the bill next in line to a higher-priority bill that was lower on the Senate calendar.[11] For example, the bill targeted by the most motions to postpone in the historic Senate was House Resolution (HR) 986 in the Forty-first Congress (1869–71), a bill to abolish the franking privilege for members of Congress. Senators apparently wanted to avoid this bill: a vote to consider it ahead of schedule failed 22–34. When HR 986 came up on the calendar, it was repeatedly skipped over in favor of other bills. In all, senators made eleven motions to postpone it, six of which were successful. HR 986 eventually disappeared into oblivion—not because it was obstructed, but because few senators seemed interested.

In short, the prevalence of filibustering in the House is not an artifact; we find the same pattern using schemes devised by other authors. Furthermore, there is near consensus that making motions to adjourn—which make up the lion's share of dilatory motions—has commonly been used as a filibustering tactic.

As an external test of my measurement strategy, I examined every use of the word *filibuster* in the *New York Times* from 1850 to 1900. A majority of the articles in which I found the term used it in its classic sense: a *filibuster* was a pirate or an adventurer, particularly one who tried to instigate or promote revolt in a foreign country. Of the 227 articles referring to filibustering in Congress, 137 use the term to discuss a filibuster, a possible filibuster, or filibuster reform in the House. While this is an imprecise measure, it does offer external validation for the claim that filibustering was more prevalent in the House than in the Senate. Moreover, the pattern of filibuster mentions

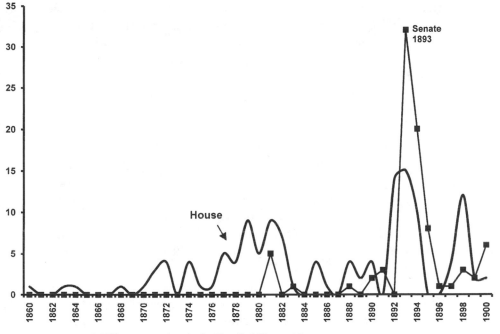

Figure 3.8. Filibuster mentions in the *New York Times*, 1860–1900.

in the *Times* shown in figure 3.8 corresponds, roughly, to the pattern noted in this chapter: increasing gradually over time and peaking in the 1880s and 1890s. The low level of mentions in the early years of the period in question probably reflects both the low level of obstruction and the gradual adoption of the term *filibuster* to describe legislative behavior. The Senate time line spikes in 1893 owing to the strong interest of the *Times* in a bill to restore the country to the gold standard—a topic of extreme interest to the financial center of the nation.

MAJOR REFORM IN THE HOUSE, 1890-94

A dominant pattern in the obstruction data is a dramatic increase in filibustering in the House during the 1880s and the early 1890s, followed by a sharp drop-off. Behind this pattern is a seminal event in congressional history: a period of obstruction-induced paralysis followed by a four-year struggle to impose majority rule in the chamber. This section recounts this battle to suppress filibustering in the House of Representatives.

After a decade of increasing obstruction in the House, the Fiftieth Congress (1887–89) was especially dysfunctional. The primary cause of this gridlock was filibustering in the House during the tenure of Speaker John Carlisle (D-KY). As Alexander (1916) explains: "By the time Carlisle reached his third term as Speaker it became so easy to muster a sufficient number of disgruntled members to delay or prevent legislation that the House, in the Fiftieth Congress, although in continuous session longer than any of its predecessors, passed only one measure except such as received unanimous consent" (62). Alexander concludes: "Carlisle's administration during the Fiftieth Congress came perilously near being a failure. . . . [D]ilatory motions, the disappearing quorum, and his refusal to ascertain the presence of a quorum by counting the House made him the slave of filibusters" (205).

The most intense filibuster was provoked by a bill to reimburse states for income taxes levied by the federal government during the Civil War—a bill that would primarily benefit Northern states. For a week in April, a filibuster led by Samuel Weaver (Greenback-Iowa) and Clifton Breckinridge (D-AR) kept the House from passing the bill.[12] Bill opponents—mostly Southern Democrats—made forty-one dilatory motions and, on fifty-two occasions, refused to vote in an effort to break a quorum. This is one of the fiercest *majority* party filibusters in House history. The bill eventually passed during the short session of the Fiftieth Congress, only to be vetoed by President Cleveland.

The House Republicans held a 51 percent majority in the Fifty-first Congress and had an ambitious policy agenda to advance: raising tariff rates, increasing pensions for veterans and widows, a federal election bill, admitting Oklahoma as a territory and Idaho and Wyoming as states, and a silver purchase bill.[13] House Republicans expected the Democratic minority to obstruct their agenda; Democratic leaders publicly vowed to veto any bill they opposed (Robinson 1930, 182–88; McKinley 1890). Furthermore, the ability of the majority party to filibuster could have also proved disastrous to the Republican Party since there was internal party opposition on several agenda items (Schickler 2001). If majority party factions were able to filibuster—or refuse to help end a minority filibuster—the Republican agenda could be jeopardized.

The Republicans elected Thomas Reed as speaker in December 1889. Instead of adopting the rules of the Fiftieth Congress on a temporary basis while the Rules Committee prepared a new set of rules (the normal practice), Reed ran the House for the first few weeks using *general parliamentary law*; since this term had little precise meaning, Reed had extra discretion in his parliamentary rulings.

Reed waited until the House began debating a contested election case, *Smith v. Jackson*, on January 29, 1890. Democrats refused to vote on the motion to consider this case, but Reed directed the House clerk to note that several Democrats were present but not voting, thereby making a quorum. After heated debate, this ruling was sustained 162–0 the next day, with no Democrats voting. On January 31, a second ruling (163–0, again no Democrats voting) affirmed the speaker's right to ignore dilatory motions. In three days, the Republicans had transformed the House. Two weeks later, a package of rules proposed by the Rules Committee codifying Reed's rulings passed the House 163–147.

During the 1890 elections, the Democrats criticized the House Republicans' drastic rulemaking and their subsequent legislative activism. They scored a dramatic electoral victory, increasing their share of House seats from 47.3 to 69.4 percent. On taking power, the Democrats (led by Speaker Charles Crisp) repealed the Republicans' rules authorizing the speaker to count a quorum and ignore dilatory motions. Within three years, the Democrats would reverse their position on both issues.

While the Democrats eliminated the rule allowing the speaker to ignore dilatory motions, the Democrat-proposed rules empowered the Rules Committee to propose resolutions that accomplished the same purpose (Follett 1974, 214).[14] At the beginning of the Fifty-third Congress, the Democrats further enhanced the power of the Rules Committee to suppress obstruction by allowing it the right to meet at any time without permission from the chamber. Together, these reforms indirectly suppressed dilatory motions by enabling majorities to prohibit them on an ad hoc basis.

The readoption of a rule for counting a quorum was more dramatic. During the Fifty-second Congress, the Democrats held about 70 percent of the seats, so they found it relatively easy to maintain a quorum in the face of Republican obstruction. Most Republicans refrained from voting on seventy-two votes but broke a quorum fifteen times. During the Fifty-third Congress, however, the smaller Democratic majority (about 60 percent of House seats) found it more difficult to muster chamber majorities since many House members returned to their districts to campaign and work. Poor attendance and Republican obstruction brought the Democrats to their knees.

After silver purchase repeal legislation passed at the beginning of the Fifty-third Congress, the Republicans began one of the most prolonged and extraordinary filibusters in congressional history: a permanent filibuster to force a change in the rules of the House.[15] The filibuster began on September 1, 1893, when the House rejected a Reed amendment to the rules that would have reduced dilatory motions, and lasted until April 17, 1894, when the Democrats proposed a quorum-counting rule. There were 157 Republican DQs on 222 roll calls and 91 broken quorums. For months, the Democrats were so committed to minority rights that they endured delay, defeat, and embarrassment rather than empower themselves. After seven and a half months, the Republicans got their wish: the Democrats proposed a rule depriving them of their filibustering tactics. The Democratic quorum-counting rule passed 213–47 (Democrats 125–47, Republicans 87–0) on April 17, 1894.[16]

These changes marked a transformation in the House. While House members have continued to obstruct, the rules changes adopted in the early

1890s effectively curtailed the two major tactics of House filibustering: dilatory motions and DQs.

CONCLUSION

This chapter makes a unique contribution to the study of filibustering. It identifies obstructive behavior and summarizes patterns of filibustering in the historic Congress. The dominant patterns are a relatively higher level of filibustering in the House and a general increase over the course of the nineteenth-century in both chambers. One finds a sharp decrease in filibustering in the House after a bipartisan majority adopted antifilibuster reforms in 1894 and a gradual decline in Senate filibustering over the last two decades of the nineteenth century.

Obviously, the relatively high level of obstruction in the historic House punctures the claims that filibustering is unique to the Senate and that filibustering is due to the Senate's unequal apportionment, the continuance of Senate rules from Congress to Congress, or the lack of a previous question motion in the Senate. We also learn from the nineteenth-century House that a legislature *can* suppress filibustering if a sufficiently determined majority is willing to pay the electoral and institutional costs of imposing majority rule.

CHAPTER 4

Filibusters in the Historic Congress

Chapter 3 measures acts of obstruction, and chapter 5 explains patterns of obstruction across time and space. It is important, however, to demonstrate that this obstruction had real consequences. This chapter is about filibusters—*systematic* struggles to block particular bills, treaties, or nominations for strategic gain. By studying filibusters, we can better understand which topics provoked obstruction in the historic Congress and how obstruction influenced legislative outcomes. I develop a strategy for identifying filibusters and then explain their variation over time, issue content, and outcomes.

IDENTIFYING FILIBUSTERS

I began by identifying the bill targeted by each act of obstruction. As a first cut, I used the bill number linked to each vote in the *Database of Historical Congressional Statistics* (Swift et al., 2000). Since many dilatory motions are not linked to bills in this data set, I went through the vote descriptions as well to identify bills connected to procedural motions, for example, "motion to adjourn, during debate on HR 1." As a third cut, I combed the *Journals* of the House and Senate and the various records of debates (*Annals of Congress*, *Register of Debates*, *Congressional Globe*, *Congressional Record*) to identify bills that were on the floor or upcoming when an obstructive action occurred.[1]

The next step is selecting a threshold for identifying a filibuster. First, I summed the obstruction scores for each bill. For example, in February 1881, House Resolution (HR) 7026, a bill to reapportion seats after the 1880 census, was stalled in the House by eight dilatory motions (+8) and three disappearing quorums (DQs) (+3), two of which were successful (+2), for a score of 13. The next step is to select a minimum obstruction score to qualify a bill as a filibuster target. Figure 4.1 displays for each chamber the number of bills with scores from 2 to 20 or more. Bills with scores of 1 are not shown; there were 494 such bills in the House and 293 in the Senate. Figure 4.1 shows the now-familiar surplus of filibustering in the House relative to the

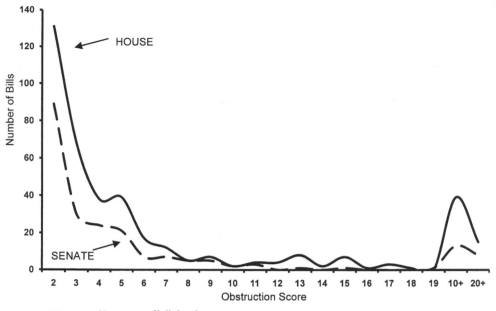

Figure 4.1. Histogram of bills by obstruction score.

Senate. Also, while a large number of bills encounter some degree of apparent obstruction, the number of bills we might consider filibustered drops sharply as the threshold increases.

While figure 4.1 helps, it is likely that any standard for defining a filibuster is imprecise. Again, there is a trade-off between identifying benign behavior as filibustering and failing to measure truly obstructive behavior. Aided by my efforts to link obstructive acts to specific bills, I selected an obstruction score of 4 as the threshold. There were some bills with scores of 3 that appeared to face a filibuster, and some bills with scores of 4 may not have been filibustered, but this threshold should, I hope, minimize the overall number of errors. The designation of a particular bill as the target of a filibuster is subject to uncertainty, especially for bills with scores at or close to 4.

FILIBUSTERS: NUMBER AND SUCCESS RATES

We begin by measuring the incidence and outcomes of filibusters over time. Figure 4.2 displays the number of filibusters in the U.S. House. As a rough measure of the effects of filibustering, I determined whether the filibustered bills passed the chamber in which the obstruction occurred. It is possible, of course, that bills might fail for reasons that have nothing to do with filibustering, that filibusters forced amendments to targeted bills, or that the set of

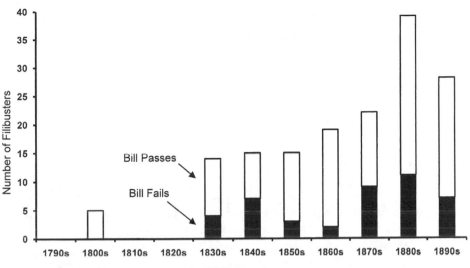

Figure 4.2. Filibuster outcomes in the U.S. House, 1789–1901.

filibustered bills is quite similar to other legislation. Readers are encouraged to treat these results as suggestive.

The historical pattern seen in figure 4.2 is familiar. The number of filibusters increases over time and then drops off in the 1890s after the major institutional changes of 1894. Second, since 43 of 157 filibustered bills failed (27 percent), we can dismiss two simplistic notions about filibustering in the nineteenth-century House. Some filibusters did not result in the targeted bills failing, so there is some potential for obstructionists to fail or to compromise. On the other hand, it seems likely that filibustering diminished the prospects for a number of bills in the historic House, particular during the Jacksonian era and the Gilded Age.

Figure 4.3 displays the equivalent data for the U.S. Senate. Overall, 21 percent (eighteen of eighty-four) of filibustered bills failed. One interesting pattern is that, while the number of filibusters gradually increases over time and peaks in the 1870s, the number of filibustered bills that fail peaks in the 1880s. This suggests that senators became more selective in their obstruction and preferred to filibuster only when their prospects of success were high. Perhaps, that is, Reconstruction-era senators filibustered to protest or delay, while Gilded Age senators filibustered primarily to influence outcomes. Note too that the number of filibusters drops off after 1891. A possible explanation for this drop-off is that public scrutiny of Senate filibustering increased during this decade, owing in part to the drastic changes going on in the House. Also, Senate filibustering was sharply criticized during and after an 1893 filibuster against a bill ending the government purchase

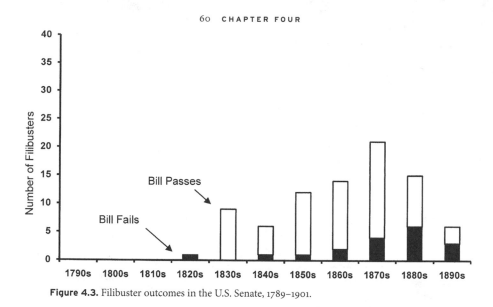

Figure 4.3. Filibuster outcomes in the U.S. Senate, 1789–1901.

of silver bullion (e.g., Lodge 1893; Von Holst 1893). This increase in public scrutiny may have increased the political costs of filibustering.

EARLY FILIBUSTERS IN THE HOUSE AND SENATE

During the First Congress, both the House and the Senate drew on the rules of the British House of Commons and parliamentary practice in the colonial legislatures and the Continental Congress (Binder and Smith 1997; Luce 1922). In the beginning, neither chamber had a specific rule for ending debate by majority vote, but this omission did not constitute an embrace of filibustering. Thomas Jefferson's *Manual of Parliamentary Practice* (1801), which was a key reference source for early senators, stated: "No one is to speak impertinently or beside the question, superfluously or tediously" (40). In lieu of a formal rule for ending debate, legislators making speeches and motions were expected to use self-restraint, and those trying to finalize a decision were expected to exercise patience. The combination of self-restraint and patience would ensure speedy decisions without artificially constraining debate.

Did this system discourage obstruction? Early accounts of the First Congress suggest that members of the House and Senate strategically dragged out discussion during debate on the location of the national capital (Burdette 1940, 14). There is little evidence in the data, however, of a sustained filibuster using dilatory tactics prior to 1807.[2]

Between 1807 and 1811, there were six filibusters in the House, as shown in table 4.1. The first case was a minor tariff bill—and, perhaps, a case of shirking rather than obstruction. Twenty of twenty-eight Federalists were absent

Table 4.1. House Filibusters, 1807–11

Congress	Description	Clausen	Obstruction Score	Outcome
Ninth	Repealing a salt tariff and extending the Mediterranean Fund (February 1807)	Government management	4	Law
Tenth	Resolution opposing trade edicts of Great Britain (December 1808)	Foreign policy	5	Pass
Eleventh	Massachusetts contested election: *Baylies v. Turner* (June 1809)	Internal/misc.	5	Pass
Eleventh	Resolution regarding conduct of the British Minister (January 1810)	Foreign policy	7	Pass
Eleventh	Reinstating trade with England and France (April 1810)	Foreign policy	4	Law
Eleventh	Banning British imports until edicts are lifted (February 1811)	Foreign policy	15	Law

for the debate on this bill to extend tariffs, but the large Republican majority carried on without losing a quorum. A second filibuster occurred at the beginning of the Eleventh Congress as the House decided whether Baylies or Turner was the rightful winner of a Massachusetts race. The Republican majority sided with Turner, who was a Republican, but a minority slowed this action with dilatory motions and a broken quorum.

The remaining four House filibusters during this era all pertain to the efforts of Great Britain and France to reduce each other's foreign trade. Presidents Jefferson and Madison, backed by Congress, opposed this policy as a breach of American sovereignty and responded by restricting U.S. trade with these belligerent countries (see Heaton 1941). This issue evoked both strong economic interests and passionate patriotism.

The most intense of these was the 1811 bill permitting trade with Great Britain once its trade edicts were lifted. The opponents of this bill used eight dilatory motions, six DQs, and long speeches to delay the bill. In the early morning hours of February 28, 1811, a frustrated Republican majority moved and approved the previous question (PQ). Thomas Gholson, a member of the Republican majority, made a point of order that debate was not allowed after the PQ had been approved.[3] When Barent Gardenier, a particularly loquacious obstructionist, rose to speak on the point of order, another member (Peter Porter) made a second point of order that debate is not allowed on challenges to the chair's rulings. All eight Federalists voted to allow debate on challenges; Republicans voted 66–5 to prohibit it. Once debate on rulings from the chair was stifled, Gholson's point of order was approved. In two quick votes, the PQ motion was, thus, transformed from a means of endorsing further debate to a tool for ending debate, although, as we have seen, the transformation of the PQ did not end filibustering in the House.

It is noteworthy that the first observed filibusters occurred in the House, not the Senate. While the volatile mix of trade and international conflict surely promoted strong opinions, it is also interesting that we do not observe filibusters in either chamber during the late 1790s, when the same issues were high on the nation's agenda. One likely reason is chamber size. By 1807, the House had 141 members, while there were just 34 senators. The larger House included cantankerous members like Barent Gardenier (Fed-NY) and John Randolph (R-VA), who expressed their intense views in long speeches and dilatory motions (Burdette 1940, 15–19).

As for the Senate, legislators and pundits often state that the first Senate filibuster was in 1841, as suggested by the Congressional Research Service list (Beth 1994).[4] A systematic search of the Senate voting record, however, reveals an earlier candidate. Late in the evening on March 2, 1831, the Senate began to consider HR 564, a bill to alter a drawbridge across the Potomac.[5] The Senate rejected five motions to adjourn by senators John Forsyth (Jackson-GA), William King (Jackson-AL), and John Tyler (Jackson-GA), with five to seven senators opposing the bill and eighteen to twenty-one supporting it. While the historical record is slender, it is possible that these senators considered this bill a reckless expenditure on internal improvements. This first filibuster was effective since the Senate finally adjourned and HR 564 was neglected for the rest of the short session.

While the defeat of HR 564 was inconspicuous, another early filibuster was a seminal event of the 1830s. In 1834, the Senate (led by Henry Clay) censured President Jackson for his policy of removing federal deposits from the national bank and distributing them to a network of state banks. Jackson and his supporters were determined to cleanse this insult from the historical record. Several state legislatures replaced their senators with pro-Jackson men or instructed their senators to vote to expunge the censure from the Senate record (Riker 1955). This effort reached fruition in 1837 when a resolution to remove the censure came to the Senate floor on January 12.

Senators debated the expunging resolution for days. To some senators, Jackson was a symbol of popular sovereignty, and the people had the right to realign their institutions and to control their elected officials; others portrayed him as a prototyrant, a demagogue who used popular support to undermine the constitutional order. Jackson supporters like Thomas Benton (D-MO) suspected that the opponents of the resolution intended to delay it as long as possible. By January 16, the Jackson senators were ready to finish the debate, and they prepared to remain in session all night with "an ample supply . . . of cold hams, turkeys, beef, pickles, wines, and cups of hot coffee" (Burdette 1940, 20). Debate continued into the evening, but the anti-Jackson coalition relented after a motion to adjourn failed, and the resolution passed 24–19. The secretary of the Senate then pulled out the *Journal* of the preceding Congress and inked out the offending passage as spectators in the Senate galleries hissed.

Another partisan debate is missing from my filibuster list: the firing and replacement of Senate printers in 1841. This is the first filibuster on the Congressional Research Service list and, consequently, often cited as the first Senate filibuster. During this era, Congress contracted out the printing of public documents to private printers.[6] The candidates for congressional printers were the two or three leading newspapers in Washington, DC, each of which was the mouthpiece of a political party or party faction. Congressional printing was a de facto subsidy for one of these printers and a major political prize. During the 1830s, each chamber chose its printer for the next Congress during the preceding short session. Thus, in February 1841, the outgoing Democratic majority selected Jackson's allies Blair and Rives, publishers of the *Washington Globe*, as the Senate printers for the Twenty-seventh Congress.

The incoming Whig majority senators were determined not to subsidize their critics for two years. One of their first proposals during the special session of the Twenty-seventh Congress in March 1841 was a resolution to fire the Senate's printers. This provoked five days of fierce Democratic criticism (Burdette 1940, 21) but apparently not an attempt to filibuster the proposal. Nor were the conditions favorable for an effective filibuster: fewer than twenty minority party members opposed the resolution, and the majority party could extend the special session until December. The resolution passed 26–18 on March 11.

In June 1841, the Senate began to choose a replacement printer, and the filibustering was unambiguous. The Democrats considered the decision to fire the previous printers illegitimate and refused to vote on the selection of a new printer. Two efforts to hire a Whig printer, Thomas Allen, failed because fewer than half the Senate participated in the vote (*Congressional Globe* 10 [June 15, 1841]: 52). The Whigs mustered a bare quorum on the third ballot without Democratic aid. These votes were not recorded as roll calls, so they are not included in my data set. If these ballots were recorded, it seems apparent from the *Congressional Globe* that they would reveal three Democratic DQs, two of which were successful, for an obstruction score of 5. Even so, it is not the Senate's first filibuster; as I have shown, there were earlier filibusters in 1831 and 1834.

WHICH ISSUES WERE FILIBUSTERED?

In chapter 2, I suggested that filibusters are more likely on issues that members care deeply about. This is a difficult proposition to test scientifically since we lack measures of how much legislators care about a proposal independent of the decision to filibuster. Nonetheless, we can gain some insight by categorizing the filibustered bills into issue areas and evaluating whether the issue composition matches our intuitions about what was important to nineteenth-century legislators.

I present the data for three eras: 1831–61, 1861–81, and 1881–1901.[7] The first era corresponds to the antebellum Age of Jackson when the Democrats and Whigs fought fiercely over economic policy but slavery increasingly dominated the national agenda, leading to the rise of the Republican Party. The second era includes the Civil War and Reconstruction and was marked by conflicts over slavery, the war, civil rights for freed slaves, and the postwar South. Finally, from 1881 to 1901, the Republican and Democratic parties clashed over trade policy with underlying debates over civil rights, economic development, and economic inequality.

I rely on the Clausen coding scheme (see Clausen 1973; and Poole and Rosenthal 1997, 259) to link each filibuster to an issue area. Clausen categorized votes into (1) government management, that is, federal budgeting and regulation; (2) social welfare; (3) agriculture; (4) civil liberties, including slavery and segregation; (5) foreign and defense policy; and (6) miscellaneous, including votes related to the rules and practice of either chamber. I matched bills to issues on the basis of the issue coding of their final-passage votes or other final-stage votes (e.g., third reading and engrossment); failing that, I used the dominant issue coding for preliminary and amendment votes.

Overview of House Filibusters by Issue Areas

Figure 4.4 displays the distribution for the House over all three periods. In each era, most filibusters are against bills related to budgeting and regulation. This includes appropriations and tariff bills, bankruptcy legislation, and bills affecting the distribution of public land. Seven bills in this category, however, pertain to the admission of states and the secession of Southern states and, thus, have significant implications for slavery and sectional rivalry. In addition, there were eleven filibusters related to civil rights and slavery during the Civil War and Reconstruction era. Another popular target of filibustering—contested-election cases—also had civil rights implications. There were eighteen filibusters linked to contested-election disputes, all classified as miscellaneous. Twelve of these occurred after 1861, and several were in Southern states where efforts to suppress voting by freed slaves were part of the dispute. Another popular target for filibustering was rules changes. Fifteen efforts to organize the House, reshape the parliamentary process, elect a speaker, or change the committee structure of the House were filibustered (see Alexander 1916; Robinson 1930).[8]

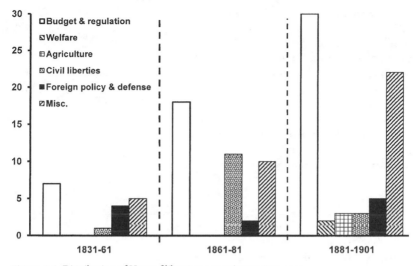

Figure 4.4. Distribution of House filibusters across issues, 1829–1901.

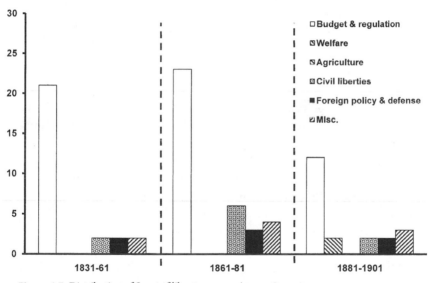

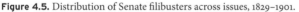

Figure 4.5. Distribution of Senate filibusters across issues, 1829–1901.

Figure 4.5 displays an equivalent breakdown of filibusters in the Senate. As in the House, the plurality of bills (fifty-six) targeted for filibusters were related to budget and regulation. Twelve of these bills, however, were related to admitting states or responding to the secession of Southern states. Unlike the House, only one of these filibusters was an election case: that of Matthew Butler of South Carolina, 1877. The primary issue difference between the House and the Senate was the relative lack of filibusters on organizational

Table 4.2. Organizational Issues Filibustered in the House and Senate

House	Senate
Slavery petition gag rule (1839)	Election of Senate officers (1881)
Slavery petition gag rule (1841)	Rule change permitting majority
Election of speaker (1855–56)	cloture (temporarily) (1891)
Election of speaker (1859–60)	
Setting aside Capitol rooms for impeachment trial (1868)	
Authorize investigation of Southern states (1871)	
Referring rule change to Rules Committee (1876)	
Establish committee to investigate elections in Florida, South Carolina, and Louisiana (1876–77)	
Rule change limiting obstruction against contested election cases (1882)	
Special rule[a] permitting a direct vote on a tariff bill (1883)	
Rule change allowing expedited approval of bills (1885)	
Rule change allowing members to add tax increases to pension bills (to cover the costs) (1886)	
Rule change suspending the call of states (1889)	
Resolution simplifying the call of committees (1893)	
Rule change to better enforce attendance rule (1894)	

[a] This was the first "special order" or "special rule" reported from the Rules Committee applying to a specific bill.

matters such as rules changes or committee authority. Table 4.2 displays a list of all rule- and organization-related filibusters. While there were well-publicized filibusters against the organization of the Senate in 1881 and a majority cloture proposal in 1891, there were more such filibusters in the historic House than in the historic Senate. The next three sections discuss the issues debated and specific filibusters in greater detail.

FILIBUSTERS DURING THE AGE OF JACKSON

From 1828 to 1845, three issues were especially likely to provoke filibusters: tariffs, fiscal policy, and public land management. Each of these policy domains involved the distribution of economic (and, hence, political) benefits and costs and provoked animosity among members and between parties.

Trade tariffs were the primary source of federal revenue, a means of cultivating targeted industries and channeling aid to specific constituents and districts. The 1828 "tariff of abominations" bill raised tariffs so high that the state of South Carolina asserted a right to "nullify" federal laws and refused to collect the new tariff. An 1833 compromise tariff bill was filibustered in both chambers but eventually became law. In 1844, the Democratic majority proposed a reduction of the tariffs, which motivated sharp speeches and a few dilatory motions. In its final stages, *supporters* of the bill filibustered while trying in vain to muster enough votes to pass the bill.

Another major economic issue was currency and banking policy. One of the major issues of the Jackson administration was the president's decision to divorce the federal government from the national bank. In 1834, House members debated and obstructed a resolution condemning Jackson's decision to remove federal deposits from the national bank and reallocate them to allied state banks. Subsequently, bills to redistribute federal revenue to state governments met obstruction in 1840 and 1842.

A third major policy topic was public land policy, the subject of six filibustered bills. The question of whether and how to sell federal land was linked to economic class, regional interests, and legislators' desire to avoid rewarding speculators while keeping federal land open to new settlers. These questions motivated two filibusters in 1832–33 and two more in 1836–37. In 1840 and 1841, the Senate debated whether and how the proceeds from the sale of public land should be shared among the states, and both proposals faced a minority party filibuster; in 1841, the Whigs succeeded in enacting their bill.

A precursor to the battles to come was an 1840 filibuster in the House against a rule prohibiting the acceptance of petitions from citizens related to slavery. While the House had adopted similar restrictions before on a temporary basis, in 1840 the antiabolition majority sought to make this rule permanent (Ludlum 1941; Remini 2006, 128–30). This move antagonized Northern legislators into making several dilatory motions.

Over the next two decades, the number of filibusters linked to slavery and territorial expansion increased. New territories, of course, were inescapably linked to the possible expansion of slavery and the balance of power between slave and free states. From 1845 to 1861, there were twelve filibusters—five in the Senate, seven in the House—related to new territories. The debate over the admission of California as a state after the Mexican-American War accounted for five of these filibusters.

Efforts to bring Kansas into the union as a slave state also sparked fierce obstruction. After the Senate passed its version of the Kansas-Nebraska Act in March 1854, the House began weeks of debate on the bill. This bill—which repealed the Missouri Compromise of 1820—was delayed by hours of debate in the Committee of the Whole, and votes on seventy-six dilatory motions by Northern Whigs (72 percent of motions) and Democrats (28 percent), especially from New York (44 percent), Maine (15 percent), and Ohio (12 percent), were recorded. The obstruction score for this bill (76) was the highest of the period in either chamber and almost three times the next highest score.

The Kansas-Nebraska Act left it to Kansas settlers to determine whether their state would permit slavery. Settlers from both sides poured into Kansas to swing the balance, resulting in civil conflict and competing territorial legislatures and constitutions. This conflict bled into congressional debate. In December 1856, the House had to decide whether John Whitfield—chosen in elections held by the proslavery government in Lecompton—was legitimately elected. Pro-Whitfield legislators, led by John Phelps (D-MO), called for seventeen roll call votes on dilatory motions to delay the House's action on Whitfield's election. Days later, Whitfield was sworn in.

The Kansas controversy also motivated an intense majority party filibuster. In February 1858, President Buchanan sent a message to Congress urging the admission of Kansas as a slave state under the Constitution written by the Lecompton legislature. When the president's message arrived in the House, an antislavery coalition of the minority Republicans and a few Democrats proposed to send the message to an antislavery special committee, while most Democrats sought to send the message to the proslavery Committee on Territories.[9] Sensing that they were outnumbered, proslavery legislators sought to delay a decision—first by adjourning for a few days, then by filibustering. Twenty dilatory motions, six DQs, and three broken quorums later, the majority party succeeded in delaying the issue until the following Monday.[10] This filibuster—the second most intense of the era—suggested that the majority party lacked procedural control over the chamber agenda on this issue.

Another nine filibusters were directly related to the emergence of the Republican Party and the dissolution of the union. Two of these were prolonged speaker elections in 1855–56 and 1859–60. The first election helped crystallize the nascent antislavery coalition (Jenkins and Nokken 2000), and the second stalemated over pro- and antislavery issues. In both cases, dilatory motions were interspersed with the repeated ballots for speaker as one faction or another sought to delay the proceedings.

Another five filibusters were directly related to slavery. In February 1859, senators debated a bill to appropriate funds to buy Cuba from Spain (Spain was not interested); filibustering prolonged debate, but the bill also lacked support and was defeated. In May 1860, a Senate debate over several proslavery resolutions was marked by six Republican DQs, which both harassed the proceedings and shielded Republicans from making a statement for the public record on the issue. During the short session of the Thirty-sixth Congress, three measures—to respond to South Carolina's secession, to resolve sectional differences, and to amend the Constitution to guarantee noninterference with slavery—overcame filibustering to pass Congress, all for naught.

Finally, Democrats filibustered two bills that the Republicans used to solidify their party coalition before the 1860 election. One bill became the Morrill Tariff Act of 1861. The House passed the Morrill bill in 1860, after which the Republican Party convention met and endorsed an increase in the protective tariff. The Morrill bill came up in the Senate in the short session of the Thirty-sixth Congress. Despite seven dilatory motions (six by Democrats) and four DQs by the Democrats (the majority party), the Morrill bill passed the Senate and became law, possibly accelerating South Carolina's break with the Union (Faulkner 1929). Second, in 1860, Congress passed a bill increasing homesteaders' access to public land. The Republicans' 1860 platform explicitly endorsed this bill. After light obstruction in the Senate (four dilatory motions), the bill passed but was killed by Buchanan's veto; the homestead bill became law in 1862 after Lincoln became president. Thus, the issues that sparked filibustering were, as anticipated, some of the most contentious questions of the age.

FILIBUSTERS DURING THE CIVIL WAR AND RECONSTRUCTION

Of the fifty-six filibusters that occurred between 1861 and 1877, half were linked to the Civil War, Reconstruction, and civil rights. Another nine were against tariff and tax bills, including four between 1861 and 1865 that were arguably tied to the prosecution of the war. Other repeat topics were railroads (four filibusters), using silver as currency (two), and appropriations (five). Five bills that faced a filibuster—four in the House, one in the Senate—failed to pass the chamber in which legislators obstructed the bills. Another nine (five House, four Senate) faced obstruction in one chamber, passed, then died in the other chamber.

One major fight concerned the decision by President Lincoln to suspend the right of habeas corpus to help suppress insurrection in Northern and border states. This decision was a key topic during the 1862 election, and, when Republicans returned to Congress for the short session, they passed a bill to shield Lincoln and executive agents from personal liability for suspending habeas corpus. The Republicans were apparently intent on passing this bill with as little discussion as possible because on three separate occasions House Democrats had to filibuster to protect their right to amend and criticize it. Finally, the House approved the conference report on March 2, 1863, and sent the bill to the Senate. When the bill arrived, senators deferred debate until 7 P.M. that evening. Republicans, led by Lyman Trumbull (R-IL), sought assurances that the bill's opponents would not filibuster if they agreed to postpone debate (*Congressional Globe*, 33, pt. 2 [March 2, 1863]: 1437–38). Trumbull should have gotten his answer in writing; at 7 P.M., Senator Wall (D-NJ) made a five-hour speech against the bill. Bill opponents combined speeches with motions to adjourn into the morning of March 3. After the fifth defeated motion to adjourn, the presiding officer (Pomeroy, R-KS) swiftly posed the question on the conference report.

Before the opponents realized what was happening, Pomeroy declared the report passed by acclamation, and Trumbull moved to consider a different bill. The habeas corpus bill thus slipped past a filibuster in the final hours of the Thirty-seventh Congress.

The use of filibustering to demand the right to debate and amend legislation was not unique to the habeas corpus bill. For example, the House minority party used similar tactics when faced with an 1866 bill requiring loyalty oaths for officials of the federal court and an 1870 resolution revising the government's contract with the Northern Pacific Railroad. In 1878, the *New York Times* suggested that this was common practice in the House: "The tactics resorted to by the [filibustering] Republicans . . . are by no means new. They have been resorted to whenever the majority has sought to crowd its measures through without giving the minority the right to be heard. The right of the minority to debate, and to offer amendments, has been insisted upon and maintained scores of times, not only by refusing to vote, and thus breaking a quorum, but by dilatory motions, in the nature of what is called filibustering" ("The Deadlock Continues" 1).

Perhaps the most significant filibuster of the era was its last. The presidential election of 1876 was a critical event in American history, with a House filibuster at the center of the dispute. The contest between Rutherford B. Hayes and Samuel J. Tilden hinged on the electoral votes of Louisiana, Florida, and South Carolina, with each party claiming victory in these Southern states (for overviews, see Morris 2003; and Woodward 1951). If Hayes proved that he was the rightful winner of all three states, then the election was his; otherwise, Tilden would win the White House. Congressional leaders hammered out a compromise solution: an independent, bipartisan commission to investigate the elections in the three states and recommend which candidate won each state. The recommendations of the electoral commission would be sustained unless both chambers voted to overturn them. The commission recommended that the electoral votes of all three states go to Hayes.

This result was unacceptable to a determined faction of about sixty House Democrats (Woodward 1951, 201). Beginning on February 24, they made repeated dilatory motions and offered gratuitous resolutions to delay the counting of electoral votes (*New York Times*, February 25, 1877, 1). Even after the electoral votes of the three contested states were accepted as valid by Congress, the obstructionist Democrats manufactured challenges to the electoral votes of other states, for example, Vermont and Wisconsin.

Behind the scenes, there were negotiations to end the filibuster. It is unclear whether the result was an explicit quid pro quo (see, e.g., Hoogenboom 1995, 274–94; Morris 2003; Peskin 1973; and Woodward 1951). However, it is clear that the Democrats' bargaining chip was the threat of continued House obstruction and that the end of the filibuster was tied to several political and policy concessions, including the removal of federal troops to maintain order in Southern states, the appointment of a Southerner as postmaster general (or, more broadly, control over federal patronage in the South), and support for economic reconstruction in the South, including the Texas and Pacific Railroad (Woodward 1951; but see Peskin 1973).

This drama came to an end on March 1. Two events led to the end of the filibuster. One was the announcement by William Levy (D-LA) that he had been assured by leading Republicans that the Hayes administration would cede political power in Southern states to Democratic forces and, hence, that further obstruction was reckless (Hoogenboom 1995). Second, Speaker Samuel Randall (D-PA), who days earlier had vowed to block the presidential vote count (*New York Times*, February 28, 1877, 1), refused to recognize any motions he considered dilatory. Randall's defiance of a sizable faction of his own party was rightly considered an act of political courage and essential to the resolution of the crisis ("Mr. Randall in 1877" 1883). Despite his opposition to the filibuster, however, the presidential count was not concluded until after 4 A.M. on March 2 in a tense, sleepy joint session of Congress (*New York Times*, March 3, 1887, 1).

The Hayes-Tilden contest was a critical period of American history, and the congressional debate illustrates some interesting features of filibustering. First, in this case, obstruction may have literally been a proxy for violent conflict. Some Democrats had announced that, if Tilden was denied his victory, they would take up arms (Woodward 1951, 110–11; but see Peskin 1973, 73). By dragging out the conflict and extracting policy concessions (real or illusory), the obstructionist House Democrats asserted the case of angry and disappointed Democrats across the nation. Second, to the extent that the Compromise of 1877 shifted Reconstruction policy, this change is the result of a filibuster in the U.S. House. Even with the procedural deck stacked against them (the House Democrats could not successfully challenge any state's returns unless the Republican-dominated Senate concurred), the ability of House Democrats to credibly threaten a descent into chaos empowered them to extort an apparent shift in federal policy toward the South.

Finally, this filibuster led to an innovation in congressional rulemaking. The first known statutory limit on filibustering was an 1887 law establishing guidelines for counting electoral votes for president.[11] During the close and often corrupt presidential elections of the Gilded Age, it was entirely likely that there would be more disputed state elections thrust before Congress. As enacted in January 1887, the bill generally gives presumption to the votes submitted by state authorities. It includes, however, a provision for challenging electoral votes as they are counted, with challenges guaranteed an immediate vote in each chamber.[12] This was the first statutory restraint on filibustering on a specific topic.

Filibusters in the Gilded Age

In the twelve years after the Hayes-Tilden controversy, there were a few major filibusters in the Senate (twenty-two total) and an escalation of filibustering in the House (thirty-five total). Neither Republicans nor Democrats had a clear advantage in national elections, so they alternated control of the U.S. House and the White House. The Republicans were the majority party in the Senate for ten of these twelve years, but their margin of control was slender. Furthermore, the legitimacy of elections in Southern states continued to be disputable. Therefore, many of the filibusters we observe during this critical era were linked to elections and campaign rules; a second major topic was tariff and taxation policy.

Although the Hayes administration had ceased enforcing election laws protecting Southern blacks, a major Senate filibuster erupted in June 1879 when Democratic majorities in both chambers attempted to eliminate the *possibility* of enforcement of election laws by the U.S. Army. They tried to attach a rider on an army appropriations bill prohibiting the use of funds to keep the army "as a police force to keep the peace at the polls" (quoted in Burdette 1940, 36).[13] On June 18, 1879, the Senate Republicans blocked the bill with fifteen dilatory motions and twenty-one successful DQs. The president pro tempore, Allen Thurman (D-OH), responded with an innovation: he counted nonvoting Republicans toward a quorum for doing business. The Republicans switched to making long, obstructive speeches and eventually relented in the early hours of June 21 (Burdette 1940, 35–39). Although the Republicans eventually allowed the Democratic rider to pass, this filibuster clearly demonstrated the willingness of senators to employ dilatory motions and DQs without shame.

Organizing the Senate, 1881

At the beginning of the Forty-seventh Congress, the party balance in the Senate stood at thirty-seven Democrats, thirty-three Republicans, David Davis (Independent-Illinois), and a "Readjuster" Democrat from Virginia, William Mahone.[14] The Republicans, however, the majority party, hoped to organize the Senate. To do so, they had to delay any organization of the Senate until state legislatures could replace four Republicans *and* persuade either Davis or Mahone to support them, with Vice President Arthur breaking the tie.

This contest led to *three* filibusters. First, Republicans blocked the Democrats' resolution to organize the committees of the Senate from March 11 to March 18, after which they organized those committees with the aid of Mahone and four new members. Part of Mahone's reward for voting with the Republicans was the chairmanship of the Senate Committee on Agriculture.

The next week, Republicans attempted to replace the key staffers of the Senate with Republicans, including a Virginia Readjuster as sergeant at arms. This was insult added to injury, and the Democrats responded with a six-week filibuster (March 24–May 6) to deny Mahone and the Republicans their political spoils (Burdette 1940, 47–51). The Democrats forced votes on 103 dilatory motions, with George Pendleton (D-OH) and Isham Harris (D-TN) making about half these motions. In the end, the Democrats successfully prevented the Republicans from installing their officers.

The third round of this conflict occurred when the Senate reconvened in October 1881. In an effort to solidify the Republicans' alliance with Mahone and the Readjusters, President Arthur nominated a Readjuster named Clifford Statham to replace the Republican postmaster of Lynchburg, Virginia. Senator Johnston, a "Bourbon" Democrat from Virginia, convinced his party to fight the nomination ("A Fight for a Post Office" 1881, 1). The main battle was October 27 and 28: in closed-door executive session, Democrats made twenty dilatory motions and broke a quorum once. In the morning, the Republicans held a caucus, conferred with President Arthur, and decided to give up the fight ("The Senate's Work Ended" 1881, 1). Days later, Arthur gave Statham his post as a recess appointment ("Notes from Washington" 1881, 5). Overall, out of 985 votes cast in the Forty-seventh Senate (1881–83), there were 117 on motions to adjourn and another 10 on parliamentary questions.

Mackey v. Dibble, 1882

On the other side of the Capitol, the House had its own election controversies to resolve. The Republicans held a slender majority of 151 out of 293 seats, so the gain or loss of a seat would have a large impact on the their ability to govern. After the 1880 elections, twenty-one candidates—many from Southern states—appealed their elections to the House (Alexander 1916, 324–26).[15]

One dispute pitted Edmund Mackey against Samuel Dibble for the right to represent South Carolina's Second Congressional District. This case came up immediately after James Chalmers (D-MS) lost his House seat to an election challenge. Chalmers publicly complained that the House Democrats had failed to filibuster on his behalf even though contested elections were understood to be party questions ("Chalmers and His Tale" 1882, 4).[16] The House Democrats fought hard for Dibble to demonstrate their resolve to protect Democratic seats. Starting on May 20, 1882, they blocked Republican efforts to award Dibble's seat to Mackey with thirteen dilatory motions and forty-four DQs—twenty-three of them successful. Frustrated and exhausted, the Republicans proposed a new rule to limit obstruction on contested-election cases. They argued that Democratic filibustering on election disputes violated the norms of obstruction (*Congressional Record* 13, pt. 5 [May 29, 1882]: 4311). When Democrats began to filibuster the rule proposal, Thomas Reed (R-ME) raised a point of order that obstruction against a rules proposal was unacceptable since it interfered with the ability of a chamber to determine its own rules. Reed won his point of order 152–0, with virtually every Democrat refusing to vote. Democrats abstained from nine of the next ten votes, with an average participation rate of 2.33 percent, but the Republicans successfully pushed Mackey's case through the House and demonstrated the majority's ability to suppress obstruction with procedural innovations.

The Force Bill, 1891

Legislation to enforce voting rights throughout the nation passed the House 155–149 on July 2, 1890, over the opposition of Southerners who feared a federal "force" bill.[17] The Senate Republican majority put this bill off until after the election, but the bill's manager, George F. Hoar (R-MA), collected signatures from every Republican promising to support the bill during the next session (Welch 1965).

When the short session began, Democrats filibustered the bill with long speeches until, on January 5, William Stewart (R-NV) moved to take up a bill permitting unlimited coinage of silver by the government. This motion passed 34–29 (Democrats 25–0, Republicans 8–29), with the aid of a Republican faction that prioritized prosilver legislation over all other bills (Wellborn 1928). After the Senate passed the silver purchase bill, Hoar won another vote on January 14, 1891, to take up the elections bill by a 34–33 margin (Republicans 33–6, Democrats 0–27), and the filibuster resumed. Beginning January 16, the Republicans kept the Senate in continuous session, but the Democrats refused to attend and successfully broke a quorum (Burdette 1940, 54–5). On January 20, Nelson Aldrich (R-RI) moved to consider a resolution that would permit simple majority cloture for the rest of the session. The cloture resolution met the same fate as the force bill: defeat by diversion. On January 26, Wolcott (R-CO) suggested that the Senate drop the cloture proposal and take up a House apportionment bill. This motion passed 35–34 with six Republican defections. The Democrats voted unanimously to take up the apportionment bill but voted unanimously against the bill on final passage. They had won the larger battle; the force bill was dead.

As Wawro and Schickler point out, this is a case of asymmetrical intensity: the Democrats wanted to kill this bill more than Republicans wanted to pass it. Republican senators were absent at critical times, and several senators defected to support "killer" motions that took the elections bill and closure rule off the Senate floor. We also learn that closure reform is *possible*, but only if senators are willing to take the necessary parliamentary steps.

FILIBUSTER OUTCOMES

The final task of this chapter is to determine which bills were most likely to be killed by a filibuster. This analysis is constrained by limited knowledge about how filibusters affected the legislative process. In part III, I present summaries of filibuster outcomes based on thousands of articles; similar sources were not available for the historic Congress. Instead, I focus on whether the proposal targeted by a filibuster was approved by the chamber in which the filibuster occurred. As discussed in chapter 2, the filibusters we observe are a function of a strategic process, and, ideally, we would analyze outcomes as part of that broader game.

What might explain filibuster success or failure? Wawro and Schickler (2006) find that coalition size is a predictor of filibuster outcomes. I use a variation on that notion. For each dilatory motion, the Pro coalition is the percentage of the chamber that votes against the motion. For each vote with a DQ (even if it is also dilatory), the coalition size is the percentage of the chamber that votes, with the intuition that any kind of vote helps defeat strategic abstention. I use the *median coalition size* for each filibuster as my independent variable: the larger the coalition supporting a bill, the more likely it is to pass. Second, I use the *obstruction score* as an explanatory variable—the more obstruction against a bill, the less likely it is to pass. In a second version of the analysis, I tested the components of these scores—dilatory motions, DQs, and successful DQs—separately to determine which kind of filibustering was most effective. I also tested for whether filibusters were more or less likely to succeed during *short sessions*, in the *Senate*, when the president was of the same party as the majority party of the chamber and whether majority party size also increased the prospects of an obstructed bill.

The results of this analysis are shown in table 4.3. Each coefficient shows the percentage change in the likelihood of the bill passing associated with a one-unit change in the value of the independent variable. Somewhat surprisingly, Pro coalition size, short sessions, and obstruction score did not have a clear effect on whether a bill passed. Obstructed bills were more likely to pass when the majority party and the president were of the same party, suggesting that either the president helped overcome the filibuster or the majority party was more determined to win when it could expect the president to approve its legislation. In the right-hand column, the different types of obstruction are estimated separately. There was no clear relation between dilatory motions and bill passage, while there was a 6.5 percent *increase* in the likelihood of passage for every attempt at quorum breaking but a 6.2 percent *decrease* in the likelihood of passage every time a party successfully broke a quorum. This result is intuitive. Given that a filibuster has occurred and a party has attempted to break a quorum, the critical test is whether the

Table 4.3. Predicting Filibuster Success or Failure

	Version 1: Obstruction Score (% Change [z-Scores])	Model 2: Obstruction Types (% Change [z-Scores])
Median coalition size	.113	−.248
	(.37)	(−.83)
Obstruction score	.3	
	(1.18)	
Majority party president	18.3	15.8
	(3.16)**	(2.87)**
Majority party size	.5	.4
	(1.41)	(1.28)
Senate	6.0	7.7
	(1.01)	(1.44)
Short session	-10.1	−8.4
	(-1.57)	(−1.42)
Dilatory motions		.0
		(.13)
Disappearing quorums		6.5
		(3.08)**
Broken quorums		−6.2
		(−2.43)*
Pseudo-R^2	.0712	.108

Note: Coefficients display the effect of a one-unit change on the likelihood that an obstructed bill passes.

* $p < .05$.
** $p < .01$.

Pro coalition can muster a quorum. If it can, the filibuster is likely to fail. If it cannot, the filibuster is more likely to succeed. These results highlight the impact of quorum breaking in nineteenth-century obstruction.

CONCLUSION

This chapter traces the number and impact of filibusters in the historic Congress and the distribution of filibusters across issues and explains which filibusters were more likely to end in the defeat of the targeted bill. The first House filibusters occurred during the years before the outbreak of the War of 1812, and the first identified Senate filibuster occurred in 1831. As chapter 2 predicts, the issues that provoked filibusters were typically the most salient issues of the day: tariffs, appropriations, slavery and civil rights, the disposition of public land, and elections and party politics. When a proposal is threatened by a filibuster, it is more likely to survive when the president is from the same party as the majority party in the legislature. Furthermore, bills are more likely to fail if the opposition breaks a quorum.

It is now clear that members of the historic House and Senate frequently filibustered to defeat legislation, to demonstrate their intense positions, and to preserve their rights to participate in debate. The next challenge is to explain why this form of opposition was more common in the House than in the Senate and why it increased over time in both chambers.

CHAPTER 5

Explaining Obstruction in the Historic Congress

The question has become simply one of physical endurance.... [T]he majority of the House, who wish to pass this bill, ... have accomplished all that they can desire. They have shown to the country their desire to facilitate legislation and to dispose of the bill in some way this afternoon.

Charles Eldredge (D-WI), speaking in Congress on May 5, 1870

This chapter explains patterns of obstruction in the historic Congress. This era of congressional history illustrates how filibustering increases as time becomes more scarce and valuable and how the introduction of an effective cloture rule can decrease obstruction. I first describe how legislators fought these "wars." I then explain my strategy for measuring the balance of power in classic filibusters—under what conditions was filibustering likely to succeed? Finally, I employ multivariate analysis to test my explanation for the rise and fall of filibustering in the historic Congress.

WARS OF ATTRITION

Robert Luce offered a glowing defense of filibustering as a contest of strength: "From the beginning of human society the supreme test of faith in principle has been the physical test.... The filibuster is a physical test. Its success depends on powers of endurance. The instances I have cited where men stood and talked for ten, twelve, fifteen hours or more, were instances of great physical strain, where vitality was endangered, health and even life were risked.... [F]ilibustering is physical sacrifice and in essence no whit different from trial by battle, the ordeal, the duel, war itself" (1922, 300). The reality of classic filibustering was often less romantic. John Quincy Adams describes the tedium of an all-night session: "There was not half a quorum present, and of them about one-half were slumbering in their seats and the other half yawning over newspapers; here and there a strolling wanderer behind the bar was pacing to and fro to keep up the circulation of the blood; two or three settees, each with a member stretched out his whole length, occupying it all, sound asleep; and groups of two or three seated before each open window, gasping, in idle conversation, for fresh air" (Adams 1969, 9:551). Filibustering subjects legislators on both sides to mind-numbing tedium, with the contest going to the team that can kill time longer.

Some factors that affect the outcome are idiosyncratic to particular bills and specific times: the number, age, and skill of the filibusterers, the time of day, absences in the majority coalition, and the salience of the issue at stake. Other factors vary over the course of a session. The historic Congress, of course, lacked air-conditioning. As spring turned to the swampy heat of a Washington summer in a stagnant chamber, wasting time became increasingly unappealing, giving obstructionists a little more leverage. Furthermore, as each two-year Congress progressed, the number of committee-reported bills waiting on the calendar tended to increase. If a chamber was efficient, the list of pending bills would be short, with few important bills awaiting action. Toward the end of the nineteenth century, however, an increasing number of bills lingered in legislative limbo, particularly in the House. Finally, obstructionists might take advantage of artificial deadlines in the legislative calendar such as the constitutionally mandated end of the short session or the end date for a special or long session chosen days or weeks in advance.

The balance of power between obstructionists and their opponents also varied over time and across chambers. These structural influences—not the idiosyncratic details that liven the narratives of specific filibusters—help us understand the main patterns of filibustering over congressional history. The challenge, however, is measuring the dynamic value of chamber time.

A common strategy for measuring the scarcity of chamber time is to assume that it varies with external demand for policy change, which presumably increases with national population, the size of the economy, the size of the federal budget, etc. Policy demand may also be linked to short-term events like military conflicts, political events such as a new party taking control of the government, or the "mood" of the public (Erikson, Mackuen, and Stimson 2002), that is, the collective desire of the American public for a more (or less) active federal government. However, the availability of time is also tied to the rules of each chamber. Legislators may respond to frustrated expectations by amending the rules of their chamber to make it more efficient. Indeed, over time, the House and the Senate have made dozens of changes, large and small, to streamline their decisionmaking.

The value of chamber time is also subjective. Legislators' willingness to hold and attend meetings of Congress depends, we assume, on the other uses they could be making of their time. The *subjective* value of time may vary with the quality of transportation back to a member's district, a member's need to supplement his congressional salary by working at home (Rothman 1966), constituents' expectations that members will personally visit federal agencies on their behalf, or the number and quality of saloons close to the Capitol. It would be impossible to measure each of these variables for each session of the historic Congress.

Instead, I develop institutional and behavioral measures of the scarcity and value of legislators' time. First, the number of legislators in the House and Senate is linked to the scarcity of chamber time. Second, the number of days with roll call votes functions as a measure of how hard each chamber had to work to keep up with policy demand. Finally, legislators' voting participation is a measure of how legislators weighed the opportunity costs of staying in the chamber to pass legislation. This approach makes it unnecessary to identify and measure every source of external workload or to identify and control for every procedural reform. To the extent that external workload increases pressure on legislative operations and internal reforms reduce that pressure, we should observe their effects by measuring legislators' behavior.

THE SIZE OF THE HOUSE AND SENATE

The Constitution provides every state with two senators and at least one representative, with additional representatives allocated by population. Technically, this formula does not mandate that the House will be larger than the Senate, but the authors of the Constitution expected the House to be larger so that it would act as the voice of popular sentiment (see Federalist Nos. 58 and 63). The first House was 250 percent larger than the Senate (sixty-five members to twenty-six), and Congress increased the size of the House significantly after each census from 1790 to 1830, as shown in figure 5.1. From 1803 to the present, the House has been about four times the size of the Senate, peaking at a five-to-one ratio in the Twenty-third Congress (1833–35). The House ballooned from 65 members in 1789 to 357 in 1901, while the Senate grew from 26 senators in 1789 to 90 in 1901. Both chambers shrank during the Civil War and then grew again as Southern states began sending legislators back to Congress.

As both chambers grew, there were simply more politicians competing for the opportunity to make speeches and bring up their own bills for consideration. This pressure was especially acute in the House, which gradually adopted limits on speeches and simplified the bill introduction process to distribute floor time more equitably (Cooper and Young 1989). Nonetheless, one effect of growing chamber size was to make floor time scarcer and valuable. A second consequence of growing chamber size was that there were simply more legislators available for a filibuster. When obstruction requires physical effort, it is easier to conduct a filibuster if there are plenty of able bodies to help.

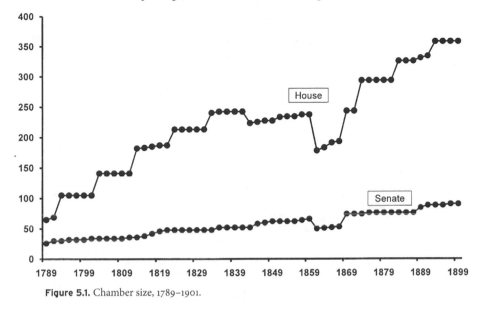

Figure 5.1. Chamber size, 1789–1901.

WORKDAYS PER SESSION

How can we adequately measure the effect of policy demand on congressional time? Scholars and journalists often associate working hard with time worked, so one expects that the number of days in session is a good measure of how hard a legislature is working to keep up with policy demand. Some scholars simply use the number of calendar days from the beginning to the end of a session (e.g., Oppenheimer 1985), but it is possible that legislators are not working on some of these days. Indeed, one chamber may be struggling through long days while the other chamber rarely meets; since both chambers must agree to an adjournment date, a simple count of days would not measure how hard each chamber worked during the same span of days. Instead, I count the number of days per session that each chamber held a roll call vote, with the expectation that a vote indicates that the entire legislature is expected to be present.

Figure 5.2 displays the number of "voting days" in each long session for the historic House and Senate. The patterns of voting days suggest that the variable measures both conflict and workload. There is an early uptick during the Fifth Senate (1797–99), reflecting a burst of activity related to foreign policy (e.g., building up the navy) and domestic security (the Alien and Sedition acts). Both chambers met and voted more frequently during the outbreak of the War of 1812. There was a noticeable trend toward more voting days from about 1825 to 1845 in both chambers, and from 1831 to 1857 the

Figure 5.2. Days with a roll call vote, long sessions.

House held, on average, thirty-four more voting days than the Senate. From 1857 on, the two chambers generally move in tandem.

Figure 5.3 illustrates the same statistic for short sessions in both chambers. Note the change in scale—while the maximum number of voting days in a long session was 157, the maximum for short sessions was 81 days. Again, the War of 1812 caused a surge of activity, this time during the short session of the Fourteenth Congress (1814–15) as the House and Senate struggled to finance the war and manage the military establishment. There is an increase in voting days starting in the 1820s, this time primarily in the House, and a surplus of voting days in the House from 1828 to 1857.

One concern is that voting days is not a "clean" measure of the increasing marginal costs of time since another cause of an increase in voting days may be *filibustering*. This puts us in the awkward position of expecting that obstruction increases as the number of voting days increases *and* that there are more voting days as filibustering increases. For reasons elaborated below, it is necessary to identify some variable that is *not* inflated by filibustering but *is* correlated with voting days per session.

As a measure of external policy demand, I use the number of presidential policy requests per session. The Constitution states that the president "shall from time to time give to the Congress Information of the State of the Union, and recommend to their Consideration such Measures as he shall judge necessary and expedient" (art. 2, sec. 3). I assume that presidents can observe variations in policy demand and act as a reasonably consistent signal of variation in policy demand. Elaine Swift et al. (2000) identify

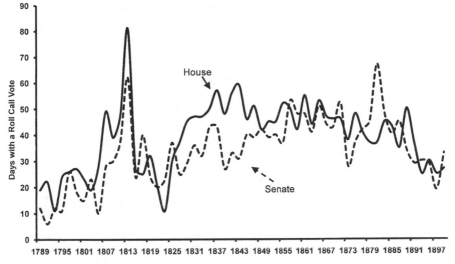

Figure 5.3. Days with a roll call vote, short sessions.

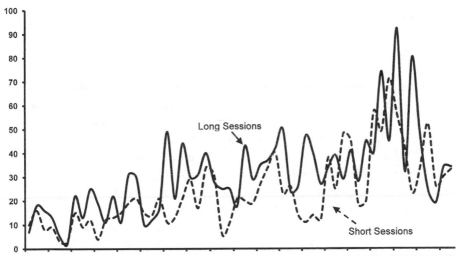

Figure 5.4. Presidential policy requests by session.

each policy request sent to Congress or included in inaugural or State of the Union addresses. I matched these requests to congressional sessions on the basis of their dates; requests that occurred between sessions were credited to the upcoming session. The number of requests per session is shown in figure 5.4.

Presidential requests increase over time, peaking in the 1880s, and dropping off in the 1890s. During the First Congress—when the structure of the federal government was being fleshed out—President Washington made 17 requests, including Hamilton's proposal for assumption of the national debt. A century later, President Harrison made 103 requests during the Fifty-first Congress. Also, the number of presidential requests during short sessions is almost as high as that during long sessions. A typical short session in either chamber has about half the voting days of the preceding long session, but the number of presidential requests decreases by only about one-sixth. This helps explain the conventional wisdom that short sessions are more pressed for time than long sessions.

Voting Attendance

Another reason that legislators value their time is that they could be back in their districts or enjoying leisure in the capital area. These personal opportunity costs probably varied over time. During the early decades of the nineteenth century, legislators typically met, resolved a relatively light workload in a few months, and quickly returned home. This arrangement minimized their unpleasant sojourns in the District of Columbia, a muddy and primitive capital in development, and permitted them to quickly return home to their constituents, their families, and their jobs. While in Washington, legislators were somewhat diligent and, if necessary, would meet at night or on Saturdays to expedite business. Over the course of the nineteenth century, however, the District became a more pleasant place to stay, and legislators began to buy houses and move their families there (Rothman 1966). The expansion of the nation's railroad system made it possible for legislators to return home in the middle of a session or even on the weekends.

We can measure the effects of increasing opportunity costs by analyzing legislators' participation in roll call votes, excluding dilatory motions and disappearing quorums. We can calculate mean participation rates by legislator, by vote, or by time period. A low participation rate suggests that the opportunity cost of attending is high and, thus, that the costs of waiting out a filibuster are high; we should, therefore, expect a negative relation between participation and filibustering.

If voting participation reflects the opportunity costs of attendance, we would expect participation to decrease in both chambers over the course of the nineteenth century as sessions lasted longer and Washington became a more livable and leavable location. Indeed, there is a negative correlation ($r = -.274$) between session length and participation. Figure 5.5 illustrates the long-term trend in participation for both chambers. It shows that participation declined in both chambers over the first century of congressional history. Interestingly, participation is higher in the House than in the Senate from 1869 to 1901, while Washington was increasingly connected to the country by rail. Also, in both chambers, there is an uptick in participation

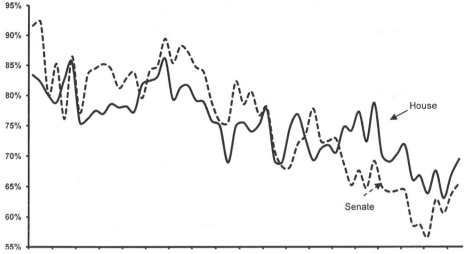

Figure 5.5. Participation by chamber, all members.
Note: Each line shows mean voting participation by Congress.

during the 1890s at the same time that presidential requests and voting days decrease.

Voting participation also varies over the course of sessions as expected. This gives us additional reason to believe that attendance reflects the opportunity costs of members' time. Figures 5.6 and 5.7 illustrate variation in attendance over the course of long and short sessions for the periods 1789–1861 and 1861–1901. The process for generating these figures was complicated,[1] but the pattern is intuitive. Each figure traces the typical attendance for each chamber at the beginning, middle, and end of each session. During the first, seventy-two-year span, participation is essentially constant for both chambers (with the House experiencing a drop in participation after the opening of the long session) until the last quartile of a typical session. As both short and long sessions drew to a close, participation dropped in both chambers— especially the House. This suggests that members began to steal away when the end was near, particularly House members who wanted to reunite with their districts before the next election. From 1861 to 1901, attendance usually sagged throughout the long session in both chambers, dipping as low as 60 percent on a typical House vote at the end of the long session. Participation at short sessions was essentially constant with no elections to lure members away, although, again, we observe an end-of-session drop-off in both chambers. This pattern helps us understand why filibustering might have been especially common at the end of the short session: not only was time limited (and, thus, scarce), but poor attendance also facilitated quorum breaking.

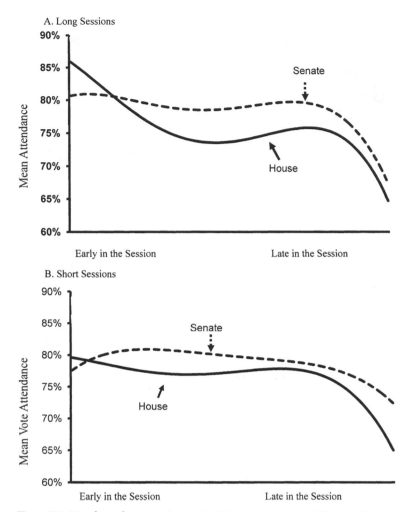

Figure 5.6. Attendance during sessions, 1789–1861. *a*, Long sessions. *b*, Short sessions. *Note*: Figures show voting attendance over the course of sessions, smoothed by a polynomial trend line (order 4).

PREFERENCES, PARTISANSHIP, AND RULES

Some scholars suggest that filibustering varies with the size and unity of legislative parties (e.g., Binder, Lawrence, and Smith 2002; Dion 1997). The filibuster model outlined in chapter 2 helps explain why these variables may be linked to the incidence of obstruction. First, filibustering may vary with the majority party's percentage share of the chamber because larger parties are better able to muster the members to maintain a quorum against a filibuster while small minority parties may find it difficult to organize a

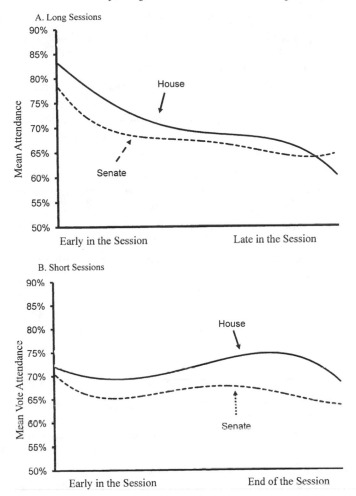

A. Long Sessions

B. Short Sessions

Figure 5.7. Attendance during sessions, 1861–1901. *a*, Long sessions. *b*, Short sessions.

sizable bloc of opposition to a majority-favored bill. Similarly, the costs of enduring a filibuster for the majority and the minority parties may vary with their "party unity" in voting.[2] If party members tend to vote together, then perhaps they will be more willing to endure a filibuster struggle together.

An alternative measure of party strength, which I call *majority advantage*, combines size and unity into a single index:

Majority advantage = (majority share × majority unity) –
(minority share × minority unity).

Sarah Binder (1997) uses this formulation, which she labels *partisan capacity*. *Majority advantage* measures the relative ability of the majority party to outvote the minority party and potentially to outlast the minority party in a filibuster contest. Another interpretation is that it measures the ability of the majority party to impose new restrictions on filibustering. Binder (1997) finds that the majority party's voting advantage is correlated with reductions in the rights of parliamentary majorities in the historic House. Wawro and Schickler (2006) claim that the ability of chamber majorities to restrict obstruction should deter minorities from violating norms against obstruction, so filibustering should decrease as *majority advantage* increases.

A final measure of partisan disagreement is the gap between the median DW-NOMINATE scores (first dimension) of the two parties. These scores are calculated using a sophisticated algorithm that assumes that legislators vote by choosing the policy alternative that is closest to their ideal policy. Over the course of hundreds of votes, the NOMINATE procedure infers each legislator's ideal point on each major category of policy, or dimension. The first dimension of DW-NOMINATE (DW-1) explains almost all the ideological component of congressional voting (Poole and Rosenthal 1997), and the absolute difference between the scores of the median members of each party is a standard measure of policy disagreement between the parties. We may also consider this intermedian gap a measure of the payoffs for winning a filibuster struggle—the greater the policy difference between the parties, the higher the stakes of a legislative struggle.

A key point about measures of party strength is that they cycle over the course of the nineteenth century. Figure 5.8 displays majority advantage statistics and DW-NOMINATE gaps for the House and the Senate. The first twenty years in both chambers were marked by high levels of majority party advantage and preference differences. However, we know that this was also a period with low levels of measured obstruction. Otherwise, the DW-1 gap grows steadily over the course of the nineteenth century, except when the two-party system breaks down temporarily in the early 1820s in the House and the 1850s in the Senate. The majority party in both chambers enjoys a strong advantage in the 1860s owing to the Republicans' large majorities, but this does not explain the boom of filibustering in the 1880s and 1890s. In sum, while parties certainly played a role in facilitating obstruction, they seem to be poor candidates to explain the major patterns of filibustering in the historic Congress.

Rules changes that make closure strategies more effective are another explanation for patterns of obstruction. In chapter 3, I discussed the 1890–94 dispute over filibustering in the House, culminating in a bipartisan rule change enabling the counting of nonvoting members toward a quorum. If rule changes do explain patterns of obstruction, we should witness a surge in filibustering during the period 1890–94, followed by a dramatic decrease in filibustering in the House after 1894.[3]

Finally, we might determine whether, controlling for all other factors, one chamber was more prone to filibustering than the other. We might expect,

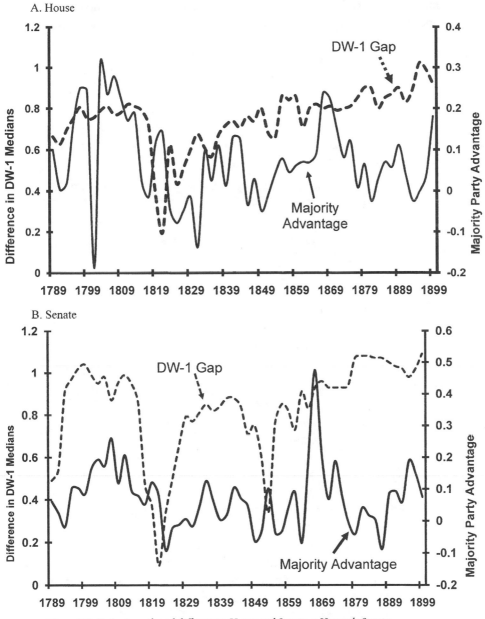

Figure 5.8. Party strength and differences, House and Senate. *a*, House. *b*, Senate.

for example, that the Senate's lax rules led to a slight bias toward filibustering once we have considered the effects of chamber size, time constraints, and major rules changes.

ANALYZING OBSTRUCTION

Now that we have reviewed potential causes of filibustering, the next step is a statistical analysis to determine which factors are most closely linked to filibustering in the historic Congress. To recap, the key variables are (with variable names in italics):

- three measures of the value of chamber time: *chamber size*, *days in session*, and *participation*;
- five measures of party strength and interparty policy differences: *majority party size*, *majority party unity*, *minority party unity*, *majority advantage*, and *DW-1 gap*;
- dichotomous variables for two key periods of House history: the *House reform era* (1890–94) and the subsequent era with a *House closure rule* (1895–1901);
- a simple test for bicameral differences: *Senate*, another dichotomous variable.

The goal of this analysis is to predict the obstruction score for each chamber during each session of Congress, as described in chapter 3. Aggregating these scores by session provides reasonably sized samples of legislative time while permitting variation over the course of each two-year Congress. Including special sessions, there are 270 sessions to explain.

Methods

One challenge for this analysis is the *truncation* of the dependent variable. In 75 of 270 cases, there was no measured obstruction, so the most common filibuster score is 0. Since obstruction scores cannot dip below 0, ordinary least squares regression could generate biased estimates and incorrect standard errors. I correct for truncation using Tobit regression, which factors in the constraint on the data-generating process.[4]

A second complication is the complex relation between the scarcity of time and filibustering. As discussed above, I expect filibustering to increase as members' attendance decreases and the number of days in session increases. However, the relation could work in the opposite direction: filibustering may force a legislature to meet for more days to wait out a war of attrition. While *participation* is rendered exogenous by purging all obstruction-related votes, *days in session* is potentially endogenous—both causing and caused by obstruction.

I use instrumental variable (IV) regression to circumvent this problem. The basic idea of IV regression is that one estimates proxy values for the endogenous variable using one or more variables ("instruments") that are exogenous to the dependent variable but correlated with the endogenous variable. In this case, the goal is to estimate the number of days each chamber would have met if filibustering had no influence, then estimate the relation between the proxy variable *days in session*^ and filibustering.

One set of instruments controls for the tendency of some sessions to last longer than others. Three dichotomous variables, *special*, *Senate special*, and *short*, control for each category of session. Long sessions are the excluded category. The final instrument is *presidential requests* per session as described above.

The regression model is, thus, a two-part process:

(1) Days in session $= \alpha_0 + \alpha_1(\text{short}) + \alpha_2(\text{special}) + \alpha_3(\text{Senate special}) + \alpha_4(\text{presidential requests}) + \alpha_n X + \varepsilon_1,$

(2) Obstruction score$_{it} = \beta_0 + \beta_1(\text{days in session*}) + \beta_n X + \varepsilon_2,$

where X is the set of exogenous variables described above, equation (1) is a linear regression model, and equation (2) is estimated using Tobit. I estimate both equations simultaneously using maximum likelihood estimation, that is, an iterative process which finds the coefficients that best fit the observed data.[5]

Results

Table 5.1 presents the results of the analysis.[6] All three versions of the regression model are a statistically significant improvement over a null model. Furthermore, a Wald test for the exogeneity of the instrumental variables suggests that *days in session* is probably *not* exogenous, so IV regression is appropriate.

The top half of table 5.1 displays coefficients for linear relations between the instrumental variables and the number of voting days per session. All four instruments help predict variation in the endogenous variable. The three session variables—*short*, *special*, and *Senate special*—are correlated with fewer days in session compared to long sessions. Each presidential policy request is associated with about one-third of an additional day. In addition, several of the explanatory variables are correlated with the number of days in session. As expected, participation is negatively linked to the number of working days in a session; a one percent increase in participation

Table 5.1. Tobit Regression of Filibuster Scores with Instrumental Variable Regression

	Model 1		Model 2		Model 3	
	Coefficient	S.E.	Coefficient	S.E.	Coefficient	S.E.
Stage 1: Predictors of days in session (linear):						
Participation	−.68	.18	−.71	.18	−.62	.19
Chamber	5.92	5.67	7.98	5.74	6.54	5.75
Chamber size	.10	.03	.10	.03	.10	.03
House reform era	−15.23	9.28	−14.61	9.43	−14.23	9.32
House closure rules	−38.87	8.77	−39.91	8.87	−41.05	8.86
Majority share	−.04	.15				
Majority cohesion	−9.00	11.97				
Minority cohesion	35.73	12.37				
Majority advantage			.07	.13		
DW-1 gap					9.97	7.78
Special	−42.65	4.88	−42.03	4.83	−42.42	4.84
Senate special	−61.33	6.12	−60.78	6.15	−61.07	6.10
Short	−40.73	2.73	−40.62	2.77	−40.73	2.76
Presidential requests	.37	.10	.33	.10	.33	.10
Intercept	88.97	21.88	105.82	17.57	93.53	20.36
Stage 2: Predictors of filibuster score per session (Tobit):						
Days in session^	.36	.07	.31	.07	.31	.07
Participation	−1.02	.25	−1.11	.26	−1.01	.27
Chamber	26.09	8.54	30.04	8.97	27.69	8.78
Chamber size	.26	.05	.28	.05	.27	.05
House reform era	43.49	11.80	48.39	12.49	48.87	12.20
House closure rules	−47.57	11.57	−46.25	12.29	−47.45	12.09
Majority share	−.05	.21				
Majority cohesion	20.40	16.60				
Minority cohesion	51.36	18.22				
Majority advantage			.05	.18		
DW-1 gap					12.10	11.99
Intercept	−24.94	31.42	23.31	26.35	8.81	29.57
Wald test of exogeneity	$\chi^2 = 4.02$		$\chi^2 = 8.50$		$\chi^2 = 8.19$	
	$Prob > \chi^2 = .0450$		$Prob > \chi^2 = .0035$		$Prob > \chi^2 = .0042$	

Note: Cells display unstandardized coefficients.

is associated with 0.7 fewer days. Stated inversely, attendance goes down as sessions last longer. Also, the larger the chamber, the more days it works: adding ten members is correlated with adding a day to each session. The last variable of note is *House closure rules*, which suggests that the suppression of filibustering in the House in 1894 had a dramatic effect on the chamber's schedule. Beginning with the short session of the Fifty-third Congress in December 1894, a typical House session was shorter by about thirty-nine

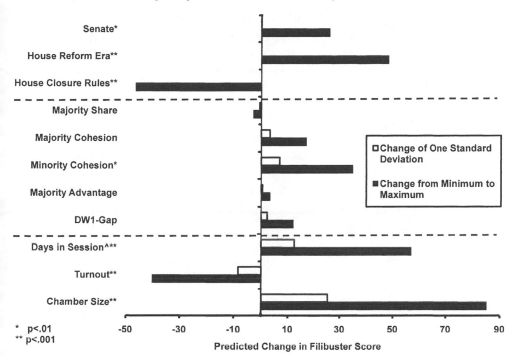

Figure 5.9. Influences on filibustering.

Note: * $p < .01$. ** $p < .001$.

days. Taken together, these patterns suggest that the first-stage regression provides a suitable proxy estimate for *days in session*.

The bottom half of table 5.1 displays the Tobit-estimated predictors of filibustering. Most of the variables have the expected effects: *days in session*^, *participation*, *chamber size*, *House reform era*, and *House closure rules* are all statistically significant and consistent with predictions. All else equal, *Senate* is correlated with additional filibustering.[7] With the exception of *minority party unity*, party-related measures do not seem linked to variation in filibustering. The positive coefficient for *minority party unity* suggests that filibustering tends to increase when the minority party votes together.

Since Tobit coefficients indicate the relation between predictors and a hypothetical, unconstrained dependent variable, it is difficult to directly interpret their substantive implications. Instead, figure 5.9 displays the predicted effect of varying the variables from their means to one standard deviation higher and from the lowest to the highest value while holding all other variables at their means. Only the latter estimate is shown for dichotomous variables. Asterisks denote statistical significance; all effects are estimates subject to error.

As figure 5.9 indicates, the most significant correlates of filibustering were variables measuring the value of time in both chambers and institutional change in the U.S. House. A one-standard-deviation change in *chamber size* is correlated with a twenty-five-point increase in filibustering, and a maximum change is associated with about an eighty-five-point increase. Next in substantive impact are *days in session* (12.6, 56.8), *House reform era* (48.4), and *House closure rule* (-46.3).[8] Finally, a one-standard-deviation increase in *participation* is associated with a 8.3-point decrease in obstruction score and a 40-point change in obstruction between the highest and the lowest values of participation. The only party-based variable that has a clear relation with filibustering is *minority party unity* (6.9, 34.9), suggesting that cohesive minority parties are better able—or more willing—to filibuster.

One danger of using these historical data is autocorrelation, that is, the level of filibustering at one time may be an echo of the previous time period. In such cases, the level of filibustering may not vary as much as it first appears to, so one may underestimate the actual variance and report false positive results. I tested a simple solution for autocorrelation: include a lagged dependent variable (at $t - 2$) in the regression model. The results (available on request) show that the lagged dependent variable is not significantly correlated with the dependent variable once the explanatory variables are considered. The lagged variable is correlated with *days in session*, but including this effect actually reduces the statistical significance of *days in session*^ as an explanatory variable. Overall, the results suggest that the regression model shown above is not compromised to a significant degree by autocorrelation.

CONCLUSION

This chapter explains patterns of obstruction across chambers and over time in the historic Congress. The central finding confirms the predictions made in chapter 2: as time became more scarce and valuable, the price for obstructing declined, so legislative minorities were more likely to filibuster to obtain their goals. Specifically, as the House and Senate grew in size, there were more members competing for the attention of each chamber and more legislators available to participate in a filibuster. Furthermore, filibustering increased as legislators met more frequently to conduct business and as legislators began to shirk voting in favor of work or leisure outside the chamber. Together, these patterns suggest that legislators are more likely to obstruct when they believe that their opponents place a high value on their time and, thus, can be beaten in a war of attrition.

Of course, the alternative to a war of attrition is an effective closure process. From 1890 to 1894, the House adopted strong reforms to reduce obstruction, but at a tremendous cost. The Republican majority of the Fifty-first Congress suffered great losses in the elections of 1890. Both parties suffered from the prolonged four-year contest over whether the draconian reforms were necessary, but, in the end, the House adopted strong closure rules that reduced obstruction after 1894. While parties and their reputations were central players in this House contest, there is little evidence that partisanship per se is correlated with filibustering. Filibustering did not significantly vary with majority party size, majority party unity, and interparty differences in preferences, although minority party unity was correlated with filibustering.

The historic House can be regarded as a particularly interesting predecessor of the modern Senate. For the first hundred years of Congress, a popularly elected legislature tolerated minority obstruction. The historic House provides an interesting case study of the life cycle of obstruction: initially obstruction is possible but rare, then it is frequent, then a majority imposes dramatic reforms, then obstruction is rare again. The chapters in the next part of this book demonstrate that the Senate has progressed from rare to nearly constant obstruction; it remains to be seen whether the Senate follows the example of the House and adopts drastic reforms as well.

III

The Modern Senate, 1901-Present

This part explains when and why the Senate transitioned from a majority-rule legislature with an occasional case of logorrhea to a sixty-vote Senate predicated on the ability of every senator to obstruct any bill at any time. The cause of this transformation was the declining ability of Senate majorities to outlast a filibuster, so the price of obstruction declined over the course of the century. Starting in the 1960s, senators gradually abandoned attrition as a strategy and began utilizing the dormant cloture rule instead. This tactical shift had far-reaching implications: not only did the number of observed filibusters shoot up, but the right to filibuster was also institutionalized in the daily operations of the Senate, creating the sixty-vote Senate that we observe today.

Part III retraces the arc of part II. Chapter 6 measures the incidence of obstruction, tracing its effects on legislative outcomes, and chapter 7 explains patterns of filibustering over time. In addition, chapter 8 explains the evolution of filibustering tactics in the Senate, especially the transition from attrition to closure as the primary response to a filibuster.

The chapters in this part offer several insights. First, through careful research, I identify many more filibusters in the Senate than have previously been cataloged. Second, filibusters have varied effects on the legislative process: not only do senators filibuster to block or modify proposals, but they also obstruct to force their own priorities onto the chamber agenda. Third, the cause of increasing obstruction is the rising value of senators' time. As senators' time became more valuable to them, they were increasingly reluctant to wait out a filibuster, and the price of filibustering declined.

We learn in this part that filibustering is not just a function of formal rules and legislators' goals. Senators must pay a price to exercise their formal rights, and the price depends on their willingness to waste time to achieve their ends. The payoffs include rewards from constituents, donors, interest groups, the media, and the president, even if the obstructionist fails. The adoption of a Senate cloture rule in 1917 and subsequent revisions to this rule neither decreased filibustering nor increased the likelihood that senators would even use the Rule 22 process. Finally, the ability of senators to hold bills hostage demonstrates that legislators can use negative power (blocking proposals) for positive ends (trading the obstructed bill for time on a different issue).

CHAPTER 6

The Growth of Filibustering in the Senate

Not only are many good measures defeated by obstruction, although demanded by decided majorities, but many schemes are engrafted upon the laws by the threat of filibuster. . . . [R]iders upon appropriations bills, and amendments wholly foreign to the subject matter of other bills, are proposed and accepted as the dire alternative to successful obstruction.

Charles Thomas (D-CO), writing in the *North American Review* in 1915

This chapter presents, for the first time, a systematic list of Senate filibusters and their consequences. This effort identifies hundreds of previously unnoticed filibusters and documents a surge of obstruction during short sessions before the adoption of the Twentieth Amendment, then a decline, then a steady increase in filibustering from 1940 to the present. These filibusters had a variety of effects: killing bills, forcing amendments, gaining floor time and opportunities to amend proposals on the floor, forcing consideration of new agenda items, and attracting public attention for the obstructionist(s).

While the underlying theory remains constant, the strategy for identifying obstruction changes dramatically as we move from the historic Congress to the modern Senate. The previous chapters focused on disappearing quorums and dilatory motions as identified in the roll call record. These were common obstructive tactics in the historic Congress and could be systematically identified over time. During the historic era, available media accounts of the historic Congress were not as systematic or reliable and, thus, could not provide a basis for identifying obstructive behavior in Congress.

In the early twentieth century, senators' filibustering tactics changed. As the *New York Times* explained in 1915, speeches took the place of procedural trickery in the modern Senate: "Filibustering in the Senate is not conducted as filibustering in the House used to be, before the Reed Rules abolished filibustering, debate, and the legislative power of nine-tenths of the membership at one and the same time. In the House a good deal could be done with parliamentary technicalities. Doubtless the Senatorial filibusters could use that weapon, too, if they chose; but filibustering is conducted there more on a sporting basis. It is a stand-up fight with speeches as weapons, oratory and not quibbling over motions to recommit, or refer, or postpone" ("The Art of Filibustering" 1915, C2). The *Congressional Record* provides a reasonably accurate account of these obstructive speeches in its hundreds of thousands of pages. However, one would have to develop a means of identifying truly worthless speaking in a chamber that tolerates superfluity in debate on an everyday basis and apply it to every page of every volume of the *Record*.

The alternative approach is to identify references to filibusters in secondary sources. Books on Congress (e.g., Burdette 1940) have provided a starting point for such efforts, and scholars have developed lists of filibusters based on selected classic texts (Beth 1994; Bell and Overby 2007). However, these texts themselves provide only illustrative anecdotes rather than a comprehensive scan of congressional history (Beth 1995). It would be preferable to conduct an original scan of news coverage of Congress over a long period of time. This chapter describes such an effort, one based on thousands of articles drawn from the *New York Times*, *Time* magazine, and other sources.

FILIBUSTERING IN THE PUBLIC SPHERE

How can we measure filibustering by reading the news? The first step is selecting available media that cover Senate politics during the modern era. While the range of media sources is vast, this choice was simplified by two criteria: I sought Internet databases (so that I could conduct textual searches) that covered a *significant span* of congressional history. These criteria led to the selection of four publications: the *New York Times* (*NYT*), *Time* magazine, *Congressional Quarterly's Congress and the Nation* series, and the *Editorial Research Reports* available through *CQ Researcher*.

The *NYT*'s daily coverage provides the backbone of this data set. I searched the *New York Times* Historical Database (available through www.proquest. com) from 1901 to 2004 for all articles containing both *Senate* and *filibuster*. This yielded 6,055 articles pertaining to filibustering in the U.S. Congress. It would be risky to rely on the *NYT* alone, however. Like many publications, the policy preferences of the paper's editorial board and the interests of its readers may skew the data set in unintended ways. For example, a fifteen-hour filibuster in 1992 by Senator Alphonse D'Amato (R-NY) merited thirteen references in the *NYT* but no mentions in my other publications. In the late 1990s, the *NYT* covered campaign finance reform intensively and frequently editorialized on the topic, while other major filibusters (e.g., on abortion, defense policy, and compensatory leave) garnered no mentions.

Variety corrects for such idiosyncrasies. One alternative source is *Time*, a classic general news magazine available from March 1923 to 2004. I searched for all *Time* articles using the word *filibuster* and found 730 articles. Another

Table 6.1. Sources for Identifying Filibusters

Publication	Frequency	Time Span	Articles Coded	Unique Cases
New York Times	Daily	1901–2004	6,055	423
Time magazine	Weekly	1923–2004	730	27
Editorial Research Reports (legislative record summaries)	End of session	1923–56	31	7
Congress and the Nation	Quadrennial	1945–2004	463	126

Note: Some publications refer to filibusters before their initial publication date.

source is *Congress and the Nation,* a series published by the Congressional Quarterly Press.[1] The first volume details legislative action on key issues for the years 1945–64. Each subsequent volume summarizes the legislative highlights of a presidential term; for example, volume 2 covers 1965–68. *Congress and the Nation*'s overview articles are well suited to document the effects of filibustering on legislation of major and medium importance. A search yielded 463 articles that use the word *filibuster.* A final source is the *Editorial Research Reports,* which summarize the legislative activity of each session of Congress from 1925 to 1956. These reports are available through the *CQ Researcher Online.* Table 6.1 summarizes these four sources.

The drawback of variety is varying coverage. For the first twenty-two years, I rely exclusively on the *NYT,* then switch to three sources, then four, then three. On the other hand, the intensity of the *NYT*'s coverage of Congress seems to decrease over the course of time, and additional sources compensate for this decline. Moreover, this concern is limited to the extent that additional sources mention filibusters that the *NYT* does not *and* that they would similarly identify new filibusters if they published from 1901 to 1923. Table 6.1 shows the number of unique cases for each publication. The *NYT* provides a healthy number of unique filibusters, with *Congress and the Nation* adding 126.

It is also noteworthy that the two periodicals in the data set had similar patterns of coverage despite differences in tone and editorial perspective.[2] Figure 6.1 displays the number of filibuster mentions per Congress for the *NYT* and *Time.* Each source has its own scale (*Time* on the left, *NYT* on the right) so that we can focus on variation over time. The two sources share three peaks of filibuster mentions: the 81st Congress (1949–50), with multiple filibusters; the 88th Congress (1963–64), with the 1964 Civil Rights Act; and the 103rd Congress (1993–94), in which Senate Republicans resisted unified Democratic control of Congress and the White House.

While it is possible that some filibusters are absent from this tally, we can be reasonably confident that the most important ones will be mentioned by

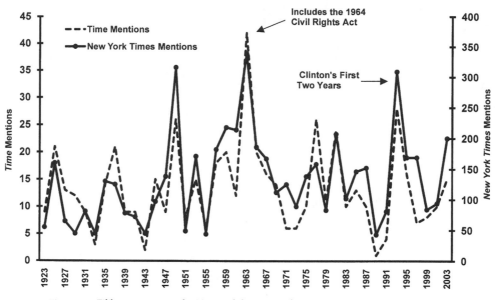

Figure 6.1. Filibuster mentions by *Time* and the *New York Times*.

at least one of the sources. As you will see, the most salient filibusters of the modern era are frequently mentioned in the news. More broadly, I expect that media attention increases with the political importance of a filibuster, so any missing cases are likely to be of limited visibility and importance.[3]

Coding Filibusters in the News

Having selected a set of articles, I then collected information from the selected articles. Table 6.2 summarizes the coding scheme used.

First, I categorized each article as either news article, editorial, opinion, letter to the editor, news summary, advertisement, legislative update or vote tally, or primary document (e.g., the text of a party platform or presidential news conference). About 600 articles made incidental use of the word *filibuster*, for example, references to the movie *Mr. Smith Goes to Washington*, to international arms negotiations, or the possibility of filibustering in the Senate.[4] Another 677 articles discuss the nature of Senate filibustering in general or efforts to reform Senate rules. The remainder, however, provided information about a filibuster against a specific bill. For every filibuster mentioned in each article, I coded for the current status, purpose, and effects of the filibuster.[5]

Second, I coded whether the filibuster was possible, threatened, ongoing, concluded, or not expected. In recent years, as we shall see, the distinction between a threatened, an ongoing, and a concluded filibuster becomes slender as cloture votes take the place of active filibusters. Articles that refer to

Table 6.2. Filibuster Article Coding Scheme

Type of Article	Filibuster Status	Filibuster Goal	Filibuster Outcome
News article	Expected/possible	Kill the target bill	Target bill defeated
Editorial	Threatened/hold	Amend the target	Amend the target
Opinion essay	Ongoing	Delay the target	Delay the target
Letter to the editor	Concluded	Take a stand	New issue scheduled
News summary	*Not* expected	Raise a new issue	Secondary bill delayed
Advertisement	Postcloture Filibuster	Delay a secondary bill	Secondary target killed
Vote tally/update		Kill a secondary target	No effect
Primary document		Force a special session	

a "hold" on a bill are coded as threats. I also noted whether the filibuster continued after a successful cloture vote.

Next, I coded for the motives of the obstructionists. Sometimes, senators' motives are simple: they wish to *block* the bill they are filibustering against (the "target" bill) or *force changes* in it. In other cases, they are *fighting for the right to offer germane amendments* to the target bill, and they filibuster to oppose efforts by the majority (often the majority *party*) to limit the amending process. In 1995, for example, Senate Democrats filibustered a constitutional amendment (a proposal needing a two-thirds threshold to pass!) so that they could offer germane amendments to it ("Senate Democrats Threaten Balanced-Budget Measure" 1995, 8). I lump such cases together with attempts to force changes since it is often unclear ex ante whether the desired amendments will pass. Fourth, senators sometimes filibuster to *force action on another, unrelated issue.* For example, in 1935, a band of senators threatened to filibuster unless the Senate held a vote on neutrality legislation; in 2001, Republican senators blocked a foreign aid bill to obtain votes on some of President Bush's judicial nominees. Fifth, senators may obstruct simply to get attention or *take a stand* (see Mayhew 2000). Sixth, legislators may filibuster one bill (the "buffer" bill) to *delay action on a second bill* (the target bill). Seventh, delay itself may be the goal of a filibuster, as when Senator Robert Byrd (D-WV) slowed a bill to create a Homeland Security Department in summer 2002 to ensure that the topic was discussed fully ("For Homeland Security Bill, a Brakeman" 2002, 17; "Homeland Security Bill Gains" 2002, 13). Finally, before the adoption of the Twentieth Amendment, senators sometimes felt it in their interest to block the passage of major legislation—especially appropriations bills—to force the president to call Congress back into session during the following spring or summer.

Third, I coded the effects of each filibuster. One possible outcome is that a filibuster has *no discernible effect.* A filibuster may lead to the *delay* of, *changes* in, or the *defeat of* a target bill; each possibility is coded separately. In many cases, the senator(s) leading the filibuster object only to a specific provision of a bill. Since 1977, for example, several omnibus energy policy bills have been blocked by senators who oppose drilling in the Alaska National Wildlife Refuge. In such cases, the goal is coded as *amend the bill,* and, if the obnoxious provision is defeated, this is also coded, as *bill amended due to filibuster.* I also coded the effects of a filibuster on other legislation when possible. If another bill or issue was forced onto the Senate agenda by a filibuster, I coded that as a *new agenda item.* If a secondary bill was *delayed* or *killed* by a filibuster, I coded that as well.[6]

There are times when the coding scheme simply fails to capture the essence of the situation. Sometimes, the Senate collapses into a complete free-for-all of filibustering, with multiple cliques of senators conducting multiple filibusters to block legislation, to hold other bills hostage as leverage, or simply to stop the Senate entirely until they get what they want. These "clusterbusters" are marked by a set of interlocking and escalating use of the power to obstruct.

FILIBUSTERS IN THE HOUSE, 1901-2004

This data collection scheme was intended to measure filibustering in the U.S. Senate. By accident, I also found evidence of filibustering on the other side of the Capitol, throughout the fifty states, and around the globe. Before focusing on the Senate, let us note that filibustering is not limited to a single legislature. In chapter 1, I mentioned that I found references to filibusters in twenty states and nineteen countries. Here, I will quickly describe the House filibusters that were noted in my sources.

Figure 6.2 displays the number of House filibusters by decade. Clearly, the imposition of Reed's rules from 1890 to 1894 did not completely eradicate filibustering in the House of Representatives. These rules made it easier to maintain a quorum while the House was debating and amending a bill by lowering the threshold for a quorum in the Committee of the Whole to one hundred members and empowering the presiding officer to ignore dilatory motions. Nonetheless, several opportunities for dilatory behavior remain in the rules. Any member can request the presence of a quorum in the Committee of the Whole and halt action until one hundred representatives are counted. During the Sixty-eighth Congress, for example, there were 309 quorum calls that consumed 150 hours of the chamber's time ("Did and Didn't" 1925). Also, if a bill comes up under an "open" rule (i.e., any member can offer any germane amendment), then opponents can filibuster by offering hundreds of amendments and forcing roll call votes on each one.

There are two reasons we do not observe more House members using these tactics. First, over the course of the twentieth century, the usage of the

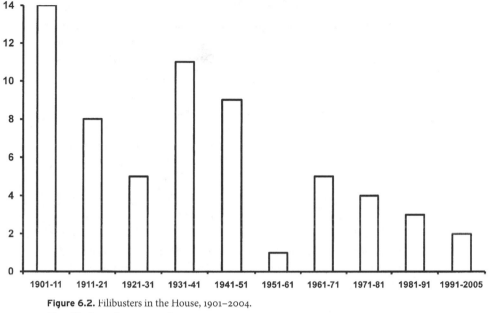

Figure 6.2. Filibusters in the House, 1901–2004.
Note: The last column spans fourteen years.

word *filibuster* shifts away from meaning "behavior that prevents action" to meaning "talking ceaselessly." Consequently, when journalists observe dilatory tactics in the House, they are less likely than their predecessors to label it a *filibuster*. For example, two recent cases missing from the list of House filibusters are unfunded mandate reform (1995), when the Democrats forced dozens of roll call votes on amendments, and agricultural appropriations (1999), when Tom Coburn (R-OK) filed over a hundred amendments to the bill (*Congressional Quarterly Almanac* 1999, 2-5–2-16). Both bills came up under an open rule. Second, if a minority of the House begins to exploit these loopholes, the Rules Committee can propose a "special rule" suspending the minority's rights until they remember that their prerogatives are subject to the good humor of the majority. Since it is comparatively easy to amend the rules of the House by majority vote, the majority party can also resort to a permanent change in the rules.

In recent years, House members (usually the minority party) tend to filibuster to achieve a short-term delay or to protest actions of the majority that are felt to be particularly abusive. In May 2007, for example, House Republicans filibustered to stave off a proposed rules change limiting "motions to recommit," which are de facto amendments to a bill. These motions may often be the minority party's best chance to offer amendments to a bill (Krehbiel and Meirowitz 2002; but see Roberts 2005), and the Republican minority had been unusually successful at winning these motions to recommit

(O'Connor 2007), leading to a rumored Democratic plan to restrict the kind of motions that could be offered (Kucinich 2007). The Republicans retaliated on May 16, 2007, with twelve dilatory motions, starting with a motion to adjourn at 11:49 A.M.[7] Within hours, the Democratic leadership dropped the proposal (it was adopted at the beginning of the 111th Congress).

The House's sixty-two filibusters include some major bills. In 1946, a bill to authorize an employment antidiscrimination agency (the Fair Employment Practices Commission) was defeated by a one-day-a-week filibuster after it came up under the House's Calendar Wednesday rule.[8] In 1968, the Republican minority in both chambers filibustered a bill to waive the equal time requirements for a televised presidential debate. House Republicans claimed that they were fighting to bring a campaign finance bill to the floor; Democrats accused them of trying to spare Nixon from a presidential debate. House Republicans used quorum calls and document reading to extend debate for twenty-seven hours straight; Speaker McCormack eventually locked the doors of the House to maintain a quorum and pass the bill ("House Votes TV Debates" 1968), only to see it die in a Senate filibuster.

FILIBUSTERS IN THE U.S. SENATE, 1901-2004: AN OVERVIEW

From 1901 to 2004, I identified 879 distinct filibusters.[9] The peaks occur in the 103rd Congress (1993–94), with thirty-eight bills endangered by a filibuster, and the 104th Congress (1995–96), with forty-seven bills filibustered. More broadly, from 1975 to 2004, there are never fewer than twenty filibusters per Congress. This is illustrated in figure 6.3, which charts the number of filibusters per Congress throughout the modern era. For comparison, figure 6.3 includes the number of filibusters included in Richard Beth's 1994 compilation.

One noticeable pattern is that the number of filibusters is elevated for the first thirty-six years of the twentieth century, then dips until the 1960s, then increases dramatically. Second, until the 1990s, there are far more filibusters in this data set than in the Beth list. The difference is starkest in the Sixty-eighth Congress (1923–25) and in the Seventy-third Congress (1933–35), with nineteen and eighteen filibusters, respectively, compared to none listed for those years by Beth. Later, the difference between my tally and Beth's is nineteen more for the Ninety-fifth Congress (1977–78) and twenty-seven more for the Ninety-seventh Congress (1981–82). Overall, for the period 1901–92, I counted 675 filibusters, while Beth counted 275. The lists concur on 206 filibusters (74.9 percent), while 69 are unique to Beth's list. Figure 6.4 shows these coding conflicts for the Beth data over time. Some of these are due to coding differences; for example, sometimes I coded *general blockade against all bills,* while Beth codes specific bills targeted by the blockade. Toward the

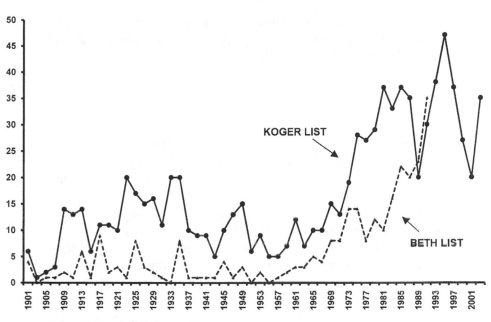

Figure 6.3. Senate filibusters per Congress, 1901–2004.

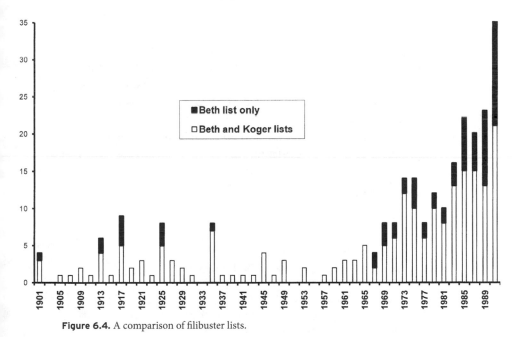

Figure 6.4. A comparison of filibuster lists.

end of the modern era, the number of discrepancies suggests that identifying filibusters in the current environment—in which senators avoid protracted floor fights—is difficult. This justifies the use of multiple sources to compensate for the evolution of Senate practice.

Top Ten List

Next, we can identify the ten most-mentioned Senate filibusters of the modern era. The more references to a filibuster in our data set, we might assume, the more important it was in its own time or in following years. These filibusters are listed in table 6.3.

The top filibuster is no surprise. The passage of the 1964 Civil Rights Act, discussed below, was a pivotal event in American history and provoked the longest Senate filibuster ever at fifty-seven days. Four more civil rights measures make the top ten list: the 1937–38 Wagner–Van Nuys antilynching bill, the Civil Rights acts of 1957 and 1960, and Rule 22 reform in 1949. The cloture reform effort of 1949 was understood at the time as the test for civil rights and, more broadly, President Truman's agenda. The filibuster of Abe Fortas's nomination as chief justice of the Supreme Court is an interesting case for the third most notorious filibuster. Fortas's defeat lingered in reporters' memories for years, with twenty-nine post-1968 mentions as Fortas's career unfolded and other controversial judges were nominated to the Supreme Court. The 1993 supplemental "stimulus" bill was noteworthy, not for its policy importance (it would have allowed an additional $17 billion in spending), but for its political impact. Contrary to expectations, the Republican minority defied a newly elected president and Democratic majorities in Congress and demonstrated that, even under unified government, senators could filibuster to block legislation (Brady and Volden 2006; Krehbiel

Table 6.3. Most-Mentioned Senate Filibusters, 1901–2004

Congress	Years	Bill	Mentions
88th	1963–64	1964 civil rights bill (HR 7152)	275
81st	1949	Cloture reform (SR 15)	122
90th	1968	Abe Fortas nomination for chief justice	115
85th	1957	Civil Rights Act (HR 6127)	109
86th	1960	Civil Rights Act (HR 8315)	100
89th	1965–66	Repeal 14(b) (right to work) (HR 77)	98
75th	1937–38	Wagner–Van Nuys antilynching bill (HR 1507)	83
69th	1927	Reed (MO) resolution to investigate 1926 Pennsylvania campaign (SR 364)	81
103rd	1993	Supplemental appropriations "stimulus package" (HR 1335)	78
105th	1997–98	Campaign finance reform (SR 1663/SR 25)	76

1998). The 1997–98 McCain-Feingold bill received much attention—including twenty *NYT* editorials—in the wake of campaign fund-raising investigations following the 1996 presidential campaign.

Short Sessions

The seventh most notorious filibuster is the mostly forgotten "Battle of the Reeds" during the short session of the Sixty-ninth Congress (1927). James Reed (D-MO) wished to extend his special committee's investigation into the 1926 elections of William Vare (R-PA) and Frank Smith (R-IL). David Reed (R-PA) wished to block the investigation so that the standing Committee on Privileges and Elections could regain control over the cases. Party control of the Senate was at stake: Republicans needed to seat both Vare and Smith to retain their majority. Reed (PA) blocked the resolution to extend the life of the committee; Reed (MO) retaliated by obstructing all other legislation until his resolution came up for a vote. This stalemate continued through two all-night sessions and lasted until the end of the session. There was immense collateral damage: several funding bills failed, including a "second deficiency bill" that was vital to government operations ("New Filibuster Holds the Senate" 1927, 1).[10]

The Battle of the Reeds exemplifies the general pattern of obstruction during short sessions, particularly at the end. With just a few days and a crush of bills to pass, any senator could credibly threaten to block one bill with extended debate and, in the process, deny floor time to many more. The cloture rule was not much help during these end-of-session rushes since multiple cloture petitions might be necessary to force a bill through and each petition requires a two-day layover. The result is a series of clusterbusters from 1911 to 1933, with most short sessions marked by some tumult as senators take advantage of the scarcity of time to block measures they despise or take hostages to force consideration of bills they favor. One famous example of this is the Ship Arming Act of 1917 (see Bawn and Koger 2008; Ryley 1975), which was easily defeated by a "little band of willful men," as Woodrow Wilson called them. The ensuing outcry against this filibuster, fanned by Wilson, led to the adoption of the Senate's two-thirds cloture rule in 1917 (Koger 2007).

These end-of-Congress crushes intensified over the first third of the twentieth century. Figure 6.5 illustrates the timing of filibuster mentions over the course of each session. The bottom axis is a timeline of the pre–Twentieth Amendment Congress, beginning with April of odd-numbered years, then an even-numbered year, then January–March of an odd-numbered year. For illustration, the period 1901–48 is broken into six periods on three charts. Each line is the sum of all filibuster mentions in the *NYT* by month across four congresses.[11]

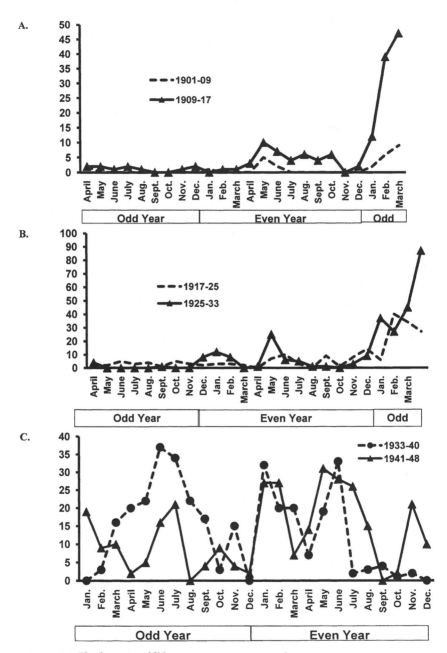

Figure 6.5. The dynamics of filibuster mentions. *a*, 1901–17. *b*, 1917–33. *c*, 1933–48.

Figure 6.5a shows us that, in the first sixteen years of the twentieth century, there was very little filibustering in the first years of congresses (the Fifty-seven Congress through the Sixty-Fourth). This is not too surprising since the Senate was typically out of session for the first eight months of each two-year span. Most reported filibustering occurred in the last three months of the congresses in this time span—about 64 percent for both periods. Note too that the number of filibuster mentions increases significantly during the eight years preceding the adoption of the Senate's first cloture rule in 1917, from 27 to 153. This pattern continues unabated after the adoption of the Senate cloture rule. Figure 6.5b shows the pattern of filibustering from 1917 to 1933. Although there are some major battles earlier in the Senate schedule, for example, the World Court Treaty in January 1926, the major pattern is a surge of obstruction during the last three months of Congress.

During this period, a proposal by Senator George Norris (R-NE) to eliminate these embarrassing short sessions and reorganize the political calendar gathered steam. This amendment, ratified in January 1933, imposed the calendar in use today: two sessions of Congress, each beginning in early January. This change had a major influence on the *timing* of Senate obstruction, as shown in figure 6.5c. From 1933 to 1948, the pattern is more episodic, with most upticks traceable to specific filibusters rather than structural incentives. The one potential pattern is that filibustering increases in June and July of each year. New appropriations bills had to be passed by July 1 of each year, and some other legislative deadlines were pegged to the beginning of the fiscal year as well. This deadline increased the credibility of filibustering threats (since the senator[s] would have to last only a fixed period of time) and created a specific set of high-value hostages.

FILIBUSTERS: GOALS AND OUTCOMES

I coded the motives of filibustering senators and the consequences of their actions. Possible motives included (1) killing the target bill, (2) killing a secondary bill, (3) amending the target bill, (4) raising a new issue, (5) taking a stand, (6) delay the target bill, (7) delaying a secondary bill, and (8) forcing a special session. If an article did not specify why a senator was filibustering a bill, the default assumption was that he tried to kill the bill. It is possible to code a single filibuster for multiple motives. This could occur if the entire team of legislators had multiple goals (say, amending the target bill and bringing up a new issue), if different subsets of the obstructionist team had distinct goals, or if senators' goals evolved over the course of their effort.

Figure 6.6 summarizes the motives of filibustering senators over the years. The top two categories are not surprising: most of the time, senators filibustered to kill legislation or to force changes in the target bill. The

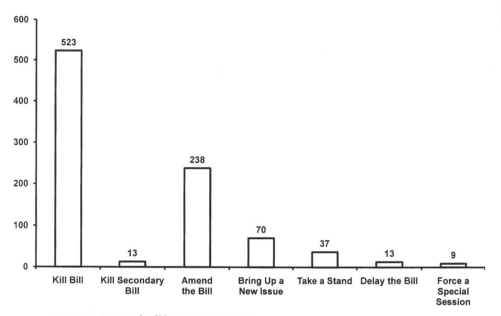

Figure 6.6. Motives for filibustering, 1901–2004.

third-highest-ranking category, however, is more interesting. In seventy cases, senators obstructed so that they could raise a new issue and have it debated on the Senate floor. *Raising a new issue* means that the filibustering senator(s) would like to either offer a nongermane amendment to a bill or force the majority party to schedule a different bill. Filibustering to take a stand appeared less than I expected. It is possible that senators who filibustered to attract public attention to themselves and their positions were unlikely to say as much to the press and that other senators were reluctant to call them out.

Hostage Taking

The practice of hostage-taking filibusters to set the agenda is rarely discussed, so I will describe some illustrative cases. In February 1931, Senator Jim Couzens (R-MI) blocked all important legislation until he had some assurance that President Hoover would veto a bill granting immediate loans to World War I veterans.[12] Couzens favored the bill and wanted some assurance that Congress would have an opportunity to override Hoover's veto; if Hoover did not actively veto the bill, it would die after Congress adjourned. At the behest of congressional leaders, Hoover agreed to veto the bill, and Congress successfully overrode the veto ("Battle of the Bonus" 1931; "Will Veto Bonus Bill" 1931).

In June 1934, the Senate was rushing through an end-of-session crush of legislation when Huey Long (D-LA) threatened to block all legislation unless the Senate passed the Federal Farm Bankruptcy Act. He filibustered to get permission to hold a conference committee meeting, then filibustered to delay adjournment after he lost the report of the conference committee (it was in his pocket). Two days later, Long threatened a blockade unless he got a vote on the bill. Long's piracy was not in vain: President Roosevelt signed the bill, and it provided farmers with shelter from bankruptcy during the dark days of the Great Depression ("Farm Debtor Bill Sent to President" 1934; "Missing Papers" 1934).[13]

In the spring of 1996, the Democratic minority wanted to vote on and pass a bill to raise the minimum wage—a popular issue opposed by small business groups that supported the Republicans. Senate Democrats offered their minimum wage hike as an amendment to a series of bills (including immigration reform and a national parks bill) and obstructed the progress of these hostage bills until they were guaranteed a vote. The Republicans eventually scheduled a minimum wage increase bill, which passed and became law. Thus, the Democrats' hostage-taking strategy led to a $0.90 per hour increase in the minimum wage ("Impasse on Wage Issue" 1996, B9; "Frustrated Dole" 1996, 19; *Congressional Quarterly Almanac* 1996, 7-3-7-9).

The use of hostage-taking filibusters richens our understanding of legislative politics. Many theoretical models of legislative politics, including the pivotal politics model, assume that issues are considered one at a time and that each policy can be understood as a continuous choice, that is, a debate over whether we should have more or less highway spending, environmental regulation, etc. The minimum wage is a classic more-or-less issue in which legislators are assumed to have an ideal minimum wage ($0, $5, $23) and vote for the wage that is closest to their own ideal (e.g., Poole and Rosenthal 1997). However, legislators can also filibuster a proposal on one issue with a demand for action on a completely different issue.

Indeed, many *germane* filibusters suggest that legislation is more complex than a point proposal on a single dimension. In the modern Congress, major bills on topics like taxes, farming, banking, defense, and energy are typically omnibus proposals. Thus, the filibusters we observe are often directed, not at the entire bill (since some of its provisions may be uncontroversial), but instead at discrete provisions like drilling for oil in the Alaska National Wildlife Refuge, funding for MX ballistic missiles, changes in the Community Reinvestment Act (banking), etc. While it is much easier to think about legislating one issue at a time, major bills are often bundles of discrete proposals with senators fighting over the parts rather than the whole.

Buffer Bills

A rare but intriguing tactic used by obstructionists is to block one bill as a proxy for blocking another measure on the agenda. For example, in March 1935, Huey Long filibustered an army appropriations bill for the express purpose of delaying a pending work relief bill. The goal was to gain time to build public support for a "prevailing wage" amendment, and Long feared that he could not last very long if he waited until the work relief bill reached the floor to begin his filibuster ("Filibuster by Long" 1935, 9). In April 1935, Southern senators delayed a bill aiding tenant farmers for the express purpose of preventing action on an antilynching bill ("Lynching Bill Foes" 1935, 1; "Filibuster Threat" 1935, 1). In February 1975, Senator James Allen (D-AL) filibustered a bill to aid Penn Central Railroad as a means of preventing debate on cloture reform. Since Penn Central operates in the Northeast, Allen hoped that delaying this bill would make Northeastern senators impatient enough to abandon cloture reform ("Senate Filibuster Stalls" 1975).

There are three reasons for legislators to filibuster buffer bills. First, if the filibustering team is small, filibustering multiple bills increases the number of speeches that legislators can offer. Second, a buffer bill can be a hostage, with inaction on the target bill as the ransom. Third, it may be more politically acceptable to obstruct the buffer bill than to obstruct the real target bill. In November 1937, for example, Southern Democrats filibustered an antilynching bill to prevent its passage. However, it was no fluke that the bill came up at that point. There was an executive reorganization bill ready for the floor that several senators opposed privately but did not want to vote against publicly, so, while senators waited for the Agriculture Committee to prepare a vital farm bill, senators conducted a futile debate on the antilynching bill. Northerners got credit for trying, Southerners got credit for blocking, and the reorganization bill was kept from the floor ("Lynch Bill Fought" 1937, 1).

Forcing a Special Session

Before the adoption of the Twentieth Amendment, one motive to filibuster was to compel the president to call a special session immediately after the short session ended. Senators forced the president's hand by blocking legislation that could not wait until the following December, especially appropriations bills that had to pass by June 30.

There were two reasons to desire a special session. Senators—especially a new incoming majority party—may simply wish to have the Senate in session so that they can monitor the president's appointments and foreign policy decisions. If Congress is not in session, of course, the president can make recess appointments, so forcing a special session is a means of maintaining Senate control over executive appointments. In February 1917, for example, the Senate Republican caucus agreed to blockade key legislation to force President Wilson to consult with them on foreign policy. Officially, the Republicans ended this strategy before the infamous ship arming bill filibuster that ended the Sixty-fourth Congress, but several Republicans participated in this effort ("Filibuster for Extra Session" 1917, 1). Second, senators may have a policy agenda that they wish to implement as soon as possible, so forcing the president to convene Congress is better than waiting until next December.

Effects of Filibusters

Figure 6.7 summarizes the effects of filibusters from 1901 to 2004. For this tally, a bill was killed by a filibuster if it failed to pass the Senate after being filibustered.[14] This includes a few cases in which less than a majority voted for cloture because some senators may have supported the bill but opposed cloture. It also includes some cases in which a bill's overall prospects were doubtful—for example, the president was likely to veto the bill—since it is difficult to anticipate the actions of the House and the president on hundreds of bills that died in the Senate. Bills were coded as *amended* if a text indicated that senators modified bills in response to filibusters.

The most common effect (343 of 878 filibusters) is that a bill jeopardized by filibustering dies. Another 222 bills were amended, and 65 were delayed.

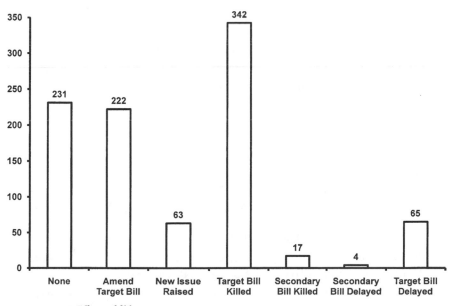

Figure 6.7. Effects of filibusters, 1901–2004.

The second most common result, however, is no effect. In 63 cases, obstruction led to another bill being scheduled.

Our theory of filibustering helps us understand why there are so many seemingly futile filibusters. One answer is simple uncertainty. Obstructionists may not know ahead of time how many senators will aid in a filibuster or the determination of the majority coalition, so they do not know whether they will succeed. The second answer is that senators may be rewarded for fighting the good fight. Filibustering is a good way for senators to attract media attention to their positions and to ingratiate themselves with constituents and organized interests. In 1986 and 1992, for example, Al D'Amato (R-NY) waged solitary filibusters on behalf of his constituents that coincided with his reelection campaigns.

Filibustering thus has significant effects on the content of legislation and on legislators' reputations. While we think of filibustering as a negative practice that inhibits policy change, senators also obstruct to *facilitate* policy change. They do so by taking bills hostage so that they have something to bargain with and by holding up legislation until they are guaranteed a fair opportunity to offer amendments.

FILIBUSTERING AND CIVIL RIGHTS, 1901-2004

For many readers, filibustering in the Senate is associated with the struggle to ensure civil rights for African Americans during the mid-twentieth century. As one would expect, my scan of Senate filibustering found that Southern senators often used the right to unlimited debate to block or weaken civil rights legislation. The historical record suggests that the Southerners' ability to frustrate progress on civil rights was based on the greater intensity of their effort.

Table 6.4 lists all *active* filibusters against civil rights measures.[15] This list excludes cases of passive obstruction, that is, filibusters that were expected or threatened but never pressed to a confrontation on the Senate floor. There were twenty passive filibusters in the data set, including antilynching bills in the Seventy-third, Seventy-sixth, Eightieth, and Eighty-first congresses, two "Powell amendment" filibusters (in the Eighty-fourth and the Eighty-sixth congresses),[16] and the Thurgood Marshall appellate nomination mentioned in chapter 8. Three filibusters by proponents of *expanding* civil rights are included and shown in italics.

Overall, table 6.4 makes clear that active filibustering contributed to the defeat of over a dozen civil rights bills. Before 1957, nine of twelve civil rights measures were defeated outright. Congress enacted modest bills in 1957 and 1960 and some other minor measures, then the landmark Civil Rights Act of 1964 and the Voting Rights Act of 1965 (Caro 2002; Mann 1996). Thereafter,

Table 6.4. Active Civil Rights Filibusters, 1901–2004

	Year (Congress)	Bill Outcome	Mentions
Antilynching	1922 (67th)	Bill failed	16
Antilynching	1935 (74th)	Bill failed	30
Adjournment resolution (hostage)	1937 (75th)	Bill scheduled	2
Antilynching	1937–38 (75th)	Bill failed	83
Poll tax ban	1942 (77th)	Bill failed	28
Servicemen voting (poll tax provisions)	1942 (77th)	Bill passed	1
Poll tax ban	1944 (78th)	Bill failed	36
War agencies appropriations—FEPC	1945 (79th)	Funding reduced	11
Poll tax ban	1946 (79th)	Bill failed	10
FEPC authorization	1946 (79th)	Bill failed	63
Poll tax ban	1948 (80th)	Bill failed	40
SR 15, cloture reform	1949 (81st)	Compromise	122
FEPC authorization	1950 (81st)	Bill failed	57
Civil Rights Act	1957 (85th)	Compromise	109
Civil Rights Act	1960 (86th)	Compromise	100
Literacy test limits	1962 (87th)	Bill failed	26
Anti–poll tax constitutional amendment	1962 (87th)	Bill passed	22
Omnibus civil rights bill	1964 (88th)	Compromise	275
Voting Rights Act	1965 (89th)	Bill passed	21
Civil rights (fair housing)	1966 (89th)	Bill failed	58
Elementary education—desegregation and busing restrictions	1966 (89th)	Compromise	1
Civil rights workers/housing bias ban	1968 (90th)	Compromise	36
Voting Rights Act reauthorization	1970 (91st)	Bill Passed	12
Equal educational opportunities— antibusing amendment	1972 (92nd)	Bill Failed	16
EEOC enforcement powers	1972 (92nd)	Compromise	11
Voting Rights Act reauthorization	1975 (94th)	Bill passed	4
Fee shifting in civil rights cases	1976 (94th)	Bill passed	1
Fair housing	1980 (96th)	Bill failed	18
Justice Department reauthorization— antibusing rider	1981–82 (97th)	Bill passed	42
Voting Rights Act reauthorization	1982 (97th)	Bill passed	14
HJR 648 continuing resolution— Civil Rights Act of 1984	1984 (98th)	Provision defeated	14

Note: Filibusters by proponents of *expanding* civil rights are shown in italics.

the Senate battled over follow-up measures to reduce discrimination in housing and to increase the enforcement powers of the Equal Employment Opportunity Commission. There were also two filibusters against proposals to restrict the transportation of students across geographic boundaries to increase racial balance (i.e., busing).

Most civil rights filibusters in the first half of the twentieth century were marked by asymmetrical intensity: the Southern senators wanted to block the legislation far more than other senators wanted to pass it (on intensity and filibustering, see Bawn and Koger [2008]). While there were several senators like Hubert H. Humphrey (D-MN) who were personally and passionately committed to the cause of civil rights, the overall commitment of many non-Southern senators to civil rights paled in comparison to the Southerners' effort.

Senators' behavior with regard to the 1922 Dyer antilynching bill illustrates this asymmetry. On one side, the Southern Democrats were "the most perfectly organized the Senate has known since the Lodge Force Bill was brought up more than a score of years ago" ("Filibuster Menaces" 1922, 2). This team utilized a new tactic: compelling the Senate clerk to read the *Journal* of the previous day and offering amendments to it. The reading of the *Journal* took precedence over all other business and prevented senators from bringing up the antilynching bill (Koger 2006a). The Southern Democrats threatened to block every other bill until the Dyer bill was completely dead. Instead of attempting attrition or reform, the Republican majority shelved the bill; the topic did not return to the Senate floor until 1935.

For non-Southern senators who lacked personal convictions on civil rights, the issue posed a political dilemma. On the one hand, an ever-increasing migration of Southern blacks to Northern cities created a new and critical constituency in the "swing states" that determined the outcome of close presidential elections and control of Congress (Valelly 2004, 149–56). One way to appeal to this constituency was to promise federal action to improve civil rights in the South. However, the South was the bedrock of the Democratic coalition, and one of the core political demands of the white political elites of that region was *inaction* on civil rights. From the 1930s on, the Democratic and Republican parties both tried to appeal to Northern blacks and Southern whites—Democrats trying to hold their fragile coalition together, Republicans trying to peel off one group or the other (Frymer 1999). From 1930 to 1956, both parties apparently tried to create the appearance of effort on civil rights while minimizing actual policy change that would drive the South to the opposing party. For example, *Time* magazine treated the filibuster against the 1944 poll tax ban as a display of bunkum:

> Everybody else knew that a cynical Senate had quietly made an election-year deal, arranged everything backstage in advance. There would be 1) no filibuster, 2) no cloture, 3) no Marcantonio bill [banning poll taxes]. By the terms of the deal, Southerners would be allowed to protest at length and get themselves on record as favoring the poll tax and "white supremacy." Republicans and Northern Democrats, prodded by church, liberal, labor

and Negro organizations, would pass around a petition to impose cloture and force a vote. When cloture failed—as it did this week by a vote of
36–44—the bill would be quietly shelved, at least until after Nov. 7. ("Today:
'The Poll Tax Peril'" 1944)

Similarly, after a bill to establish a permanent Fair Employment Practices
Commission failed, the *NYT* columnist Arthur Krock placed the blame on
the supporters of the bill, who would neither vote for cloture nor keep the
Senate in continuous session, preferring to keep "banker's hours" ("Filibuster That Kept Banker's Hours" 1946, 23).

One manifestation of electoral calculations was the timing of Senate
action on civil rights. Most of the bills listed in table 6.4 above were debated
in election years, even though it was widely known that their consideration
would provoke a filibuster when legislators were eager to finish and return
home to campaign. A sophisticated strategy for sincere advocates would
have been to schedule these bills as soon as a new Congress began so that a
pro–civil rights majority would have ample time to wait out a filibuster during the slow opening months of the Congress.

Second, civil rights legislation was sometimes proposed or scheduled
for purely tactical reasons. In November 1940, for example, pro-Roosevelt
Democrats wanted to block two bills that Roosevelt opposed (one revised
the National Labor Relations Act; the other allowed judicial review of federal agency regulations). They considered bringing up an antilynching
bill so that Southern obstruction would consume the last month of the
Seventy-sixth Congress—conservative filibustering for liberal ends ("Senators Pressed" 1940, 17). While they did not follow through, this example
suggests that some of the support for this proposal was insincere.

Additionally, the inability of senators to invoke cloture on civil rights prior
to 1964 is puzzling. There were only eleven states in the former Confederacy,
with a total representation of only twenty-two senators. Of those, senators
from Tennessee were often inclined to support civil rights bills, while senators from West Virginia, Oklahoma, Kentucky, and Maryland sometimes
voted against civil rights bills and even joined in filibusters against them.
This left a core of only fifteen to twenty-five senators adamantly opposed to
civil rights. By themselves, these Southern senators never had enough votes
to prevent cloture on civil rights. Why did the Senate not simply force civil
rights bills through the Senate using the cloture rule?

There are two recurring answers: principle and horse-trading. Some
senators claimed to oppose the use of the cloture rule in general, which
meant that, despite their support for civil rights, they could not impinge
on free debate in the Senate (see chapter 8 below; and Binder and Smith
1997, 92–105). On the other hand, there are occasional claims that a group

of non-Southern senators made some sort of bargain to vote against cloture in return for Southern support for their pet policy proposals. Caro (2002) claims, for example, that a key bloc of Western senators agreed to vote against cloture on the 1957 civil rights bill in exchange for legislative action on a bill related to the Hell's Canyon dam project. Similarly, W. E. B. DuBois suggested that a coalition of Southerners and Westerners agreed to let the 1922 antilynching bill die in exchange for limits on Japanese immigration ("Fifty Years of Crusading" 1940, 81).

Taken at face value, these answers highlight the tenuous support for civil rights in the Senate. In the first case, senators are claiming that their opposition to using a prerogative granted by the rules of their own chamber exceeds their opposition to having citizens lynched or denied the right to vote. Senators who bargained their votes on civil rights valued other policy rewards more than they did progress on civil rights.

A final indicator of the weak intensity of support for civil rights in the Senate is the relative absence of *pro*–civil rights filibusters. Above, we noted the use of hostage taking to barter for consideration of new issues. During the first six decades of the twentieth century, senators were certainly aware of this strategy. Indeed, in 1937, advocates of an antilynching bill successfully extracted a guarantee of floor time for their bill in exchange for allowing the Senate to adjourn the session ("Record of the 75th Congress" 1937). This is the only such episode in the data set, however. Instead, senators and interest groups supporting civil rights legislation pegged their hopes on reforming the Senate cloture rule, an effort that was similarly constrained by apathy (Zelizer 2004). Senators who were passionate about civil rights per se might have been more successful obstructing to extort floor time and guaranteed final-passage votes for civil rights bills.[17]

The drought of civil rights legislation ended with the 1957 Civil Rights Act. Though this act is remembered as weak and flawed compared to its successors, it had the distinction of being the first civil rights law since 1875. The course of the 1957 civil rights bill has been well documented (e.g., Caro 2002; Mann 1996) as Southerners used the threat of obstruction to extract compromises but never overtly filibustered the bill or tried to prevent its passage. Why did Southern senators not kill it by filibustering, just as they had blocked a dozen other bills since 1922? There are several reports that fear of a strong cloture rule deterred a more active filibuster. The 1949 cloture rule exempted proposals to change the rules of the Senate from the cloture process. Senators and interest groups dissatisfied with the rule mobilized efforts to liberalize it in 1957 (Binder and Smith 1997; Wolfinger 1971; Zelizer 2004). Although their attempt failed 38–55, this margin represented a seventeen-vote increase over the previous effort in 1953. Majority Leader Lyndon Johnson (D-TX) noted this increase in the size of the reform coalition and feared that cloture reform

would gather more steam if the Senate continued to block civil rights bills
(Mann 1996, 183–84). Johnson convinced the Southerners that they needed
to let a modest civil rights bill slip through the Senate; otherwise, the reformers would impose majority cloture in 1959 and pass whatever civil rights bills
they wished (Caro 2002, 864).

This argument may explain the Southerners' restrained tactics against
the 1957 civil rights bill on the Senate floor. To be sure, Southerners made
long speeches against it and used the implicit threat of a filibuster to extract
concessions, but they refrained from an all-out effort to kill it (Caro 2002).
When the bill emerged from a conference committee, the Southern senators
formally decided to refrain from filibustering. The fear of majority cloture
was reportedly a key part of this decision:

> Southern Senators decided that a filibuster would be both futile and dan-
> gerous: it might result in a harsher bill, it might bring about a change in the
> Senate's cloture rule, and it would certainly build up ill will that could only
> harm the Southern cause in future years. ("The Last, Hoarse Gasp" 1957)

> Senators James O. Eastland and John C. Stennis, Mississippi Democrats,
> said in a statement that the Southern bloc had agreed at a strategy confer-
> ence this week that a filibuster would only make closure easier to obtain in
> the future. ("Russell Assails Nixon" 1957, 1)[18]

This is the backdrop for the longest solo filibuster in Senate history: Strom
Thurmond's twenty-four-hour, eighteen-minute solo effort on August 28
and 29, 1957, against the civil rights conference report. With a few short
interruptions, Thurmond spoke continuously until his voice dwindled to a
dull whisper. Not a single Southerner joined in the effort, and Thurmond
did not request any aid before beginning his speech. The filibuster generated
the impression that Thurmond was fighting for the South while the other
senators snoozed, and, when he was done, Herman Talmadge (D-GA) came
to the floor to criticize his "grandstand of longwinded speeches," which
would "in the long run wreak unspeakable havoc upon my people" ("The
Last, Hoarse Gasp" 1957).

An alternative explanation for the success of the 1957 bill is that the Southerners let it pass so that the Democrats could shore up their support with
African American voters. In the 1956 election, African American support
for President Eisenhower increased around 20 percent over 1952, the largest
swing of any demographic group. Black voters were a critical swing group in
the Midwest and Northeast and helped Eisenhower win five Southern states
(Glantz 1960; Irving 1957; Mann 1996, 178–81). Consequently, Democratic
leaders thought that progress on civil rights was critical to the party's electoral fortunes. Southern senators may have allowed a modest bill to pass so

that their party could retain control of the Senate and compete for the White House in 1960. In order for this to be true, they would have had to believe that passing a civil rights bill would make a critical difference to the party's future and that they would gain more from the party's collective fortunes than they would lose by allowing a bill to pass.[19]

Nonetheless, the balance of evidence seems to tilt toward this bill as a case of reform deterrence. One of LBJ's policy aides during this era endorses this explanation: "Johnson persuaded Russell that a filibuster, if it were successful, would so embitter the nonsouthern Democrats that they would change the rules on the filibuster and there was a fair chance that there would be a majority cloture as a result. And so, far better to negotiate, never to describe it as a filibuster, always to say negotiations are going on and that sort of thing" (McPherson 1985, 16). An early LBJ biography echoed this explanation:

> Russell would scarcely make so critical a strategic decision out of his sentiment for his old protégé. The real reason lay in the fact that Russell totally agreed with Johnson's warnings about the danger to Southern self-interest of a filibuster now that the coalition was crumbling—on two scores. If the Southerners successfully filibustered the bill to death, the country would rise up in anger and demand that the filibuster rule be changed, causing the South untold misery in the future; but if the civil rights bloc succeeded in breaking a filibuster, the defeat would open the bill to amendments by triumphant liberals far more unacceptable to the South than a mere voting rights bill. (Evans and Novak 1966, 127–28)

It seems that the threat of reform was at least part of the explanation for the passage of the 1957 Civil Rights Act.

Lyndon Johnson stressed the psychological value of the 1957 and 1960 acts as preparation for the idea that Congress might occasionally adopt civil rights measures (Caro 2002), but the 1964 Civil Rights Act was a turning point for civil rights legislation by making it federal policy to enforce nondiscrimination in employment and public accommodations. Why did Congress finally pass a major civil rights bill in 1964? A key factor is an enormous increase in public interest in civil rights legislation. President John F. Kennedy proposed the core of the bill in June 1963, but the bill's visibility increased dramatically after Kennedy's assassination. In his first address to Congress as president, Lyndon Johnson urged Congress to pass civil rights legislation as a tribute to Kennedy (Mann 1996, 383). Also, media coverage of incidents of racial oppression raised public interest outside the South (Caro 2002; Mann 1996). In Washington, DC, civil rights groups announced efforts to clearly label and defeat their opponents on the basis of their votes on the 1964 civil rights bill (Harvey 1973, 8), and they were joined by national

("Statehood for Alaska and Hawaii" 1965). These concerns interacted: partisan balance could be achieved by inducting both states, but the addition of four votes to the Senate rather than two at a time heightened Southern concerns.

Over the last four decades, senators have been especially prone to filibuster campaign finance reform legislation. Obviously, senators' interests as incumbents and partisans are at stake, so they are likely to take campaign finance reform seriously. Their interest in the issue increased with the cost of campaigning and the difficulty of fund-raising as well as in reaction to publicized scandals like President Nixon's 1972 campaign (Zelizer 2004). During the 1960s and 1970s, filibusters blocked bills to subsidize campaign spending and/or limit campaign spending. In partisan terms, these reforms favored Democrats, while the status quo tended to favor Republicans. During the 1990s, the primary goal of campaign finance reform was to ban "soft money" donations to formal party committees.[23]

The Senate's battles over S. 25, a ban on soft money authored by John McCain (R-AZ) and Russ Feingold (D-WI), illustrated the tactics of modern filibustering. In 1997, Senate Democrats sought action on the issue to highlight a key contrast with Republicans (who tended to oppose reform) and to distance themselves from the activities of the 1996 Clinton campaign (Zelizer 2004). Majority Leader Trent Lott brought up S. 25 after President Clinton threatened to bring Congress back into session if it adjourned without voting on campaign finance reform. However, Republicans offered a killer amendment that required labor unions to obtain the consent of their members before using dues for political purposes. Lott shielded this proposal by offering several amendments to the bill and to his own proposal. Since only a limited number of amendments can be considered at one time, the Democrats could not offer their own proposal or amend Lott's amendment; this tactic is known as *filling the amendment tree*. Since they lacked the votes to defeat Lott's amendment, Democrats filibustered the amendment and filed cloture petitions on the bill. After five failed cloture votes (three on the bill, two on Lott's amendment), Lott pulled the bill from the floor and decried the Democrats' filibuster of their own bill (*Congressional Quarterly Almanac* 1997, 1-27).

Subsequently, Democrats offered the soft money ban as an amendment to other major legislation. When a highway spending bill came up in October 1997, Republicans shielded the bill by filling the amendment tree. Democrats responded by blocking a vote on the bill, taking it hostage until the Senate voted on campaign reform (*Congressional Quarterly Almanac* 1997, 3-21). After a similar confrontation over education tax breaks, Republicans agreed to bring the McCain-Feingold bill to the floor in 1998 (*Congressional Quarterly Almanac* 1997, 7-7). In February 1998, the roles reversed, but the outcome remained the same. Lott offered his "Paycheck Protection Act," McCain offered his bill as an amendment, and cloture votes on both failed.

church organizations that had previously remained on the sidelines (Mann 1996). Notably, citizens and groups attached importance to whether the bill was filibustered. There were threats of civil disobedience and labor union strikes and fears that, if the bill was defeated by a filibuster, African Americans would become radicalized or even violent ("No Longer a 'Problem'" 1963, 148). Finally, the Democratic platforms of 1960 and 1964 committed the party to further action on civil rights in voting, schools, housing, and employment. The Republican platform of 1960 exceeded the Democratic platform in the length and specificity of its promises, but the party's 1964 platform was brief and vague on promoting civil rights.[20]

The combination of demonstrations, party promises, and Johnson's linkage of civil rights to Kennedy's legacy generated unprecedented attention given to civil rights legislation in the Senate (Valeo 1999, 98–103). As figure 6.8 illustrates, the expected filibuster was mentioned in over a hundred articles before it officially began in March 1964, and high-intensity coverage continued until the bill passed. As a result of this shift in public attitude, senators who were previously indifferent and willing to logroll with Southern senators now found that alliance with the South would be costly in their home states (Mann 1996, 410; Valeo 1999, 113). On the other hand, the political rewards to Southern senators for opposing the civil rights bill were decreasing. The attitudes of Southern whites toward desegregation were softening; an August 1963 poll by Louis Harris found that 54 percent

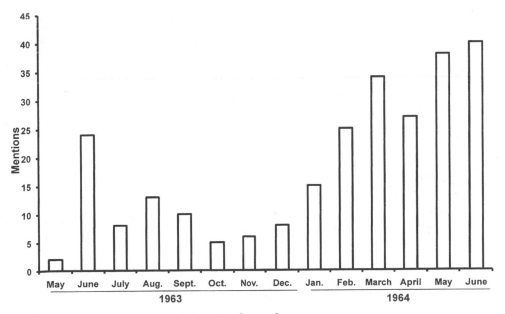

Figure 6.8. 1964 Civil Rights Act mentions by month.

of *Southern* whites favored desegregating public accommodations (Mann 1996, 366). Even Richard Russell (D-GA), the leader of the Southern bloc, conceded that the bill would probably pass ("Message Viewed as Election Key" 1964, 1).[21] And so it did, after the longest filibuster in the history of the U.S. Senate: fifty-seven working days (seventy-five days overall). Chapter 8 returns to the 1964 Civil Rights Act to review the tactics used by the opponents and the proponents of the bill.

FILIBUSTERING AND PARTISAN ADVANTAGE

The preceding section focused on a policy topic on which many senators (and their constituents) had feelings so intense that they were willing to filibuster for weeks on end. There are other veins of intensity in public affairs that provide recurring incentives to filibuster. This section describes another such vein: measures that would (or so senators thought) directly affect senators' political interests by altering electoral rules or passing judgment on contested Senate elections.[22]

I begin with a list of active filibusters in table 6.5. There are thirty-five active cases shown, with another nine passive cases. This is a relatively large set of filibusters, suggesting that senators are keenly interested in their own elections, the relative influence of their states, and partisan advantages built into the rules of the electoral game.

One interesting cluster is four filibusters by senators seeking to preserve their states' political representation. In 1929, there were two filibusters (one during a short session and one during a subsequent special session) against a bill to establish a permanent system for reapportioning House seats across states after every census. The reason is simple: since Congress failed to pass a reapportionment bill after the 1920 census and the 1929 proposals would cap the size of the House at 435, a number of states would suffer a net decrease in representation if the bill passed. Senators from Mississippi (which would lose two seats), Alabama (which would lose one), and Virginia (which would also lose one) led the fight against the bills ("Legislative Record of the 70th Congress" 1929; "Old Twins" 1929). The remaining two filibusters (to which can be added a passive filibuster in the Ninety-fifth Congress) were against Electoral College reform. Again, some senators opposed these plans because their states' influence would be reduced under a more popular system.

Statehood for Alaska and Hawaii was delayed by a decade of filibustering that was the result of two concerns. First, Southern senators were reportedly concerned that senators from these states with significant non-Caucasian populations would be likely to vote for civil rights legislation ("Truman Asks" 1950). Second, senators expected that Hawaii would support *Republicans* for Congress and president but that Alaska would be a *Democratic* state

Table 6.5. Active Filibusters Linked to Electoral Advantage

Description	Year (Congress)	Mentions	Outcome
Bill admitting Oklahoma, New Mexico, and Arizona as states	1903 (57th)	2	Defeated
House reapportionment bill	1911 (61st)	1	Defeated
Direct election of senators	1911 (61st)	5	Lost a vote on passage
Resolution to unseat Lorimer	1911 (61st)	3	Lost a vote on passage
Six-year limit on presidential terms—constitutional amendment	1912 (62nd)	1	Defeated
Harris nomination—Census Bureau	1913 (63rd)	3	Delayed
Female suffrage constitutional amendment	1918–19 (65th)	6	Delayed
Female suffrage constitutional amendment	1919 (66th)	2	Delayed
Reed (MO) resolution to investigate 1926 campaign	1927 (69th)	81	Defeated
Reapportionment bill	1929 (70th)	2	Defeated
Reapportionment bill	1929 (71st)	1	Passed
Hatch Act II	1940 (76th)	6	Passed
Senator Bilbo election	1947 (80th)	15	Compromise
Resolution to investigate Kansas City voting	1947 (80th)	8	Defeated
Alaska/Hawaii statehood	1950 (81st)	14	Defeated
Alaska/Hawaii statehood	1954 (83rd)	17	Defeated
Alaska/Hawaii statehood	1958 (85th)	9	Alaska passed, Hawaii lost
Foreign aid—reapportionment rider	1964 (88th)	29	Defeated
American League Baseball—Dirksen anti-reapportionment amendment	1965 (89th)	9	Delayed
Electoral College reform	1970 (91st)	23	Defeated
Debt limit increase–campaign finance reform rider	1973 (93rd)	21	Defeated
Campaign finance reform	1974 (93rd)	15	Passed
Campaign finance reform—conference report	1974 (93rd)	1	Passed
New Hampshire contested election	1975 (94th)	5	Defeated
Electoral College reform	1979 (96th)	4	Defeated
Campaign finance reform	1987–88 (100th)	35	Defeated
Hatch Act revision	1990 (101st)	1	Passed
Campaign finance reform	1990 (101st)	2	Delayed
Campaign finance reform (public financing)	1993–94 (103rd)	54	Defeated
Voter registration ("motor voter")	1993 (103rd)	17	Amended
Campaign finance reform	1996 (104th)	13	Defeated
Campaign finance reform	1997–98 (105th)	76	Defeated
Campaign finance reform—Beck amendment	1997–98 (105th)	1	Defeated
Campaign finance reform	1999 (106th)	40	Defeated
Campaign finance reform	2001 (107th)	35	Passed

Lott then withdrew his bill. Finally, in September 1998, McCain offered his bill as an amendment to the Interior appropriations bill but withdrew it after another failed cloture vote.

This debate illustrates several features of modern filibustering. First, senators took bills hostage to trade for action on bills they preferred. Second, the primary actors in this dispute were parties. The Senate majority leader has the power to propose bills and to file amendments, while the Senate minority leader can block bills and extract concessions to the extent that he or she can rally the minority to vote as a bloc against cloture. Binder and Smith (1997, 90–92) note increased partisanship in cloture votes, and, in this polarized environment, party leaders become key actors in instigating and resolving filibuster disputes. Third, the practice of filling the amendment tree is apparently a recent development (see Evans and Oleszek 2001) and has mixed benefits. On the one hand, it allows the majority party to preclude an unwelcome amendment, but this comes at the cost of antagonizing the minority and inviting a filibuster. Finally, cloture votes are the beginning and the end of the contest. Lott did not keep the Senate in session indefinitely to obtain a vote on his amendment, nor did McCain and the Democrats seek to do so for their bill. Both sides accepted the sixty-vote threshold as normal.

The broader implication of this contest and the other electoral filibusters is that senators are able and often willing to block proposals that advantage one party's or one state's fortunes over another. The optimistic spin on this pattern is that federal election laws and Senate elections are the product of consensus rather than the exploitation of narrow political advantages. Change occurs when senators agree, when they compromise, or when they are too embarrassed to maintain their positions and, thus, finally allow reform to pass. On the other hand, this means that status quo inequities can persist as long as a sizable minority of senators votes to protect them.

FINAL-PASSAGE VOTE MARGINS

A final measure of the effect of filibustering is the size of winning coalitions on final-passage votes. How many senators voted for (against) bills that passed (failed)? If the margin of victory is small, then filibustering presumably had little effect since a narrow majority of senators was able to override the opponents of the bill. On the other hand, bills that appeal to a broad range of senators should pass with little trouble. In the pivotal politics model (Brady and Volden 2006; Krehbiel 1998), the minimum coalition size is defined by the cloture rule: 67 percent of the Senate from 1917 to 1975 and 60 percent thereafter. In chapter 2, I modify this approach so that the minimum coalition size depends on the majority's response strategy and the number of senators necessary for a prolonged filibuster.

I use all final-passage votes from 1901 to 2000 on bills and resolutions that were subject to obstruction and required a simple majority to pass; budget resolutions, treaties, constitutional amendments, and other bills that are statutorily immune from obstruction have been excluded from this analysis.[24] Most previous works on pivotal politics focus on final-passage votes on "major" legislation (e.g., Chiou and Rothenberg 2003, 2006; Krehbiel 1998; Wawro and Schickler 2006). My use of *all* passage votes reflects my interest in Senate decisionmaking in general and my concern that, for my purposes, a select set of major legislation might furnish a biased sample. This would be the case if senators tended to be more competitive or more consensual on major legislation than they are on ordinary legislation. Furthermore, the fact that the Senate held a roll call vote at all on final passage of a bill is a signal that the bill is somewhat important; truly minor legislation usually passes without a recorded vote. At the same time, readers should note that the number of votes on final passage increases significantly over the course of the twentieth century; for example, there were as many final-passage votes in 1995 (forty-eight) as there were from 1901 to 1911.[25]

Here, we are interested in what these votes tell us about the effects of filibustering in the Senate. Let us begin by comparing differences across sessions before and after the adoption of the Twentieth Amendment. Figure 6.9a shows the median passage vote coalition size from 1901 to 1933 for long sessions (triangles) and short sessions (circles). The median changes a great deal from Congress to Congress since there are relatively few votes per session (never more than ten during short sessions). To show the overall patterns, there is a trend line for each session.[26]

There are two main patterns in figure 6.9a: a gradual increase in winning coalition size and a growing difference between long and short sessions. During long sessions, the median coalition size increases from 65 percent (Fifty-seventh Congress) to 78 percent (Seventy-second Congress). For short sessions, the median increases from 62 percent in 1903 to 85 percent in 1933. The difference between long and short sessions increased over time; a typical increase from one Congress to the next was 0.73 percent for short sessions and 0.32 percent for long sessions.

After the adoption of the Twentieth Amendment, median coalition sizes dips for a while, then continues to increase. Notably, the distinction between the two sessions dissipates. Figure 6.9b illustrates these patterns. The slopes of the two trend lines are virtually identical, suggesting that, after the adoption of the Twentieth Amendment, patterns of filibustering were similar across the two sessions.

Figure 6.10 shows the distribution of final-passage margins by decade for bills that passed from 1901 to 2006. For this analysis, I calculated the percentage of senators on the winning side (out of all senators voting) and

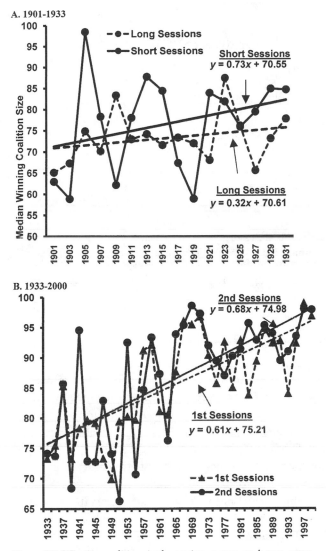

Figure 6.9. Winning coalition size by session. *a*, 1901–33. *b*, 1933–2000.

Note: The actual time unit is a Congress, so the year shown is the first year of each Congress.

then grouped votes together in 10 percent ranges (50–60 percent, 60–70 percent, 70–80 percent, 80–90 percent, and 90–100 percent) and aggregated by decade. So figure 6.10 compares the proportion of near majority (50–60 percent) and near unanimous (90–100 percent) votes over time, with other ranges for comparison. One major pattern is a significant drop in the number of close votes after 1960. From 1941 to 1950, 13.3 percent of all passage votes were won by 50–60 percent of the chamber, declining to 9.6 percent

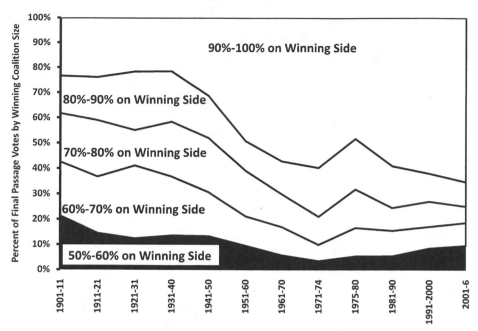

Figure 6.10. Winning coalition size in the Senate.

and then 5.8 percent over the next two decades. Meanwhile, the proportion of near unanimous votes increased from 31 percent during the 1940s to 49 percent in the 1950s and 57 percent in the 1960s. These patterns continued into the twenty-first century.

The implication of these patterns is that Senate decisionmaking changed significantly during the middle decades of the twentieth century. Legislation was more likely to pass with broad support and less likely to pass with the opposition of large minorities. While there are many factors that may contribute to this transformation, an increased capacity for senators to filibuster is probably a contributing factor.

Figure 6.10 suggests that many bills pass with less than a filibuster-proof majority. Figure 6.11 illustrates this pattern more precisely by showing the percentage of subcloture passage votes by period from 1917 to 2006. In this figure, each period represents an institutional era, the eras marked by the initial cloture rule (1917–33), the initial rule after the adoption of the Twentieth Amendment (1933–48), the 1949 rule (1949–58), the 1959 rule (1959–74), the 1975 rule (1975–86), and the current cloture rule (1987–2006). Figure 6.11 shows, for each period, the percentage of all passage votes lower than the existing cloture threshold. For example, about 40 percent of all passage votes were decided by less than a two-thirds margin from 1917 to 1933 and by one-third of all votes from 1933 to 1948. There is a spike in subcloture votes

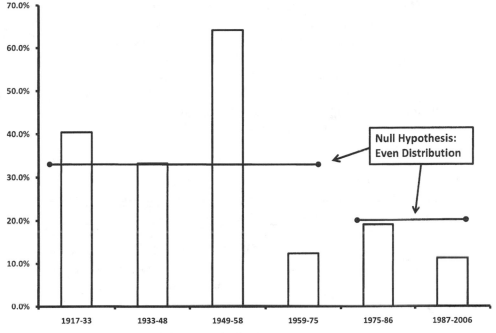

Figure 6.11. Percentage subcloture votes by decade, 1917–2006.

Note: Asterisked votes occurred after the Senate reduced the cloture threshold to three-fifths.

after the 1949 rule that is due, in part, to the fact that absentees counted against cloture. There is a noticeable drop-off in the proportion of close votes beginning in 1959; 64 percent of passage votes in the previous decade were subcloture, while just 12 percent were close in the period after 1959. For additional comparison, I have included a "null hypothesis" line indicating the percentage of all votes that we would expect to be subcloture if passage coalitions were evenly distributed from simple majority to unanimity. Through 1949, the actual results approximate the null prediction, then tail off from 1949 to 1974. After 1975, there are a substantial number of subcloture votes—around 19 percent—but this declines after 1986 to about 11 percent of all votes. The decline in the number of close votes over time implies that Senate legislation is increasingly written and amended to attract the support of large, diverse groups of legislators.

CONCLUSION

This chapter begins our study of the modern Senate. It introduces a data set of Senate filibusters based on a systematic scan of multiple media sources. There is, as anticipated, a dramatic increase in filibustering over time as measured both in the count of filibuster events and in the increasing size of bill passage coalitions in the Senate. The next two chapters explain why we observe this boom in Senate obstruction. This chapter provides two clues to the answer. First, there is little change in the rate of obstruction after the adoption of the 1917 cloture rule; if anything, filibustering increases during short sessions. Second, there is a noticeable change in both the number of filibusters and passage coalition size after the adoption of the Twentieth Amendment, which eliminated the old congressional schedule in favor of the current scheme with two annual sessions. Together, these patterns suggest that formal closure reforms have less influence on obstruction than do shifts in the ability of majorities to outlast minorities in wars of attrition.

This chapter also justifies our interest in filibustering. Most of the time, filibusters lead to the defeat or modification of the target bill. Senators have also filibustered to force new issues onto the legislative agenda, a practice known as *hostage taking*. Two sets of filibusters—on civil rights and electoral issues—illustrate how filibustering is common on important and salient issues and has a powerful impact on the course of American politics.

CHAPTER 7

Explaining the Rise of Filibustering in the Senate

This chapter provides the first half of the answer to the core question of this book. Why did Senate filibustering explode in the latter half of the twentieth century? The answer is based on the theory presented in chapter 2: Obstruction increases as the price of a filibuster decreases, which occurs as the value of time increases. This chapter tests this claim and compares it to other explanations for the explosion of Senate obstruction. I find a clear link between filibustering and a general increase in the value of Senate floor time, measured as the concentration of votes in the middle of the Senate workweek and the number of days with a roll call vote. I do not find much support for alternative accounts: neither partisan polarization, threats of reform, nor the adoption of the 1917 cloture rule provides a consistent explanation for the emergence of the sixty-vote Senate or change in obstruction over time.

EXPLANATIONS FOR PATTERNS OF SENATE FILIBUSTERING

Prior research on the growth of Senate filibustering suggests that obstruction has boomed owing to rules changes in the Senate, partisan polarization, growing workload and time constraints, and/or threats of institutional change. These influences are not necessarily competing; each can be understood as an element in the theory of obstruction outlined in chapter 2.

Workload and Chamber Time

A central claim of this book is that filibustering increases when legislators stop trying to outlast the obstructionists. In the case of the modern Senate, the motivation for this tactical shift is that the workload of the Senate has increased to the point that wasting time is more costly than accepting the outcome of a cloture vote. More generally, the opportunity costs of wasting the time of the Senate as a collective body and of senators as individuals increased as travel opportunities increased, Senate staffs swelled, and Washington, DC, became a more livable city.

Bruce Oppenheimer (1985) stresses the role of increasing workload as a cause of increased filibustering. He notes that the workload of the Senate, measured by the length of Senate sessions and number of pages of the *Congressional Record*, committee meetings, recorded votes, and bills under consideration, grew over the course of the twentieth century. This growth in workload meant that senators had to produce a steady stream of legislation if they were going to keep up with the demands of a growing country and federal government. By the 1960s, they began using cloture votes to respond to obstruction, which lowered the costs of filibustering and invited further obstruction. While several authors have endorsed Oppenheimer's account (e.g., Binder and Smith 1997, 14–15; Koger 2002; Sinclair 1989, 126; Smith 1989, 94–96), most subsequent research has ignored its implications, perhaps because filibustering and the value of time are exceedingly difficult to measure.

How shall we measure the value of time? Previous chapters discuss the value of time and measure it in the historic Congress, but, here, we face the same challenge in a different context. Again, it is preferable to avoid *external* measures of workload expectations because the value of time also depends on the (in)efficiency of the legislative process and the outside opportunities (jobs, recreation, casework, fund-raising, etc.) available to legislators.[1] Instead, I use internal measures of the value of chamber time.

For the historic Congress, I used chamber size, absenteeism in floor voting, and days with a vote to measure the subjective value of chamber time. Chamber size does not vary much over the twentieth century. In 1901, the Senate had ninety members, then ninety-six in 1913, then one hundred from 1961 to the present. The number of days with a roll call vote continues to be a good measure of how well the Senate is coping with its workload and how expensive an additional day of work would be. This statistic is shown in figure 7.1, with the calendar days (i.e., from the first to the last day of a session) and the days in session (i.e., the days on which the Senate met) shown for comparison.[2]

On the other hand, senators' interest in outside activities does not translate into absenteeism throughout the twentieth century. At the turn of the century, railroad travel had become commonplace. Air travel, in particular, left its mark on the Senate, as senators took advantage of the opportunity to fly back to their home states or to travel the world on fact-finding, diplomatic, or pleasure trips (Valeo 1999). As senators' outside options improved, it became more difficult to muster the numbers necessary for a war of attrition. The contest over a 1962 communications satellite bill illustrates this point: "In frantic attempts to muster a quorum on a summer Saturday, Senate Democratic leaders summoned Senators to Washington from as far away

Figure 7.1. Days in session: calendar days, workdays, voting days.

as Mackinac Island in Lake Huron, even dispatched a Navy PT boat to fetch three Democrats from the nuclear merchant ship Savannah, cruising off Norfolk, Va. . . . The quorum was achieved only at 3 P.M., five hours after the session started, when North Dakota's Republican Senator Milton Young, still wearing his windbreaker, arrived from a Virginia golf course to round out a quorum" ("Head Winds" 1962). At the same time, senators did not want to miss important votes or debates on issues that were important to them and their constituents, so they worked with their party leaders to make the schedule of the Senate coincide with their travel plans.

One manifestation of this pattern was that senators increasingly clustered their votes in the middle of the week. The "Tuesday–Thursday" club in Congress began as a cluster of Eastern seaboard legislators who traveled home by train or car on the weekend (see Nokken and Sala 2002). In time, the number of legislators commuting to their home districts on the weekends grew to the point that their travel plans dictated the chamber schedule. As figure 7.2 illustrates, during the modern era, the Senate did an increasing portion of its work from Tuesday to Thursday. The line marked with triangles shows the percentage of all voting days in each session that were Tuesday, Wednesday, or Thursday. If the Senate met and voted on every day of the week but Sunday, this statistic would be 50. The line marked with circles shows the percentage of all votes held on Tuesday, Wednesday, or Thursday in a given session. Both measures tell the same story: the contemporary Senate

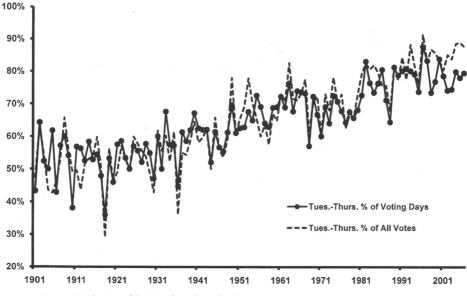

Figure 7.2. The rise of the Tuesday–Thursday Senate, 1901–2006.

operates as a three-day-a-week chamber so that senators can do other work (or none) the rest of the week.

The number of voting days in a session and the percentage of votes held from Tuesday to Thursday are both useful indicators of the value of Senate time. The former reflects the extent to which senators are working more days to cope with their legislative duties; the second reflects the subjective value that senators attach to legislative work relative to alternate uses of their time. Although they are correlated ($r = .6377$), I use both because they reflect distinct notions of the value of time.

Institutional Reforms

Another explanation for variation in filibustering is institutional change: over time, senators adopted new rules and practices that restricted or promoted obstruction. These reforms change the key terms of my model—the probability of success using closure or attrition and the exchange costs associated with each strategy.

The 1917 Cloture Rule

What was the effect of the first cloture rule in 1917? Several authors suggest that the rule, adopted in response to public criticism, was intended to have little effect on Senate operations and, in practice, did not (Burdette 1940; Haynes 1938; Koger 2007). Burdette, for example, says: "If anyone supposed that a provision for cloture would bring an end to filibustering, even by a small minority, events in succeeding years have proved him a poor judge of Senatorial characteristics. Intense filibusters have been waged exactly as before" (1940, 128).

Wawro and Schickler (2006), however, make the case that the 1917 rule should significantly reduce filibustering. In their account, the cloture rule enabled senators to pass bills that would otherwise have been jeopardized by filibusters—particularly at the end of a Congress: "The cloture rule alters the strategic calculations of legislators so that [legislative entrepreneurs] should build bigger coalitions in order to head off potential filibusters, and those who might have engaged in obstruction before might instead channel their resources into other activities that have more promise of a substantive return" (219). If senators had perfect foresight, we would almost never observe filibusters unless they are "revealing information" about the intensity of their preferences by engaging in a doomed filibuster (219). In practice, we would also expect some filibustering owing to uncertainty. The net effect, however, is to reduce the number of filibusters because senators presumably have some ability to anticipate filibusters and head them off and would-be obstructionists will avoid losing battles (218).

The Twentieth Amendment

A second major reform was the Twentieth Amendment to the Constitution. As discussed later in chapter 8, this amendment revised the congressional schedule to replace long and short sessions with two sessions beginning in January.

(Double) Tracking

Another innovation that scholars link to increased filibustering is a tactic that the Senate began using around 1970: debate filibustered bills for a few hours a day, and then pass less contentious bills the other hours of the day (Binder and Smith 1997, 15; Binder, Lawrence, and Smith 2002, 411; Fisk and Chemerinsky 1997; Oppenheimer 1985, 406). This eliminates attrition as a viable response since it is difficult to wear down an obstructionist team a few hours at a time. Like Wawro and Schickler (2006, 261–62), however, I am inclined to treat this innovation as a minor reform that is symptomatic of a broader shift from attrition to cloture as the dominant response to obstruction but that has little independent effect.

1975 Cloture Reform Proposal

One would expect that lowering the cloture threshold from two-thirds of voting senators to three-fifths of the entire chamber (whether voting or not) would reduce the minimum size of winning coalitions. Indeed, Krehbiel (1998, 89–90) finds that presidential party changes after 1975 result in a significant decrease in the size of passage coalitions on major legislation.[3]

In short, prior research suggests that institutional variation is a cause of historical shifts in filibustering. However, each of these works explore the effects of only one or two changes, and only Binder, Lawrence, and Smith (2002) also consider measures of workload or time constraints as an alternative explanation for historical variation. Without a measure of workload, researchers may mistakenly conclude that an institutional reform is responsible for long-term trends on the basis of a simple "before-and-after" test. Instead, I tested for the effects of Rule 22 reforms and the Twentieth Amendment by segmenting the era 1901–2004 into six major periods: 1901–17, 1917–33, 1933–48, 1949–59, 1959–75, and 1975–2004.

Partisan Polarization

Party unity plays a small role in my model of obstruction. Unified minority parties may be more likely to band together to stave off cloture, while unified majority parties may be better able to organize an attrition effort or vote for cloture. The recent increase in filibustering coincides with an increase in partisan polarization in the U.S. House and Senate. Binder and Smith (1997, 15–17) suggest that polarization *causes* filibustering; the more members of each major party disagree with the members of the opposing party, the easier it is to organize a coalition of forty-one senators to filibuster a bill. Their multivariate analysis of Senate filibusters from 1917 to 1996 finds a correlation between increased partisanship in the Senate and filibustering.

Binder, Lawrence, and Smith (2002) measure party "strength" as party size interacted with party unity in voting. Below, I use this measure, which I call *majority advantage*:

> Majority advantage = (majority party chamber share × majority party unity) – (minority party chamber share × minority party unity).

I also test an alternative measure of polarization: the absolute difference between the Democratic and the Republican median first-dimension NOMINATE scores. This latter measure is a common measure of polarization because it is designed to capture the difference in policy views between a typical member of each party (McCarty, Poole, and Rosenthal 2006). Both variables are shown in figure 7.3. Note that both party strength and

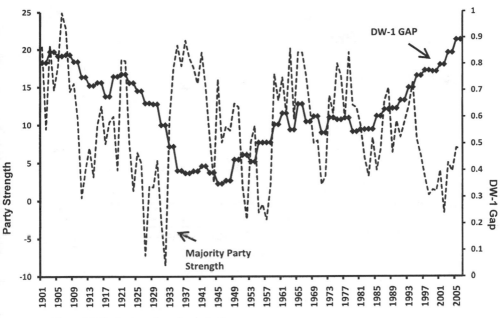

Figure 7.3. Party strength and polarization.

polarization are high at the beginning of the twentieth century, when filibustering was rare. This makes it less likely that party polarization is the primary cause of Senate filibustering, but it may play a minor role in explaining
senators' behavior.

We should note the distinction between the claim that partisan polarization *causes* an increase in the number of filibuster and the claim that the filibusters that occur for other reasons are increasingly fought along party lines.
Binder and Smith (1997, 90–92) show that cloture voting has become more
partisan, while Evans and Oleszek (2001) document the partisan strategy
and negotiations behind modern filibustering. It is clear that filibustering
has become more partisan in form, particularly since the Senate became
a sixty-vote chamber. When filibusters are wars of attrition, the necessary
condition for a meaningful filibuster is a cluster of senators (five to twenty)
with intense policy preferences who are willing to wage an active filibuster.
If cloture is the primary response to obstruction, the necessary condition for
success is a sufficiently sized minority composed of anyone willing to vote
against cloture, with no further effort required. In practice, this often means
that a filibuster can be successful if one party unites to vote against cloture.
Thus, it is possible to claim that filibustering has become more partisan in
form without also claiming that polarization is a direct cause of *additional*
filibustering.

SENATE NORMS AND REFORM THREATS

Some authors suggest that filibusters are restrained by informal norms. In this account, the rules of a legislature may permit obstruction, but the right to filibuster is constrained by collective expectations about whether and when obstruction is permissible. Any legislator who violates these norms may be sanctioned by his or her fellow legislators. In the theory presented in chapter 2, internal sanctions are included in the costs of filibustering, so, obviously, filibustering should decrease as sanctions increase. Previous research on the Senate has highlighted the important of informal norms in the historic and the "textbook" Senates (Matthews 1960; Wawro and Schickler 2006; White 1955) and their decay over the latter half of the twentieth century (Foley 1980; Sinclair 1989).

Wawro and Schickler (2006), in particular, emphasize the role of informal norms as a constraint on filibustering. In their account, the socially sanctioned use of obstruction is to test the relative *intensity* of the majority and the minority on a given question, with the result that an intense minority may be able to trump an indifferent majority. The ability of the Senate to enforce this norm will vary with the "size and stability of the group" (56). While the size of the Senate is relatively stable over the course of the twentieth century, the stability of the membership does vary from Congress to Congress and, thus, may be a measure of the ability of senators to punish illegitimate filibustering.

Furthermore, filibustering may be deterred by threats of institutional change. If a majority of a legislature can credibly threaten to alter the rules and precedents of the Senate to suppress a filibuster, it can intimidate minorities into refraining from filibusters that they would otherwise support (Binder, Madonna, and Smith 2007; Koger 2004, 2008; Mayhew 2003; Wawro and Schickler 2006).[4] In chapter 2, this is presented as a distinct strategic option for a majority, and, given full information, the minority may refrain from filibustering to avoid losing its right to filibuster in the future.

The key term is *credible*. There are two conditions for a reform threat to be credible. First, there must be a majority willing to alter the rules of the game to restrict filibustering. This is only half obvious. A bill or nomination that is being blocked by a filibuster may be supported by a majority of legislators, but that does not mean that every legislator supporting the bill will also support procedural reforms required to overcome a filibuster. The greater the additional costs of institutional change, the more likely it is that legislators will be deterred from imposing institutional reform. It is likely that the incremental costs of reform—public disapproval, reduced opportunity to filibuster in the future, and diminished collegiality—will be steep (see Koger 2002, 2007). Second, institutional reform—with all its costs—must

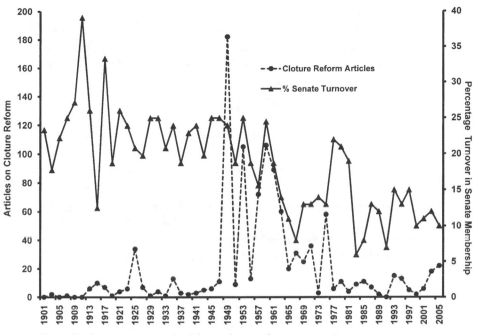

Figure 7.4. Senate turnover and articles on cloture reform, 1901–2006.

offer greater payoffs than attrition or cloture. That is, even if a simple majority of a legislature would prefer reform to surrender, the coalition may prefer
to try a less costly strategy, in which case a threat of reform is not credible.

Although it is difficult to find a precise measure, we should incorporate
reform threats into our analysis of Senate filibustering. I use the number of
articles about cloture reform in the filibuster coding data set to measure the
severity of the reform threat. This measure reflects both whether senators
or outside observers were discussing cloture reform and the extent of media
attention to the topic. As shown in figure 7.4, this measure generally corresponds with major efforts to reform Rule 22, particularly during the mid-
twentieth century (Zelizer 2004). Figure 7.4 also shows turnover in Senate
membership as a percentage of the chamber for the modern era. Turnover
generally declines over the time period, making it easier to inculcate and
enforce Senate norms.

Summary and Methods

Altogether, we have variables to measure the marginal value of chamber
time, key reforms, party polarization, internal sanctions, and threats of
reform.[5] The next task is to choose an appropriate method for analyzing
the number of Senate filibusters over time. There are two basic challenges.

First, we are trying to understand how many times something happens in a given time period, so we should use a technique that is appropriate for count variables. The classic technique for such data is Poisson regression, unless, as is the case here, the data are "overdispersed," that is, the variance exceeds the mean or the cases are not independent.

Second, our dependent variable is a time series, so we should be sensitive to the possibility that the number of filibusters in one Congress is, to some extent, an echo of previous time periods. There are good reasons to suspect that filibustering is "contagious" over time. First, an unresolved filibuster from one session may be revived at the next session, for example, antilynching legislation in 1937–38. Second, to the extent that filibustering is sanctioned (or rewarded) internally (by other senators) or externally (by constituents or interest groups), these sanctions are probably linked to whether senators consider filibustering normal or the conditions that define appropriate filibustering. These shared expectations are probably based on recent events; if there was lots of filibustering in the previous session, then filibustering in the current session is probably acceptable as well.[6] A simple test for autoregression confirms that there is a temporal relation between one session and the next one.[7] However, it would be preferable to avoid including the number of filibusters from the previous session as a control variable since this would introduce a great deal of multicollinearity with the explanatory variables—that is, it would be more difficult to parse out what is causing senators to filibuster.

In light of these challenges, I use an autoregressive Poisson estimator for this analysis. This estimator first calculates a simple Poisson regression, then corrects for autodispersion and lags the error term from the first regression in a second-stage equation (Schwartz et al. 1996).[8] I present several variations on the regression model below, but the base model is as follows:

Filibusters per session = β_0
+ β_1(turnover) + β_2(reform news) [*norms and reform threats*]
+ β_3(voting days) + β_4(Tuesday–Thursday vote percentage)
  [*value of time*]
+ β_5(DW-1 gap) + β_6(party strength) [*polarization*]
+ $\beta_7\varepsilon'_{t-1}$ [*lagged first-stage error*]
+ β_8(short [1901–17]) + β_9(short [1917–33]) [*sessions*]
+ β_{10}(1917–33) + β_{11}(1933–48) + β_{12}(1949–58) + β_{13} (1959–75)
  + β_{14}(1975–2004) [*periods*]
+ β_{15}(time trend)
+ ε [*residual error*].

Note that the error term includes all other variables, events, and personalities that also explain why we observe each particular filibuster.

RESULTS

The results confirm the relation between the scarcity of floor time and the increase in filibustering. On the other hand, party strength, Senate norms, and reform threats have little systematic effect. Furthermore, the 1917 and 1975 cloture rule reforms had effects that contradicted our expectations, as did preference polarization in the Senate.

Table 7.1 summarizes the results of this analysis. We begin in column 2 with a simple version of the model that includes all the continuous variables. This version suggests that the primary determinants of the number of filibusters per session are the number of voting days in a session and the extent to which senators cluster their votes in the middle of the week.

What happens when we account for variations in sessions and cloture rules, shown in the second model? The second version of the regression model (shown in col. 3) incorporates the two most important institutional variables: short sessions and the 1975 reduction in the cloture rule threshold.[9] I include dichotomous variables for short sessions before (1901–17) and after (1917–33) the adoption of the Senate cloture rule. Although the catalyst for the adoption of the 1917 rule was an end-of-short-session filibuster (Koger 2007), short session filibustering essentially *doubled* after the adoption of the 1917 rule. This pattern is inconsistent with the notion that the 1917 rule enhanced certainty for Senate entrepreneurs by providing a means for them to suppress obstruction during short sessions. In addition, there is a pattern of increased filibustering after the Senate changed the cloture threshold from two-thirds of voting senators to three-fifths of the entire chamber in 1975. These three variables help explain a great deal of the variation we observe.

Interestingly, adding institutional variables—particularly a variable for the period 1975–present—in the second model changes *DW-1 gap* to a statistically significant *negative* relation. This means that, as the ideological gap between the two parties grew, filibustering *decreased*. This is contrary to our expectations; why do we observe this relationship? The short answer is that polarization was high at the end and the beginning of the twentieth century. While other variables account for the surge of filibustering in the late twentieth century, this variable predicts the low level of filibustering in the early twentieth century.

A similar pattern arises when we add variables to measure the effects of major changes in the rules and schedule of the Senate. The third version also includes dichotomous variables for the period after the adoption of the Senate cloture rule (1917–33), the Twentieth Amendment (1933–48), and cloture reform in 1949 and 1959. The major surprise is that there is virtually no change in our findings. All else equal, none of these reforms seem to have

Table 7.1. Causes of Filibustering, 1901–2004 (Autoregressive Poisson Estimation)

	Expectation	β (S.E.)	β (S.E.)	β (S.E.)	β (S.E.)
Constant		−.242	.611	.182	.536
		(.696)	(.612)	(.740)	(.602)
Turnover (%)	+	.006	.013	.018	.017
		(.012)	(.010)	(.010)#	(.010)#
Reform threat	−	−.004	−.001	.000	−.001
		(.003)	(.002)	(.003)	(.002)
Voting days	+	.009	.007	.007	.006
		(.002)***	(.002)***	(.002)**	(.002)**
Tues.–Thurs. vote (%)	+	2.779	1.772	1.421	1.233
		(.700)***	(.659)**	(.748)#	(.779)
DW-1 gap	+	−.221	−1.268	−.860	−1.165
		(.458)	(.413)**	(.568)	(.419)**
Majority advantage	+	.000	.000	.000	.000
		(.000)	(.000)	(.000)	(.000)
Lagged shock	+	.157	.200	.173	.219
		(.090)#	(.096)*	(.098)#	(.096)*
Short sessions, 1901–17	+		.508	.695	.607
			(.298)#	(.379)#	(.313)#
Short sessions, 1917–33	+		1.036	.998	1.017
			(.230)***	(.277)***	(.230)***
1917–33				.291	
				(.344)	
1933–48				.558	
				(.394)	
1949–59				.209	
				(.429)	
1959–75				.557	
				(.402)	
1975–present			.893	1.369	.750
			(.151)***	(.395)***	(.179)***
Time trend					.006
					(.005)
R^2		.4241	.6411	.6363	.6438

Note: $N = 115$.

# $p < .1.$ * $p < .05.$ ** $p < .01.$ *** $p < .001.$

had any significant effects on the rate of filibustering once we incorporate measures of the value of time.

As a final reality check, I include a version of the model with a simple time trend variable, starting with 1 in 1901 and increasing until the 116th session in the dataset. This is shown in the right-hand column of table 7.1. The trend variable is not statistically significant and does not improve our ability to explain Senate filibustering. When we include this variable, *Tuesday–Thursday vote percentage* is no longer statistically significant. This is not surprising since the two variables are correlated at $r = .8349$, so we are practically including the same variable twice.[10]

Overall, this analysis is interesting for the claims it dispels as well as those it confirms. The results do *not* show that any change in the Senate cloture rule from 1917 to the present has *reduced* filibustering. Indeed, short session filibustering increased after the 1917 rule was adopted. The most significant reform, lowering the cloture threshold to 60 percent of the Senate in 1975, may have increased filibustering, although we might also attribute that increase to the broader acceptance of cloture as a normal and preferred response to obstruction. Other reforms, such as the adoption of the Twentieth Amendment in 1933 and cloture rule reforms in 1949 and 1959, seemed to have little impact on the incidence of obstruction.

The results are also inconsistent with the claim that the recent increase in filibustering is attributable to the concurrent increase in partisan polarization in Congress. *Majority advantage*, the measure used by Binder, Lawrence, and Smith (2002), is not a significant predictor of filibustering in any version of the equation. This may be because I use a different measure of filibustering or a different estimation technique, but another critical difference is that this analysis includes the years 1901–17. This was a period of historically high polarization and low filibustering, a fact that undermines the claim that these two phenomena are linked. Indeed, one measure of polarization, *DW-1 gap*, is negative in several specifications. The underlying idea is that partisanship is a long-term cycle in American politics: polarization ebbs and flows while the polity evolves, so, if we study a long segment of American history, it is easier to distinguish between trends and cycles.

There is some support for the notion that filibustering is constrained (or not) by internal sanctions. The strongest evidence is the positive effect of the error from the previous session. Again, this may be partially due to filibuster-prone bills remaining on (or passing from) the Senate's agenda. However, we can also interpret this positive correlation across sessions as a measure of senators' tolerance for filibustering; the obstruction from the previous session may be an indicator of whether filibustering is punished or tolerated. In addition, there may be a slight relation between Senate turnover and filibustering, but this is unclear. Furthermore, it does not appear that, as measured, the threat of reform is much of a systematic deterrent against filibustering, although there have been some clear cases of deterrence.

While rules, norms, and parties contribute to our analysis, the primary determinant of filibustering is the opportunity cost of wasting the time of the Senate on a war of attrition. One measure of this cost is the number of days in each session with a roll call vote. In each version of the model, this is a strong predictor of the number of filibusters; the more days senators meet to do legislative work, the less willing they are to wait out a filibuster. A second measure reflects the subjective value of legislative work relative to outside options. Specifically, as the percentage of Senate votes that occur from Tuesday to Thursday increases, senators are less willing to remain in and around the Senate chamber for a prolonged filibuster. Filibustering increased with this clustering of votes.

CONCLUSION

This chapter began the task of explaining why filibustering has exploded in the modern Senate. Overall, the results suggest the importance of floor time. As senators spent more days in session and tried to fly away on the weekends, filibustering increased. Filibustering during short sessions also increased after the adoption of the Senate cloture rule, suggesting that this rule had little effect on the behavior that it was supposedly created to prevent. Both these results are perfectly consistent with our theory, which predicts that Pro's costs of an attrition strategy increase as chamber time becomes more scarce and, thus, more valuable. Chapter 8 proves that this is exactly what happened: as time became too scarce to wait out a filibuster, senators began to accept cloture as a necessary and proper response.

CHAPTER 8

From Attrition to Cloture: Institutionalizing the Filibuster

Here is a fight of words against time, of men against inevitability, of voices against the ebbing strength that portends eventual silence.

Charlotte Observer editorial, February 28, 1960

Obstruction by the threat of endless debate has become so common that for all practical purposes the three-fifths vote required by Senate rules to close debate has become the margin needed to do anything.

Anthony Lewis, writing in the New York Times on October 10, 1994

The remaining task is to explain how and why filibustering exploded in the Senate over the latter half of the twentieth century. This chapter explains the evolution of Senate filibustering from rare public contests to institutionalized supermajority rule. From chapter 7, we know that the underlying reason is the growing value of senators' time; as the number of voting days in session increased, and as the Senate's work was increasingly compressed into three-day workweeks, filibustering increased. The link between the value of time and filibustering is based on senators' *responses* to a filibuster. This chapter provides the final piece of the puzzle by tracing the responses to and tactics of filibustering in the modern Senate.

The main narrative is that votes replaced intensity as the critical commodity of Senate lawmaking. Attrition was the primary response to filibustering prior to the adoption of the Senate cloture rule in 1917, and it continued to be the primary response for the following four decades. The adoption of the Twentieth Amendment to the Constitution eliminated the short sessions, which had become filibustering free-for-alls, and restored the effectiveness of attrition. By the early 1960s, however, it was clear that attrition was not effective in the modern age: increasing workload, peripatetic membership, and growing dissatisfaction with the racial status quo convinced senators to prefer closure as a response to obstruction. Instead of allowing filibusters to play out on the Senate floor, they adopted informal practices to communicate and negotiate potential filibusters.

This chapter also illustrates three broader ideas about the nature of political institutions. The first is that the effect of formal political rules depends on whether actors behave in accordance with the intent of their rules (see Mill 1861/1991, 13). In the Senate, the ability to invoke cloture is of little use unless senators are willing to file cloture petitions, vote for cloture on proposals they support, craft bills that will attract a cloture-sized coalition, and preserve the intent of the rule in the face of new challenges.

The second idea is that an institutional change—in this case, the Senate's cloture rule—can have effects that are *important* but not *immediate*. In other work, I have found that the Senate cloture rule was initially adopted for symbolic purposes and was intended to have minimal short-term effects (Koger 2007). Subsequently, senators rejected opportunities to lower the cloture threshold to a simple majority while allowing obstructionists to utilize tactics that were immune from the cloture process (Koger 2006a). Not surprisingly, then, the immediate effects of the rule were minimal. However, senators eventually considered using the cloture process as attrition became less effective as a strategy.

Finally, one of the constraints on minority rights is the ability of majorities to revoke those rights. As discussed in chapter 2, legislative minorities may refrain from obstruction if they expect that the majority will respond by restricting the right to filibuster. These cases are rare, but there have been a few in Senate history. This chapter describes these cases, including the fight over judicial nominations from 2003 to 2005 during which Republicans threatened to exercise the nuclear option of simple majority reform.

FILIBUSTERING, REFORM, AND ATTRITION, 1901–17

Prior to 1917, the Senate had no formal rule for ending debate and forcing decisive votes. Instead, the dominant response to a filibuster was attrition: the majority would attempt to wait until the minority was exhausted. In addition, there was also an apparent episode of reform deterrence. As I coded articles for this project, I noted all articles on reforming the Senate and kept notes on any deterrence that may have occurred. This search turned up seven possible cases from 1901 to 2005. The first was a curious dip in filibustering during the Fifty-eighth Congress.

There were six filibusters during the Fifty-seventh Congress, all during the short session of 1902–3. This includes a famous incident in which "Pitchfork" Ben Tillman (D-SC) came to the Senate floor on March 3, 1903, with a satchel of books that he piled on his desk. Tillman then noted that, unless an item for his home state remained in the general deficiency appropriations conference report, he would filibuster the entire bill. Tillman got his money, and the bill passed (Burdette 1940, 72). This anecdote, however, was part of a larger clusterbuster. The *New York Times* (*NYT*) describes the last hours of the Fifty-seventh Congress:

> A notable occurrence, however, was the incidental remark from time to time of Senators in reference to measures suggested for consideration, "but then this bill will not pass." This was said by Republican as well as Democratic Senators. It was spoken of every measure that was called up, except such as were the subject of conference. The unblushing frankness with which Senators declared that there would be no vote on any contested bill was unusual and unprecedented. There have been many periods when partisan feeling has produced a bitter and revengeful situation in the Senate, but it is almost beyond recollection that there has been such an avowed condition of deadlock. ("Strife Marks Closing Hours" 1903, 2)

This stalemate stemmed from a dispute over admitting Oklahoma, Arizona, and New Mexico as states. Democrats sought statehood for these states, but several Republicans filibustered ("Statehood Lines Break" 8). In response, Democrats filibustered a Panama Canal treaty, a banking reform bill, and a bill lowering tariffs on Philippine goods; the entire set of bills died at the end of the session ("Dead-Lock in Senate Remains Unbroken" 1903, 1; "Strife Marks Closing Hours" 1903, 2).

Senators considered closure reform in the aftermath of this clusterbuster. The *NYT* reported that "there has been more talk of cloture during the past fortnight than for years," and William Allison (R-IA) introduced a resolution calling on the Rules Committee to consider the topic of closure reform. Although "not one of [the members of the Senate Rules Committee] is in favor of cloture," the *NYT* states, "all are convinced that there has been grievous abuse of the traditional unwritten law of the Senate and that the country demands a change" ("Proposition to Limit Debate" 1903, 5). Afterward, the *NYT* does not mention closure reform again for years.[1] Since the Rules Committee was opposed to closure reform, this threat does not appear to be credible. Nonetheless, this threat preceded the restoration of calm; there were no recorded filibusters in the Fifty-eighth Congress.

There are numerous cases of attrition during this era (see, e.g., the discussion of the Federal Reserve Act of 1913 in Bawn and Koger [2008]), but I will focus on one critical fight: the 1915 Ship Purchase Act.[2] After the 1914 elections, President Wilson proposed legislation to alleviate a shortage of ocean ships by establishing a government corporation to purchase and operate merchant vessels. Many senators opposed government involvement in the shipping business and also worried about providing Germany with cash and facilitating the shipment there of nonmilitary goods like cotton (Garraty 1953, 308–11; *Congressional Record* 56, pt. 8 [June 8, 1918]: 7537).

Despite these concerns, the Senate voted 46–29 to consider the shipping bill on January 4, 1915, on a mostly party-line vote. Republicans announced their intent to filibuster. They claimed that President Wilson called for party caucuses to pressure Senate Democrats, and, thus, the Senate, to adopt his legislation hastily and without change. Gilbert Hitchcock (D-NE) said: "There would have been no Democratic caucus if it had not been for outside influences." Theodore Burton (R-OH) noted that the partisan and business pressure on Democrats was greater on the shipping bill than on any previous Democratic agenda item (*Congressional Record* 52, pt. 4 [February 13, 1915]: 3711). On the other hand, some Democrats alleged that a "shipping trust" opposed the bill (*Washington Post*, February 16, 1915, A2), giving the Republicans extra incentive to fight the bill.

The Senate began continuous debate on the shipping bill on January 18. The Democrats caucused six times from January 16 to January 23 to revise the bill and to bind all Democrats to support the compromise bill as a party measure. Over the next several days, Republicans used dilatory motions, prolonged speaking, and disappearing quorums to prevent a final vote on the bill. Of the nineteen votes taken during this week, most Republicans were absent from twelve, and the Republicans broke a quorum eight times. Six amendments to the bill were tabled by mostly party-line votes, demonstrating to Republicans the futility of deliberation. The *NYT* framed this as an attrition contest: "The Republican senators, as on previous night sessions, abandoned all efforts to conceal obstructive tactics, and as the evening wore on it was apparent that another endurance test was on. While some of the Democrats doubted that there would be insistence upon the point tonight, it was declared that all-night sessions certainly would be resorted to in the near future" ("Democrats Refuse to Alter" 1915, 13). Days later, George Norris (R-NE) nicely summarized the state of the Senate: "Things have come to such a pass here now that on every bill that is presented there must be a test of physical strength, the old trial by battle. This is a relic of barbarism. We often boast that this is the greatest deliberative body in the world, and we have no cloture and unlimited debate. But unlimited debate under present conditions is the most inhuman and cruel cloture in the world. It is a cloture against everything except debate. It kills time and it kills the members of this body as well" ("Desertions Deal Blow" 1915, 1).

Finally, on February 1, seven Democrats allied with the Republicans to send the bill to committee (Burdette 1940, 107). Another five Democrats voted with Republicans on preceding procedural votes, suggesting even broader discontent within the majority party.[3]

Instead of conceding defeat, Democrats began filibustering while rounding up absent members from around the country and negotiating with dissident Democrats and progressive Republicans (Ritchie 1998, 194; Burdette

1940, 107). A week later, three Democrats returned, and the roles reversed again—Republicans obstructing, Democrats pushing for a vote.

On February 12, the Democrats agreed to attempt a closure rule. This proposal, supported by the "unanimous resolve" of the Democratic caucus (*Washington Post*, February 14, 1915, A1), would add a provision to the standing rules of the Senate calling for a final-passage vote on the Ship Purchase Act by February 19. This effort lost steam when Senator Cummins (R-IA) offered an amendment invalidating the rule if a party caucus bound members' votes on a bill. An attempt to table this amendment failed 45–47. Rather than lose a direct vote on Cummins's amendment, Democrats conceded both the proposed cloture rule and the shipping bill.[4]

All told, the ship purchase filibuster stretched across twenty-six days and 702 pages of the *Congressional Record*, including a 118-page day (January 29) and an 83-page day (February 8).[5] Both sides obstructed to delay a final decision as they struggled to convert votes and manipulate attendance to win a final vote. As Mayhew (2003) noted about the 1937 court-packing bill, this was a struggle for the median voter rather than an effort to build a supermajority; this is also consistent with Wawro and Schickler's (2006) finding that slender majorities often won before the adoption of the cloture rule.

While a minority of senators blocked this bill, it is likely that only a minority of the Senate genuinely supported it. Only thirty-five of fifty-three Democrats went to the Democratic caucus meeting and voted to make the bill a party measure; opponents of a bill typically avoid such votes. As Senator Hitchcock (D-NE), stated: "Not one half of the senators upon the Democratic side of the chamber believe in this bill as it is now before the Senate" (*Congressional Record* 52, pt. 4 [February 13, 1915]: 3707).

This contest was a critical event in the history of the Senate because it crystallized views about filibustering. On the one hand, Woodrow Wilson soon began to push for a closure rule (see Koger 2007). On the other hand, this episode demonstrated that obstruction could be legitimately used to thwart majorities manufactured by binding party caucuses.

Midsession Filibusters

During this period, senators were increasingly willing to attempt midsession filibusters. Figure 8.1 illustrates this pattern. The large dots (measured on the left-hand axis) indicate the number of filibusters during special and long sessions for each Congress. The line shows the mean number of days left in session when each filibuster begins.[6] If senators are taking advantage of their colleagues' eagerness to quit and go home at the end of a session, then this statistic should approach zero; if they are filibustering throughout the session, then it will increase.

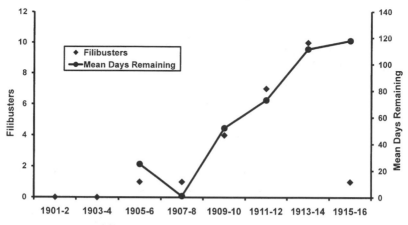

Figure 8.1. Timing and filibusters in early and long sessions, 1901–1917.

Figure 8.1 shows there were no filibusters in the long sessions of the Fifty-seventh and Fifty-eighth congresses. There was a fleeting mention of a filibuster against the 1906 Hepburn Act, then the 1908 banking bill, which began the day before the end of the long session of the Sixtieth Congress. Over the next three congresses, filibustering increases steadily and begins ever earlier. In the Sixty-third Congress, the Republican minority delayed several items on President Wilson's agenda during 1913 and 1914. In the Sixty-fourth Congress, there was just one early filibuster as the Senate agenda shifted toward defense and foreign affairs and the Democratic caucus was less aggressive about forcing party bills through the Senate.

CLOTURE AND ATTRITION, 1917-33

On March 8, 1917, the Senate amended its Rule 22 to include a formal process for closing debate on a measure by a two-thirds vote. Although it would be two and a half years before the Senate voted on cloture, there was immediate interest in trying out the new option. In June and July 1917, President Wilson suggested using closure to force through a bill regulating food supply as the country mobilized for war ("Wilson Warns Foes" 1917, 1). In August 1917, senators Hale (R-ME) and Shafroth (D-CO) gathered the required sixteen signatures on a cloture petition to end debate on a bill raising taxes to pay for the war effort, and another thirty-nine senators promised to support cloture on the bill ("War Tax in Snarl" 1917, 3). In both cases, the minority retreated before any petition was filed. These early episodes suggest that senators were reluctant to be labeled obstructionists after the public outrage against the 1917 ship arming bill filibuster and during a national war effort. A cloture vote, even if it failed, would be used as proof that a filibuster was ongoing.

Notably, the cloture rule was not used against a clusterbuster at the end of the Sixty-fifth Congress. Over the last two weeks of the short session, it was clear to observers that Republicans were blocking key bills to force Woodrow Wilson to call a special session ("Borah to Tour" 1919, 1). The Republicans had won a majority of Senate seats in the 1918 elections and wanted the Senate in session to enact Republican priorities and to monitor Woodrow Wilson's negotiations to end World War I. Toward that end, they blocked seven appropriations bills, nominations for controller of the currency and attorney general, and bills related to water power, luxury taxes, public buildings, immigration, and Prohibition enforcement. As this legislative massacre drew to a close on March 4, Vice President Thomas Marshall banged his gavel and declared the Senate adjourned "sine Deo" (without God) instead of "sine die" (without day) ("Congress Ends" 1919, 1). The record of the Sixty-fifth Congress suggests that, while the political costs of filibustering could be steep, the new cloture rule provided little defense against short session obstruction; the combination of time constraints and multiple target proposals rendered the rule ineffective.

Senators first applied cloture on the Treaty of Versailles in November 1919. The Senate began debating the treaty in July 1919. Sixteen weeks, twenty-eight votes, and 1,060 pages of debate later,[7] treaty supporters moved for cloture. On November 12, the Democrats and the Republicans circulated separate cloture petitions.[8] The Democratic petition (with thirty-five signatures) applied to Republicans' "reservations" or amendments to the treaty, while the Republican petition (with sixteen signatures) applied to the treaty and all amendments ("51 Senators Sign" 1919, 1).

When Hitchcock (D-NE) submitted the Democrats' cloture petition, Cummins (R-IA) was presiding and ruled that the petition was invalid because it applied only to reservations to the treaty and not the "pending measure," that is, the treaty itself. This ruling was upheld on a nearly party-line 44–36 vote (Republicans 42–0, Democrats 2–36). Later, Lodge (R-MA) submitted a petition signed by thirty Republicans that applied to the treaty and all amendments (Burdette 1940, 131; "Adopt Reservation" 1919, 1). In time, this minor snag would nullify the rule: once the term *pending measure* was narrowly defined, it became easy to block a bill when it was not formally on the floor of the Senate. Two days later, the Senate approved cloture for the first time by a 78–16 vote. Four days and forty votes later, the resolution to approve the treaty came to a vote and failed, 39–55; thus, the cloture vote represented an agreement that further debate was pointless rather than supermajority support for the treaty.

In all, there were eleven filibusters during the Sixty-sixth Congress. Senators attempted cloture again in February 1921 on an emergency tariff bill and failed 36–35 (Republicans 27–7, Democrats 9–28); amending continued for two more weeks before the bill finally passed. From 1921 to 1933, there were eighty-eight filibusters, nine cloture votes, and three successes. After the initial eagerness to use the new rule, cloture became the exception rather than the norm. What happened?

Aversion to Cloture

Senators rarely attempted cloture because they developed a general aversion to voting for it. Two filibusters from the Sixty-seventh Congress may have helped shift senators' preferences. First, the November 1922 filibuster by Southern senators against the Dyer antilynching bill reminded those senators that broad majorities of the Senate might vote for civil rights measures if given the chance, meaning that Southerners might lose more than they gain if the Senate began applying cloture against all filibusters. Over time, some Southerners began to view cloture voting as a logroll—if I don't vote to end your filibuster even though I disagree with you, you don't vote for cloture against me.

Two months later, senators were reminded why they were reluctant to adopt a cloture rule in the first place: when they face pressure from outside external actors, actions may speak more sincerely than votes. Even though the issue had contributed to Republican losses in the election of 1922, President Harding was determined to enact a bill subsidizing the sale of merchant ships during the short session of the Sixty-seventh Congress. The bill passed the House November 29 amid charges that Harding had "bought" the margin of victory by dangling promises of patronage jobs before lame-duck Republicans, especially incumbents defeated in the 1922 election (see Goodman and Nokken 2004). In the Senate, Democrats and progressive Republicans insisted on delaying the bill until the Sixty-eighth Congress. Early on, it appeared that Republican leaders would bow to this opposition ("Half the Session Gone" 1923, 20), but, on February 7, Harding made a *second* address to the Congress imploring senators to pass the bill.[9] Senate leaders dutifully brought the bill to the Senate floor on and off until Harding finally accepted defeat on February 27 ("Harding Abandons Ship" 1923, 7). To the victors, this was a justified filibuster to prevent illegitimate action. Even if a majority of the Senate was willing to vote for the bill, this majority might be based on side payments rather than conviction, and it likely would not represent the majority of public opinion as expressed in the 1922 election.

Senators' attitudes toward cloture crystallized in 1925. When the Sixty-ninth Congress convened, senators were confronted by a new vice president, Charles Dawes, who openly disdained the Senate's filibustering tradition. Dawes proclaimed the Senate's rules an outrage against democracy and, since senators used filibusters to extort appropriations, an invitation to swindle (Burdette 1940, 224–26; Haynes 1938, 415–39; Koger 2006a). A *NYT* poll found that six senators (one Democrat, five Republicans) agreed with Dawes's majority-cloture plan, twenty-two (all Republicans) probably supported it, seventeen (fourteen Republicans, three Democrats) were uncertain, six (all Republicans) probably disagreed, and forty-five (thirty-seven Democrats, eight Republicans) disagreed ("Senate Poll" 1925, XX1). Two Republican Party leaders were uncertain (Curtis and Wadsworth), and a third, Watson, was opposed; every Democratic Party leader opposed cloture reform. The balance of members' private preferences may have been closer to eighty senators opposed (Haynes 1938, 418). The *NYT* concluded that Dawes's proposal was doomed to "almost certain defeat" ("Senate Poll" 1925, XX1).

From that point, news stories begin to refer to senators who are generally opposed to using or voting for the Senate's cloture rule. During a filibuster against joining the World Court in early 1926, proponents of the bill were reluctant to file for cloture because they feared that some members of the pro-Court coalition might vote against cloture as a matter of principle or political expediency ("Move to Fix Date" 1926, 4; "Vote or Talk" 1926, 14). This concern was well-founded: roll call votes on cloture (approved 68–28) and then ratification of the World Court treaty with reservations (76–17) revealed nine senators who voted *against* cloture but *for* the treaty, as if they were opposed to cloture per se. Of these "principled" senators, four were Democrats (three from Southern states), and five were Republicans (two from Nebraska and one each from Vermont, Arizona, and Colorado).

In *Politics or Principle?* Sarah Binder and Steve Smith (1997) take on the difficult task of testing whether there were senators who opposed cloture on principle. They reason that principle per se should be uncorrelated with ideology and, thus, that, if conventional measures of ideology (specifically, D NOMINATE scores) correlate with support for cloture, then we can conclude that principled votes against cloture are just a thin veil for legislators' policy preferences. In fact, they find that ideological measures are correlated with support for cloture and infer that senators are driven by politics, not principle. How can we reconcile this analysis with frequent references to the anticloture disposition of some senators in news stories?

The answer, I suggest, is to think of principle as a *penalty* for supporting cloture. In many cases, this penalty would not be enough to deter a vote for cloture or may not sway the votes of senators who opposed cloture because they are openly opposed to the underlying bill. The "cloture penalty" may have been crucial, however, for senators who could honestly say that they would vote for the target bill if it came to a vote but whose support for the bill was lukewarm.[10] Ideology would be a strong predictor of senators' votes in such a case, with (say) liberal senators voting for cloture, conservative senators voting against it, and many moderate senators also voting against it because they do not support the target bill strongly enough to pay the extra price of voting for cloture.

Nor is the cloture penalty merely a matter of conscience. As suggested above, senators may have practical motives to vote against cloture: they fear that other senators might invoke the rule against them on other issues. For senators with practical motives, voting against cloture was like cooperating in a prisoner's dilemma: (almost) everyone is better off in a cloture-free Senate, so, as long as a sufficient portion of the chamber cooperates by voting against cloture, cooperation against using the rule can be sustained.[11]

One successful cloture vote suggests that opposition to cloture was probably tactical rather than principled. In February 1927, senators faced two filibusters: the McNary-Haugen farm bill and the McFadden banking bill. Supporters of the two bills struck a deal: if the farm bill proponents supported cloture on the banking bill, the banking bill proponents would refrain from a filibuster against the farm bill. Both sides honored their deal: the Senate invoked cloture on the bank bill 65–18, then passed the farm bill without an active filibuster ("Legislative Summary" 1927; "Bank Bill" 1927).[12]

Occasionally, senators recognized the Rule 22 threshold without formally applying cloture. Arizona's two senators gave up a filibuster against Boulder Dam appropriations rather than force and lose a cloture vote ("Fight $10,660,000" 1930, 5). In January 1933, Huey Long relented in a filibuster rather than lose a cloture vote ("Agreement in Senate" 1933, 1). Days later, a cloture vote on the same issue failed 58–30; as *Time* noted: "The vote did not mean that Huey Long had 30 die-hard supporters on the floor but only that many a Senator is opposed in principle to any form of gag" ("Pitiable and Contemptible!" 1933).[13] Indeed, two senators voted against cloture only because they knew that the Senate would limit debate by unanimous consent immediately after the cloture vote ("See Long Beaten" 1933, 3).

One manifestation of senators' antipathy toward cloture was the gradual weakening of the rule and reductions in its scope. As discussed in chapter 6, during the 1922 filibuster against an antilynching bill, Southern senators blocked the reading of the *Senate Journal* with dilatory amendments. While there was a minor precedent preventing dilatory motions until after the reading of the *Journal* is complete, the Republican majority made no apparent effort to apply the cloture rule to this situation.[14] The effect of this filibuster was to expand the pending measure loophole in Rule 22: a filibuster that prevents a bill from becoming the pending measure cannot be stopped by a cloture vote. Earlier in 1922, a Democratic filibuster against a tariff bill exposed another vulnerability in the rule: there is no limit on the number of amendments that senators can file before cloture is invoked, and, after a successful cloture vote, the opponents of a bill can call up a limitless number of amendments for roll call votes (Koger 2006a). Together, these events suggested that the cloture rule was ineffective against a determined minority. A cloture vote could signal that two-thirds of the Senate was impatient, but it could not ensure that a filibuster would stop.

The Attrition Option

Since the cloture rule was unpopular and ineffective, senators continued to rely on attrition as their primary response to obstruction. This is implicit in Wawro and Schickler's (2006) analysis of the effects of the cloture rule: their tests of a "cloture effect" focus on short sessions before and after the 1917 rule, assuming that the cloture rule would have little use during long sessions, when it was comparatively easy to wait out a filibuster.[15] For example, when a few senators threatened to filibuster the Supreme Court nomination of Pierce Butler in 1922, Senate leaders brought up the nomination on December 21. The small band of opponents quickly backed down from a filibuster right before Christmas, and the Senate approved Butler after just four hours of debate ("Butler Confirmed by Senate" 1922, 11). Years later, the mere threat of round-the-clock sessions ended a filibuster against the repeal of Prohibition ("Repeal Vote Today Set" 1933, 1). Note that, in this case, the majority was able to make a credible threat of attrition with three weeks left in the short session.

One case of senators' preference for attrition was the debate on the London Naval Treaty in July 1930. President Hoover called a special session in the hot summer for the sole purpose of passing the treaty, but a small band of senators led by Hiram Johnson (R-CA) filibustered it. The proponents of the treaty had the votes to invoke cloture and pass the treaty but waited it out: "To be gagged was exactly what Senator Johnson and his followers most wanted from the majority. Republican Leader Watson had in his desk a petition signed by 35 Senators to invoke cloture and thus kill the filibuster. But Senator Watson was too good a tactician to martyrize Senator Johnson and friends with this extreme parliamentary measure. The mere threat served him better" ("Treaty Ratified" 1930). In this case, the threat of cloture reduced the obstructionists' fervor by guaranteeing their loss, but the majority accepted delay rather than apply the cloture rule.

The Twentieth Amendment

While senators were reluctant to vote for cloture, the rash of short session filibusters during the 1920s fed the movement for reform. Rather than revise the cloture rule, George Norris (R-NE) advocated a constitutional amendment to eliminate short sessions,[16] which would make attrition a viable strategy throughout each Congress (Norris 1926).[17] The Senate passed Norris's resolution six times from 1923 to 1933, all by overwhelming margins. Owing to opposition from Republican presidents and House leaders, however, the House was slow to deal with this issue; the first House floor vote did not come until 1928, when the Norris resolution lost 208–157. The resolution finally passed the House after the Democrats gained a majority in the Seventy-second Congress. The Twentieth Amendment was ratified on January 23, 1933, with high hopes that the Senate's agenda would no longer be jeopardized by clusters of filibusters.

THE EMERGENCE OF THE TEXTBOOK SENATE, 1933-48

The effects of the Twentieth Amendment on Senate obstruction were not immediately obvious. There were twenty filibusters in the Seventy-third Congress (1933–35) and twenty more in the Seventy-fourth (1935–37). Indeed, after surveying Senate filibusters from 1933 to 1939, Franklin Burdette concluded: "Obviously filibustering is still a successful instrument in the Senate of the United States" (1940, 206). In 1937–38, however, the number of Senate filibusters declined to ten, followed by nine in the Seventy-sixth Congress (1939–40). Indeed, it would be thirty years before there were twenty or more filibusters in a two-year Congress. This section surveys the beginning of this "textbook" era of low obstruction, during which many of the popular notions about Senate filibustering took hold. A key lesson is that the effect of the Twentieth Amendment depended on the adoption of complementary tactics as political actors learned to take advantage of the new congressional schedule.

The Long-Suffering Senate

Why did filibustering thrive after the Twentieth Amendment passed? One answer is that the new congressional schedule (expected to reduce filibustering) was adopted at the same time that the congressional agenda was swelled by President Roosevelt's New Deal legislation and other relief measures, making time scarce and, thus, valuable throughout the calendar year. In addition, these years were marked by one of the most colorful obstructionists in American history: Huey Long (D-LA). Long did not begin serving as a senator until 1932, and he died after being shot in September 1935. In the intervening three and a half years, he had a lasting impact on Senate history and American politics.

Although Long was a Democrat, he was at odds with Senate majority leader Joseph T. Robinson (D-AR) and Franklin Roosevelt. Long's solution to the economic crisis was a massive redistribution of wealth, and he also sought control over federal patronage jobs in Louisiana. After a fight with

Robinson in 1932, Long resigned from his committee assignments so that he could focus his attention on Senate floor debate (Gould 2005).[18]

Long was a prolific obstructionist. Of the forty filibusters from 1933 to 1936, Long was a named participant (i.e., individually or as part of a team of two or three) in half: twelve in the Seventy-third Congress and eight in his abbreviated second term, the Seventy-fourth Congress. Some of Long's highlights:

- June 1933: blocks a presidential reorganization plan;
- April 1934: blocks the nomination of Daniel Moore as tax collector for Louisiana;
- June 1934: blocks adjournment for the year until the Senate acts on a farm relief bill (the bill passed, but Roosevelt pocket vetoed it);
- June 1935: attempts to block renewal of the National Industrial Recovery Act (NIRA) with a fifteen-and-a-half-hour "speech" (the bill passed with some modification);
- August 1935: forces (with others) passage of the first Neutrality Act by threatening to block adjournment for the year.

The most famous of Long's filibusters was his effort to block the renewal of the NIRA in June 1935. The ostensible goal was to attach a rider to the bill requiring Senate confirmation for all federal employees making over $4,000 a year, although grandstanding may have been a motive as well (Krock 1935a, 22). His solo filibuster lasted fifteen and a half hours; it was shorter than La Follette's 1908 marathon but perhaps the most *colorful* filibuster in Senate history. Since Long was not prepared to speak all night, he ran out of pertinent comments and discussed the Constitution, his uncle, Roquefort dressing, his "share-the-wealth" movement, the U.S. postmaster, his fights with Louisiana oil companies, tariffs, silver, oyster frying, and (most famously) the right way to make potlikker stew (ingredients: turnips, turnip greens, salted meat). When he ran out of ideas, he began taking suggestions from the press gallery (*Congressional Record* 79, pt. 8 [June 12, 1935]: 9091–9175; "Huey for 15 Hours" 1935, E1). To senators who were loyal to their institution, Long's flamboyant disrespect was unacceptable. Three days later, for example, Senator Ashurst condemned his reckless rhetoric in a speech on the Senate floor (*Congressional Record* 79, pt. 8 [June 15, 1935]: 9364–65).

Long's NIRA spectacle was the last straw for several senators, who formed a "suffer Long" club determined to deny the Louisiana senator any refuge from the trials of obstruction. Three weeks earlier, senators had successfully outlasted a Long filibuster against a resolution to allow President Roosevelt to deliver a veto message to Congress in person: "Floor leaders had determined early in the afternoon to 'sit out' the filibuster, if it took all night. 'I want to see just how long he (Senator Long) intends to make an ass of himself," [Majority Leader] Robinson said" ("Congress Will Hear Veto" 1935, 1). Long was defeated when he used up his two speeches on the issue.

During the NIRA filibuster, a band of senators sat out Long's speech and objected to all unanimous consent requests and motions to recess, denying him a graceful exit from the Senate floor. The "suffer Long" movement included Senators Guffey (D-PA), Black (D-AL), Moore (D-NJ), Radcliffe (D-MD), Minton (D-IN), Schwellenbach (D-WA), and Bilbo (D-MS), all of whom urged Senate leaders to play hardball with Long ("Long's Filibuster" 1935, 2). They were joined by Alben Barkley (D-KY), who threatened to propose a precedent that would take Long (and other obstructionists) off their feet if they propose or yield for a quorum call or motion (*Congressional Record* 79, pt. 8 [June 12, 1935]: 9137), and Vice President Garner allegedly encouraged the effort (Krock 1935a, 22).

Despite the galvanized opposition against him, Long had one more infamous filibuster left. On August 26, 1935, the Senate had an agreement to adjourn sine die at midnight. At 6:30 P.M., Long began filibustering against a $93 million catch-all deficiency appropriations bill until the House added price supports for wheat and cotton. Huey had the upper hand; he could easily last five and a half hours. Moreover, senators refused an opportunity to remove him from the floor for speaking ill of the House of Representatives, suggesting that he had not completely exhausted the Senate's commitment to free debate (Burdette 1940, 187–89). Long lasted until midnight, killed the entire bill, and delayed the implementation of several new social programs, including social security and the Labor Relations Act ("Saturday Night & After" 1935). Two weeks later he was shot and killed in Louisiana.

The Club and Senate Norms

The next twelve years were marked by the emergence of a strong set of norms in the Senate that constrained members' behavior and enhanced the reputation of the Senate. Matthews (1960) lists these norms as: (*a*) apprenticeship, that is, new senators keeping a low profile while they learned about their jobs; (*b*) focusing on legislative work rather than seeking out media attention; (*c*) specializing on a few topics, especially the issues covered by each senator's assigned committees; (*d*) courtesy toward each other; (*e*) reciprocity, that is, helping out other senators with their requests; and (*f*) institutional patriotism, that is, supporting and honoring the Senate as an institution. While historical evidence on the emergence of these norms is scanty, they might be considered a repudiation of Huey Long, who began grandstanding as soon as he arrived, rejected committee work, filibustered on various issues, insulted his colleagues, and used the Senate floor as his personal stage.

When applied to filibustering, these norms imply that senators should not filibuster frivolously or for the sake of public attention. Ideally, all filibustering speeches should be germane to the target bill; at the least senators should not recite recipes or fiction on the Senate floor. Southern senators, for example, tended to make germane speeches against civil rights bills (the 1942 poll tax ban is an exception), especially after Richard Russell became their leader (Mann 1996).[19]

Why would senators adhere to these norms? After all, it might be beneficial to grab headlines with a spectacular and colorful filibuster. One answer may be senators' renewed willingness to sit out filibusters and to threaten senators who persist in abusive filibusters with new reforms. This is an extension of the "suffer Long" movement. A second incentive to adhere to the norms of the Senate is the emergence of a "club" of elite senators who held positions of influence and who could use their power to punish or shame those who violated the norms of the Senate. In 1949, for example, Hubert Humphrey experienced social shunning when he first arrived in the Senate after convincing the Democratic convention to adopt a strong civil rights plank (Caro 2002; Mann 1996).[20]

Statutory Restraints on Filibustering

Another innovation that limited filibustering was the creation of new expedited procedures, beginning with the Reorganization Act of 1939. This law ensured a simple majority vote to disapprove a presidential plan to reorganize the federal bureaucracy (Burdette 1940, 228–29; Binder and Smith 1997, 186–88). Like the Electoral Count Act of 1887, this law was motivated by a specific filibuster. Reorganization plans had been filibustered in the Senate in 1933 and 1938; as discussed in chapter 6, the 1937 antilynching bill was scheduled to keep Roosevelt's reorganization plan off the Senate floor. Reorganization plans often inflicted political pain in the name of efficiency, and some senators preferred to avoid such choices. In 1933, furthermore, Roosevelt waited to submit his plan until immediately before the Senate planned to adjourn for the summer, and some senators objected to his apparent gamesmanship ("Towards Adjournment" 1933).

Filibustering and Attrition

The combination of the Twentieth Amendment, a renewed commitment to attrition, statutory safeguards for high-priority legislation, and social sanctions for inappropriate filibustering led to a decline in filibustering. After forty filibuster incidents from 1933 to 1936, there were just fifty-five cases from 1937 to 1948. This reduction included fewer efforts to influence the

Senate agenda. From 1933 to 1936, seven filibusters were intended to raise a new issue, but there were only two such attempts from 1937 to 1948.[21]

Attrition and compromise remained the primary responses to filibustering. For example, in 1947, the Republican majority held night sessions to try to outlast filibusters against a resolution to investigate vote fraud in Kansas City ("Taft Surrenders" 1947, 1) and against an effort by liberal Democrats to delay a veto override vote on the Taft-Hartley Labor Act ("The Majority Rules" 1947). In 1938, the Fair Labor Standards Act was modified in response to a filibuster threat by Southern senators so that there would be regional differences in the minimum wage ("Record of the 75th Congress" 1938). In 1942, as Southerners were avoiding the chamber to help break a quorum, Majority Leader Alben Barkley had absent senators arrested and brought to the chamber ("Filibuster!" 1942).

While the number of senators required to mount a filibuster varied with circumstances, a few sources mentioned fifteen to twenty as a reasonable minimum ("No Drifting" 1938; "Conferees Clash" 1939, 1). Another estimate is that it would take a full month to outlast such a team, for example, Southern senators blocking a 1948 poll tax ban ("Ohioan Arrives to Cheers" 1948, 1).

If such a small number of senators can filibuster, why (other than the physical costs) were there so few filibusters? One reason is public condemnation of filibustering. Classic war-of-attrition filibusters were newsworthy public events, which increases the political implications of a filibuster. If the public sides with the obstructionists, they win; if not, their reputations suffer. There are several references to the importance of public opinion to filibuster contests. Arthur Krock portrays public opinion as a key factor in the Court-packing fight, as public sympathy for one side or the other could sway swing votes (see Krock 1937, 22). *Time* highlighted the role of public opinion in senators' decisions on a 1939 neutrality bill and then noted: "While delaying tactics probably mean victory for the Isolationists, the U.S. public will stand for no filibuster" ("Big Michigander" 1939). In 1941, opponents of the Lend-Lease bill overtly tried to "expand the game" by slowing the bill down and appealing to the public, but they found that general public opinion was against them ("Filibuster Threat Renewed" 1941, 10). Similarly, in October 1941, opponents of revising the Neutrality Act considered filibustering but abandoned the fight rather than lose publicly ("New Ship Clauses" 1941, 12). Public opinion thus acted as an effective constraint on obstruction.

Cloture and Reform, 1933–48

Senators used the cloture rule sparingly in the textbook Senate. There were cloture votes on seven bills: the 1937–38 antilynching bill (two votes); poll tax bans in 1942, 1944, and 1946; a bill authorizing the Federal Employment

Practices Commission (FEPC) in 1946; a resolution approving of a loan to Britain in 1946; and a bill to change labor laws in 1946. All eight votes failed.

Why was cloture rarely used? As Arthur Krock said of the rule: "It is mild; it can be circumvented; and senators hesitate to apply it against one member or a group for fear of reprisals against themselves when some hated measure invites their own dilatory tactics" (Krock 1935b, 20). Some senators who were generally against voting for cloture sought to avoid cloture votes on issues they genuinely cared about. When the Court-packing bill was obstructed in mid-1937, for example, senators avoided a cloture vote because they anticipated that an antilynching bill would come up later and, if they voted for cloture on the Court-packing bill, they would lose the ability to explain their votes against cloture on a civil rights bill as a matter of principle ("President Speeds Court Bill Vote" 1937, 16) or they might make enemies who would exact retribution on the next cloture vote ("New Court Bill" 1937, 35). Furthermore, senators had an incentive to concede rather than lose a cloture vote. In 1944, Southern senators compromised on FEPC funding rather than risk a precedent-setting cloture vote on civil rights ("Sabath Continues Battle" 1945, 1).

Furthermore, senators were reluctant to attempt cloture because the rule was ineffective. As in 1922, Southerners resorted to filibustering the approval of the *Journal* to block a 1937–38 antilynching bill, a 1942 antilynching bill, and a 1946 bill to authorize the FEPC. According to the Senate's interpretation of Rule 22, this tactic was immune to the cloture process, a decision that was affirmed in 1946. In 1944 and 1946, Barkley filed "snap" cloture petitions on bills to ban the poll tax because he anticipated similar tactics by determined Southerners. In addition, in 1944, Southerners prepared over a thousand amendments to the poll tax ban so that they could drag out voting indefinitely if cloture was invoked ("Senate Prepares" 1944, 21). The neutering of Rule 22 culminated in an August 1948 precedent by Arthur Vandenberg stating that cloture does not apply to a motion to proceed to a bill. The Republican majority gave up on cloture and conceded defeat but vowed to change Rule 22 when they returned in 1949 ("Southerners Win" 1949, 1).

This was not the first time the Republican majority had discussed cloture reform. At the opening of the Eightieth Congress, the threat of cloture reform ended a filibuster intended to help Theodore "The Man" Bilbo (D-MS) keep his Senate seat. From 1935 to 1946, Bilbo was one of the loudest and most virulent opponents of civil rights legislation. During his 1946 primary campaign, he called for "every red-blooded white man to use any means to keep the niggers away from the polls. If you don't understand what that means you are just plain dumb" ("Prince of the Peckerwoods" 1946).[22] Subsequently, Mississippians and citizens across the country called on the Senate to invalidate Bilbo's primary election results ("Demand Ouster of

Bilbo" 1946, 17). Days before the inauguration of the Eightieth Congress, the Justice Department announced that it had been investigating Bilbo's questionable relationships with defense contractors for months ("Top Republicans" 1947, 1).

Republican leaders decided to exclude Bilbo from swearing in as a senator ("Top Republicans" 1947), which requires a simple majority vote. Southern senators began to filibuster the effort to exclude Bilbo. The Republicans did not believe that they could use the cloture process, however, because Bilbo was not a "pending measure" ("Bilbo Is Held Off" 1947, 1). After a few hours:

> Taft made himself heard long enough to call first for a recess until noon of the next day (Saturday). Then, he said in cold anger, he would wait until Monday. And then, "if those who are now blocking the organization of the Senate have not changed their minds, I propose to keep the Senate in session to break this. Use of the filibuster on such an occasion for such an inconsequential purpose is so unjustifiable that if you do not change your minds you are going to face a complete change of the rules of this Senate, face a change that will bring about cloture on any subject. We cannot begin a session facing the threat of a filibuster on every measure we may bring up." ("That Man" 1947)

In our terms, Taft threatened a strategy of attrition, then reform.

Southern Democrats apparently considered this threat credible since the Republican Conference had authorized Taft to craft its anti-Bilbo strategy ("Southerners Balk" 1947, 1). They soon capitulated: Bilbo was excluded but retained his salary. The *NYT* attributed this outcome to "the apparent willingness of the Republicans, with some Democratic support, to fight a filibuster to the bitter end, and possibly to amend the Senate rules so that cloture could thereafter be imposed by simple majority vote" ("A Satisfactory 'Compromise'" 1947, 22). Southerners had been prepared to filibuster "indefinitely," including one senator's threat to read aloud the entire Senate committee report on Bilbo's election, but, once Taft threatened to reform Senate rules, the Southerners yielded ("Filibuster Plan Outlined" 1947, 2).

THE SENATE IN TRANSITION, 1949-60

The Republican majority of the "Do-Nothing" Eightieth Congress did not get a chance to follow through on their promise of cloture reform. Instead, it fell to a deeply divided Democratic majority party to revive the cloture rule or bury it. An easy opportunity to restore meaning to Rule 22 failed on March 11, 1949, when senators decided in a 41–46 vote that the cloture rule does not apply to motions to take up a bill. Subsequently, proreform senators struck a bargain with Southern senators to revise Rule 22. As rewritten, the cloture rule applied to all motions and measures *except* resolutions to revise Senate rules, but two-thirds of all senators (absent or present) would be required to invoke cloture ("Compromise Closure Rule" 1949, 1; Zelizer 2004).

This new rule was very successful. It was intended to make Rule 22 difficult to invoke, and, over the next ten years, senators attempted to use the rule three times—and failed three times. In 1950, two attempts to invoke cloture on an FEPC authorization bill failed 52–32 and 55–33, illustrating the difficulty of mustering sixty-four votes for civil rights legislation.

The third failed cloture vote was on the Atomic Energy Act in 1954. Interestingly, the obstructionists were liberals—senators like Wayne Morse (Ind-OR) who ordinarily criticized filibustering and pushed for a strong cloture rule. Senate majority leader William Knowland (R-CA) was blindsided by this filibuster and called for round-the-clock sessions, including cots in the Senate cloakroom. However, Knowland and the supporters of the bill were ill prepared for an attrition battle and quickly tired of the fight. Desperate, Knowland filed a cloture petition. At this point, conservative Democrats led by Lyndon B. Johnson (D-TX) distanced themselves from the liberal opposition and moved to end the contest. They cared little about the bill but feared any change to the procedural status quo, that is, sincere voting on cloture or a successful filibuster that fueled efforts to strengthen Rule 22 ("Democrats Split" 1954, 1). After cloture failed 44–42 (with conservative senators opposing it to keep the rule ineffective), Johnson negotiated an amicable settlement. The obstructionists settled for a fair opportunity to offer their amendments without the all-night sessions and tabling motions imposed by Knowland ("Log Jam Broken" 1954). Once Knowland relented, the bill passed in a day.

Although the cloture rule was difficult to use, attrition continued to be an effective response to obstruction by small numbers of senators. In June 1950, the Senate outwaited a twelve-hour filibuster by Harry Cain (R-WA) against a bill extending rent controls. Senators allowed Cain bathroom breaks while they waited him out in absentia: "By suppertime, each side had reduced itself to a corporal's guard, left behind in case of a break. The rest slipped off to dinner parties or catnapped on cots in the cloakrooms. Some fortified their spirits with quick nips of bourbon" ("12 Hours, 8 Minutes" 1950). Once Cain had made his public stand, he allowed a vote on the bill.[23]

In October 1950, a band of liberal senators filibustered a vote to override Truman's veto of the anti-Communist Internal Security Act. They wanted to delay the vote so that Truman could rally public opinion and round up senators to sustain his veto. One obstructionist, Langer (R-ND), literally collapsed from exhaustion on the Senate floor and had to be carried off on a stretcher. After a day, however, it was clear that public opinion was unchanged: "The [telegraph] wires from the hinterland had warmed hardly at all and most of the telegrams that did come in bore the parrot tracks of organized pressure groups" ("Dawn over Capitol Hill" 1950). The filibuster collapsed, and the Senate overrode Truman's veto.

In 1953, the Republican majority faced a filibuster by a band of liberal Democrats against a bill granting states control over their offshore coastland, a goal endorsed by the Republican platform. The opponents' "educational campaign" lasted almost four weeks and spread a half million words across a thousand pages of the *Congressional Record*. Majority Leader Bob Taft considered all the weapons in the majority's arsenal. He prepared a cloture petition but did not file it, and the Senate Rules Committee reported a resolution to restore the pre-1949 cloture threshold of two-thirds of those *voting* ("Taft Maps Move" 1953, 20; "Senate Unit" 1953, 20). Both efforts faltered because the Southern Democrats who supported the bill were adamantly opposed to voting for cloture or strengthening Rule 22. Instead, Taft settled on a strategy of attrition. On April 27, he announced that the Senate would begin twenty-four-hour sessions the next day, and Senate workers retrieved cots for senators to sleep on {"Offshore Bill Foes" 1953, 1). The next day, the obstructionists accepted a final vote on the bill rather than wage a war of attrition ("Offshore Oil Vote" 1953, 1).

In 1959, senators revised Rule 22 to lower the threshold for cloture to two-thirds of the senators present and applied Rule 22 to resolutions that altered Senate rules. This reform had little immediate effect on senators' strategies, however. Senators used the new rule for only one of the seven filibusters during the Eighty-sixth Congress: the 1960 Civil Rights Act.

After ten days of debate on the Civil Rights Act, Majority Leader Lyndon Johnson attempted to exhaust the Southerners with round-the-clock sessions. From February 29 to March 8, 1960, the Senate was in session for 157 hours, held thirteen roll call votes and fifty quorum calls, and filled over 650 pages of the *Congressional Record* ("Statistical Summary for 1960," Mansfield Archive, XXII, 28, 6).[24] During this marathon, Morse (now D-OR) made an attempt to collect signatures for a cloture petition that met an abrupt end. After Morse announced that he had a petition to sign, Thruston P. Morton (R-KY), who was acting as the floor monitor for pro–civil rights Republicans, crossed the chamber and ripped the petition into dozens of pieces ("Morton Rips Up Petition" 1960, 1). Morton believed that a cloture vote, if held too soon, would doom the bill by locking in senators' positions before the bill's supporters had formed a two-thirds majority. Eventually, however, a faction of the pro–civil rights group filed a cloture petition, and Johnson, piqued at the premature move, called off the twenty-four-hour sessions ("Senate Calls Off 24-Hour Sessions" 1960, 1). The cloture attempt failed 42–53.

Weeks later, the Senate renewed the civil rights debate with a recently-passed House bill as the base text. The Democratic Policy Committee (DPC) discussed cloture prior to this debate and decided that it was a no-win strategy. If a cloture attempt failed, there would be "another heated debate on the Senate rules in January [1961]." If cloture was invoked, "it would certainly be succeeded by a number more petitions for cloture," but it was unlikely because "there were many Senators outside of the South who did not like to invoke cloture" (Democratic Policy Committee Minutes [hereafter DPC Minutes], March 29, 1960).[25] In the end, no cloture votes were held on the House civil rights bill and, after ample debate, it passed 71–18.

THE EMERGENCE OF THE SIXTY-VOTE SENATE, 1961-2004

The contest over the 1960 Civil Rights Act illustrated the futility of attrition against a phalanx of Southern senators. It was unrealistic to expect a majority of the Senate to remain in the chamber indefinitely while obstructionists killed time in two man teams. The world of the 1960s Senate was a different place: increasing workload, peripatetic membership, and growing dissatisfaction with the racial status quo. Senators began rethinking the Senate's tradition of unfettered debate.

After the 1960 election, leadership of the Senate Democratic majority passed from Lyndon Johnson to the mild Mike Mansfield (D-MT). Mansfield and Johnson had distinct views of Rule 22 and legislative strategy. As the fight over the 1960 Civil Rights Act demonstrated, Johnson and the DPC believed that attrition was still a viable response to filibustering, especially in light of senators' general preference to avoid using the cloture rule. More broadly, Johnson was willing to use any tactic available to achieve his goals, such as shortening or lengthening the time allotted for a roll call vote, offering unexpected motions and amendments, and timing votes to take advantage of senators' absences (Caro 2002).[26] To Mansfield, on the other hand, attrition had proved ineffective against organized filibusters, and the spectacle of cots, bathrobes, and extended speeches damaged the reputation of the Senate.[27] Furthermore, Mansfield treated every senator as his equal, and he respected their prerogatives; he would not avail himself of Johnson's devious tactics to succeed.[28] For both reasons, cloture was preferred to attrition: it *might* be more effective, and it was a transparent response.

Of course, the preference for cloture was not a matter of personal taste. Mansfield had voted twice on cloture (1954 and 1960), both times against it. Instead, his views on cloture reflected the realities of Senate life: senators faced a growing set of policy problems to deal with and increasing public expectations for government action (Stimson 2004), leading to longer sessions. Also, senators were increasingly nomadic, roaming the country to cultivate political alliances and traveling the globe on fact-finding missions.

It was unrealistic to expect that these globe-trotting senators could stay in the Senate to outlast obstruction on a variety of issues. Finally, Mansfield was concerned that, in the modern age, round-the-clock Senate sessions turned the chamber into a media zoo, with senators posing for the peanuts of public attention.

Furthermore, Mansfield's campaign to normalize cloture indirectly reflected a collective choice by senators. Mansfield's sixteen-year tenure as majority leader is the longest in Senate history. Senate Democrats reaffirmed Mansfield every two years, and, if a majority was discontented with his parliamentary tactics, they could have replaced him. Nor did Mansfield strong-arm his colleagues into voting for cloture since he was reticent to use the tactics that made Lyndon Johnson powerful but despised.

Mansfield's Early Contests

At the beginning of his tenure as majority leader, Mansfield was not completely averse to attrition. In August 1961, the Senate waited through Senator Proxmire's quixotic nineteen-hour filibuster against Lawrence O'Connor's nomination to the Federal Power Commission. A month later, Mansfield filed a "snap" cloture petition on a proposal to revise Rule 22. He had promised to schedule the proposal but was skeptical about its prospects, so he forced a quick vote to avoid wasting time.[29] Senators rejected cloture 37–43 ("Drive to Curb Filibusters" 1961). Days later, Mansfield headed off a filibuster against a migratory labor bill by threatening a serious attrition effort ("Congress Delays" 1961). In 1962, the Senate passed a constitutional amendment to ban poll taxes without cloture, but only because Southern senators were unwilling to invest their full effort in a filibuster once they had registered their opposition for public consumption ("Friendly Filibuster" 1962). Later, a Kennedy proposal to reduce literacy requirements for voting encountered more determined Southern obstruction, with weak support from the administration, the Democratic leadership, and the Republican Party ("Everybody's Getting Fat" 1962). After cloture failed 43–53 and 42–52, Mansfield moved to table the bill so that conflicted senators had an opportunity to vote for the bill by defeating the motion 33–64. Twenty-one senators (fourteen Republicans, seven Democrats) voted against cloture and against tabling the bill, suggesting that they supported civil rights (publicly) but opposed cloture on a civil rights bill.

While cloture on civil rights remained taboo, in August 1962 senators approved cloture for the first time in thirty-five years. Curiously, the obstructionists were liberal Democrats opposed to a bill proposed by President Kennedy. The bill established a public-private corporation to launch and operate communications satellites. The opponents filibustered this "Comsat" bill for weeks because they considered it a giveaway of public resources to AT&T. Eventually, Mansfield assembled a coalition to invoke cloture, 63–27. While several conservative Democrats voted nay, seven others agreed to skip the vote so that Mansfield could reach the critical two-thirds majority *of those voting* ("Silence in the Senate" 1962).

This single vote transformed cloture politics in the Senate. Of the twenty-one senators who cast principled votes against cloture on the literacy test bill, thirteen Republicans and one Democrat switched to support cloture on Comsat. Of the thirty-one senators who voted against both cloture and the literacy bill, ten supported cloture on the Comsat bill. Subsequently, senators in general, and these twenty-four switchers in particular, would have a difficult time voting against cloture on principle, and the trust that sustained strategic opposition to cloture was broken by the Comsat vote. Also, this overt filibuster by Senate liberals who had railed against filibustering for a decade suggested that obstruction was simply an ordinary tactic that *all* senators used to get what they wanted.[30]

A possible beneficiary of the Comsat debate was Thurgood Marshall, who had waited months for the Judiciary Committee to act on his nomination. Days after the Comsat bill passed, Kennedy urged the Judiciary Committee to report Marshall. Senate liberals threatened to discharge Marshall from the committee, and some Republicans threatened a cloture vote ("Senate Tax Bill" 1962, 1). The committee acted swiftly, and no filibuster materialized ("Progress on Marshall" 1962, 190). No article directly links Marshall's swift approval to the Comsat filibuster, but Southerners may have feared a civil rights cloture vote after the Comsat vote.

The 1964 Civil Rights Act

The 1964 civil rights bill marks a transition from attrition to cloture. Although the filibuster that it occasioned is the longest on record, it was not an endurance contest in the classic sense. There are several excellent accounts of the passage of the 1964 Civil Rights Act (e.g., Harvey 1973; Mann 1996; Valeo 1999), but we have a special interest in the tactics used to overcome Southern obstruction. The filibuster ended by cloture, but senators' willingness to vote for cloture was uncertain and contingent on the amount of debate that preceded the vote.

From the outset, Mansfield sought cloture. In a June 1963 memorandum to President Kennedy, he wrote: "There is only one practicable way [passage of a civil rights bill] can be assured, by counting 67 votes on cloture for whatever bill is pushed" ("Civil Rights Strategy in the Senate," Mansfield Archive, XXII, 103, 14). Democratic leaders began whipping votes on cloture by June 1963 (Robert G. Baker to Mansfield, "Civil Rights Possibilities," June

27, 1963, Mansfield Archive, XXII, 28, 6) and had conducted several polls by June 1964. Cloture was not a unanimous choice, however; at various times, President Johnson, Senator Hubert Humphrey, and some civil rights groups expressed a preference for wearing out the Southerners ("Humphrey Asks Speed" 1964, 17; Valeo 1999, 105).

Mansfield, working with Richard Russell (the leader of the Southern bloc) cleared the Senate agenda of other major bills (e.g., tax reform, agriculture, military procurement) before bringing up civil rights legislation so that there would be ample time for debate.[31] Once this must-pass legislation was through, the opportunity costs of floor time were low, and senators were prepared to spend the rest of the session passing a civil rights bill (Whalen and Whalen 1985, 97). Mansfield also objected to all committee meetings while the civil rights bill was on the Senate floor. This deprived Russell of the power to selectively inconvenience committees and ensured that disappointed senators blamed the obstructionists for committee inaction (Valeo 1999, 142–43).

The Senate debated the bill for fifty-seven working days, the longest filibuster on record. Oddly, this "longest debate" was not an effort to wear the Southerners down. In a conventional attrition contest, the majority remains quiet so that the minority has to occupy the floor continuously. One drawback of this strategy is that one side of the debate gets all the attention. Instead, bill supporters fought a public relations struggle with Southern obstructionists. Bill proponents organized speakers to monitor the debate, refute Southerners' claims, and defend the bill (Mann 1996, 395–99). Hubert Humphrey (D-MN) and Thomas Kuchel (R-CA) circulated a newsletter tracking the status of the bill so that proponents could muster a quorum at a moment's notice.

The real contest for civil rights was waged in closed-door negotiations to form a supermajority coalition in support of cloture. The probill leaders were confident of fifty to sixty votes but needed ten to fifteen Republican votes to invoke cloture. Humphrey negotiated with the Republican leader Everett Dirksen for these votes. On its face, this is similar to a standard pivotal politics account: bill supporters negotiated with the filibuster pivot to craft a compromise bill. However, the policy concessions made to obtain Dirksen's support were largely cosmetic (Mann 1996, 421). Instead, historians describe Dirksen's primary payoff as public credit for pondering, perfecting, and rescuing civil rights legislation (Mann 1996; Valeo 1999). With the Illinois senator's support, the Senate invoked cloture on June 10, 1964.

Filibustering continued after the Senate invoked cloture. Sam Ervin (D-NC) staved off final passage by forcing votes on over a hundred amendments filed before cloture was invoked. Since the cloture rule ca. 1964 did not count voting time toward the time limits in Rule 22, the cloture rule provided no defense against this tactic. A close observer suggests that Ervin's "last stand" was purely for the consumption of his constituents; once his solitary antics were reported in North Carolina media outlets, he relented (Valeo 1999, 161–63).

The 1964 Civil Rights Act was one of the most important bills ever passed by Congress. A century after the Civil War, it finally committed the nation to racial and gender equality, prompted the realignment of the South to the Republican Party, and cemented the loyalty of African Americans to the Democratic Party for generations (see, e.g., Carmines and Stimson 1989; and Rohde 1991). It also marked a transition in filibuster politics. Senators had finally invoked cloture on a civil rights bill. Now that this taboo was broken, they were able to think about cloture and filibustering as it touched a variety of issues. Liberals continued to propose reforms, and some senators continued to oppose cloture on any issue, but senators had finally invoked cloture on a civil rights bill.

Mansfield considered the filibuster an essential element of the passage of the 1964 act. It gave Southerners an ample opportunity to make their case, allowed civil rights proponents to demonstrate the intensity of their commitment, and ensured that a large final coalition voted for cloture. The Senate debate helped convince Southern whites that their senators had fought the good fight and promoted Southern acceptance of the act:

> You will recall that the [1964 civil rights] debate proceeded on this Senate floor 83 days. I cannot help but wonder what might have been the result if a majority could have imposed cloture on that debate. I know it could have been accomplished in a month or less. I doubt very much if the bill would have been nearly as comprehensive. I do not believe that this law's observance today would be nearly as uniform, nearly as great a source of pride for all Americans without that debate. . . . The fact that the law is now fully observed in all parts of the country attests abundantly to the vital service performed in this chamber. (*Congressional Record* 115, pt. 2 [January 27, 1969]: 1868)

Even though the debate changed few minds, weeks of legislative resistance may have substituted for years of opposition by Southerners and local officials.

Filibustering and Cloture, 1964–74

For the next decade, there was no serious effort at attrition in the Senate. From 1965 to 1974, there were sixty-eight filibuster events in the data set. Of these, twenty-eight came to a cloture vote. The rest were resolved by surrender, compromise, or circumvention, but not attrition. Figure 8.2 illustrates

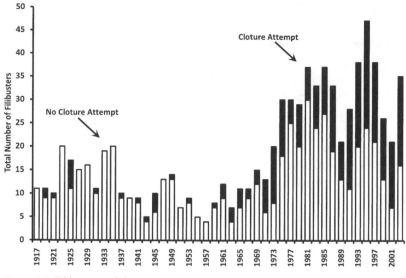

Figure 8.2. Filibusters and cloture, 1917–2004.

this pattern. In this figure, each bar shows the total number of filibusters per Congress, the black portion of the bar indicates the number of filibusters on which there was a cloture vote, and the white portion is the number of filibusters resolved by some other means. After a fifteen-year drought, there is an increase in the use of cloture during the 1960s and a further increase during the 1970s and after. This reflects Mansfield's view that "there is no remedy for [filibustering] in around-the-clock sessions or any other kind of parliamentary buffoonery or quackery. The only rational remedy under the present rules remains the procedure of cloture" (*Congressional Record* 115, pt. 2 [January 27, 1969]: 1867).

Some senators were slow to adopt this attitude toward cloture. During the 1969 cloture reform debate, Mansfield lamented that principled voting against cloture was negating the purpose of Rule 22 and feeding calls for reform: "Carried to the extreme, a refusal by a substantial body of members to vote for cloture even when such a vote would accord with their position on the substantive issue tends to reduce the Senate to a debating society and it might well precipitate in time a drastic reordering of the constitutional structure of the government. . . . Indeed, a score of determined members or even fewer can tie up the Senate, not for weeks, not for months, but indefinitely" (*Congressional Record* 115, pt. 2 [January 27, 1969]: 1867). When the Senate voted on William Rehnquist's nomination to the Supreme Court in 1971, for example, a cloture vote failed 52–42, but a motion to table the nomination (implicitly a test of senators' preferences) failed 22–70. Nineteen senators voted against cloture and against tabling the nomination.[32]

One response to principled voting was holding multiple cloture votes. Of the twenty-eight bills that merited a cloture vote from 1964 to 1974, there were multiple cloture votes on twenty. There were apparently several motives to hold multiple votes on the same question. First, some senators may have felt that they had honored their generic opposition to cloture if they waited until the second or third attempt to vote for cloture. Second, a vote was a lazy means of whipping votes; the easiest way to find out how members would vote on cloture on a given bill was to hold a vote on cloture. Given the information provided by a defeated cloture vote, bill supporters could decide whether the base of support was large enough to continue trying and, if so, with whom to bargain. This occurred with the ill-fated 1966 Civil Rights Act, when Mansfield announced ex ante that the first cloture attempt would probably fail but that the debate would continue if the bill obtained fifty-five votes or more ("Senate to Vote Tomorrow" 1966, 1). Third, even when there may be no real hope of winning, Senate leaders may schedule cloture votes to satisfy the demands of a key interest group or draw attention to a salient issue; for example, in 2003, Republicans scheduled seven votes on the appellate court nomination of Miguel Estrada, with a narrow majority supporting the nominee on each vote. Fourth, there was some uncertainty about senators' participation from day to day, so, if a cloture attempt loses by a narrow margin, for example, 64–33, the proponents of the bill may be tempted to simply roll the dice again and hope that some of the votes against cloture do not show up. The 1975 cloture rule eliminated this practice by tying cloture to a fixed percentage of the chamber.

THE ORIGINS OF THE SENATE HOLD SYSTEM, 1953–70

While filibustering tactics and responses were evolving on the Senate floor, a revolution in Senate operations was going on behind closed doors. Party leaders instituted a vetting process for the unanimous consent calendar that slowly evolved into a system of invisible obstruction.

In the contemporary Senate, individual senators signal their intent to filibuster legislation or nominations and expect, within limits, their party leaders to respect this threat. The standard means for doing so is a letter requesting a "hold." Senators request that bills be held from floor debate for a short time for a variety of reasons: they may wish to read and analyze the bill, to delay floor debate while they are out of town, or to negotiate with the bill sponsor about a specific provision (Sinclair 1989, 130–31). Some hold letters, however, express a senator's intent to filibuster a bill and request that party leaders refuse any unanimous consent agreement on that bill without consulting the filibustering senator.[33] Majority leaders will typically respect short-term hold requests from their own members, but they may challenge long-term filibuster threats by holding cloture votes to test the sincerity of senators' threats and the size of filibuster coalitions.

The emergence of the hold system was a criticial development. Without holds, senators had to maintain a constant vigil on the Senate floor to prevent the passage of, or the limitation of debate on, bills they oppose by unanimous consent. Holds also tend to decrease the external sanctions for filibustering. Since holds are private communications, senators can reveal their holds to groups and individuals who approve and remain anonymous to everyone else.[34] For legislation on which the political sanctions would otherwise be negative, this is a significant change in the calculus of obstruction.

It is unclear when the hold system began. Senator Byrd (D-WV) coordinated the system as majority whip in the early 1970s (Davidson 1985; Evans and Lipinski 2005), and this is often considered the origin date.[35] Archival evidence supports the claim that Byrd coordinated the hold system for Democrats. In December 1970, Byrd wrote to Mansfield that, "as it is now, each Senator can request some time of the Majority Leader or Minority Leader in order to study and to prepare amendments to a bill" (Mansfield Archive, XXII, 101, 11), and, in June 1972, he reported to Mansfield: "Several senators have a hold on [House Resolution (HR) 13324, the maritime authorization bill]. . . . Senator McIntyre has a hold on it—and several other senators. . . . [I]t looks like it might be an organized hold" (Mansfield Archive, XXII, 65, 14).

However, there is strong evidence that senators placed holds long before the 1970s. The earliest known reference to a hold is in the DPC Minutes for August 5, 1958. Lyndon Johnson refers to a letter he received from Senator Chavez (D-NM) requesting that HR 7168, a bill setting policy for construction contracts, be held until he had completed some hearings. The DPC granted this request and held the bill. Mansfield also received hold letters in the early 1960s. On January 19, 1961, Senator Proxmire (D-WI) wrote to block consent agreements on the nomination of John B. Connally for secretary of the navy, citing a desire to speak to the committee chairman and give a floor speech (Mansfield Archive, XXII, 67, 21). On March 10, 1964, Frank Church (D-ID) wrote to Mansfield to object to S. 829, which restricted potato farming. Church threatened to offer and debate an Idaho-related amendment "most thoroughly," after which he would "expect to debate the bill itself until its evils are understood or my strength fails" (Mansfield Archive, XXII, 65, 12).

Furthermore, a DPC offshoot called the Legislative Review Committee (LRC), also known as the Calendar Review Committee, also received objections to legislation. From time to time (often every Monday), the Senate would go through its calendar in sequence and pass minor legislation by unanimous consent. In lieu of requiring every senator to be present for these "calendar calls," the LRC would (*a*) independently review bills and block or amend those that were inconsistent with party principles and (*b*) act as a proxy for other party members by vetoing bills on request.[36] The latter role is most interesting here: other Democratic senators communicated their opposition to passing legislation to senators on the LRC or to DPC staff.[37] The LRC would block these bills in a manner that obscured the identity of the objector (McPherson 1985, 1). In February 1953, Lyndon Johnson proposed the LRC to the DPC to provide a social good for party members: LRC members would scan bills on the Senate calendar waiting for floor consideration and block those that should not pass quickly (DPC Minutes, February 3, 17, and 24, 1953). Ripley (1969) notes that the role of the LRC declined over the course of the 1960s. Once Johnson and Mansfield began allowing the LRC members to participate in DPC meetings, they became policy players instead of service providers. Furthermore, classic calendar calls occurred less frequently as Mansfield increasingly arranged with the minority party leader to pass bills by unanimous consent.

The DPC noted the effects of accommodating senators' requests to schedule legislation around their absenteeism: "Senator Russell said he objected strongly to the practice of holding up bills because a Senator would be out of town and he considered it a new development which flowed from the elimination of the old system of pairs" (DPC Minutes, March 6, 1959).[38] Russell repeated this claim weeks later (DPC Minutes, April 27, 1959).

The nature of the DPC's concern is indirectly apparent in the roll call record. Figure 8.3 displays the percentage of all recorded votes[39] from 1941 to 1970 on which senators were recorded as paired or absent. The percentage of all votes that are paired fluctuates from 1941 to 1958, but there is no obvious trend over time. On the other hand, there is a significant drop in absenteeism, from 22.5 percent of all senators registering no position in 1950 to 3.8 percent absent in 1959. The DPC discussion suggests that this decrease in absenteeism is not due to increased diligence on the part of senators. Instead, senators worked to make the Senate's agenda conform to their individual travel schedules. Russell's comments about the decline of pairing were aimed at these jet-setters who imposed on the Senate schedule rather than simply pair off with another senator. This pattern intensified during Mansfield's tenure as majority leader (Valeo 1999, 71, 81).

At the same time, many senators became more active legislative entrepreneurs. During Mansfield's tenure, a typical senator offered an increasing number of amendments on the Senate floor on an increasingly diverse range of issues (Sinclair 1989; Smith 1989). To accommodate the combination of spotty attendance and legislative activism, Mansfield and his successors began negotiating complex unanimous consent agreements so that senators would be guaranteed chances to offer their amendments at mutually convenient times

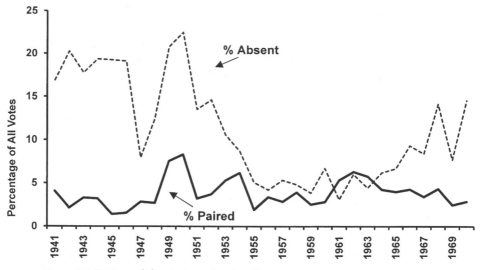

Figure 8.3. Pairing and absenteeism in Senate voting, 1941–70.

(Ainsworth and Flathman 1995; Smith and Flathman 1989). These agreements—and not the calendar system provided by Senate rules—became the primary means of structuring the day-to-day schedule of the Senate.

Republicans insisted on having a full opportunity to influence unanimous consent agreements. In 1973, for example, the Republican Conference formally requested that the Democratic leadership notify the Republican leadership and the ranking minority member of the affected committee before entering into any unanimous consent agreement that would prevent the offering of nongermane amendments (Scott to Mansfield, January 16, 1973, Mansfield Archive, XXII, 101, 10). Second, it instructed its leader, Hugh Scott, to enforce a rule requiring appropriations legislation to wait three days before floor consideration (Scott to Mansfield, March 27, 1973, Mansfield Archive, XXII, 68, 4). Together, these actions enhanced the ability of ranking members and rank-and-file Republicans to participate in the agenda-setting process.

REFORM, ANARCHY, AND CLOTURE
IN THE SENATE, 1975-86

In March 1975, senators revised Rule 22 so that a three-fifths majority of the Senate is required to invoke cloture. Instead of making cloture a more powerful option, however, the short-term effect of this rule change was to provoke postcloture filibusters, drastic countermeasures, and follow-up reforms.

A key figure in this turbulent period was James B. Allen of Alabama. Allen was one of the last of a stereotype: a superbly mannered conservative

Democrat, opposed to civil rights measures and many other progressive proposals, and a parliamentary expert. As Alabama's lieutenant governor, he presided over the state senate for eight years. As a U.S. senator, he spent long hours mastering the rules and precedents of the Senate (Gould 2005, 266–68). As a result of this training, "he exhibited an amazing knowledge of the Senate rules, an admirable tactical sense, and the patience and endurance needed to stay on the floor all day long for nearly two weeks and make certain his opponents didn't grab a procedural advantage" (Rich 1974, A2). In particular, he was superb at identifying potential dilatory motions and using them.

During the Ninety-third Congress (1973–74), Allen successfully blocked campaign finance and tax reform proposals, both attached to increases in the national debt limit (Rich 1974). In 1975, he led the fight against cloture reform. After this loss, he used his talents more aggressively. He led six other filibusters during the Ninety-fourth Congress. In at least three cases (antitrust litigation reform; cost shifting in civil rights cases; federal aid to New York City), he engaged in postcloture filibustering by provoking parliamentary votes and calling up amendments after cloture had been invoked ("Civil Rights Attorneys' Fees" 1977; "Senators Open Partisan Debate" 1977, 13).

Allen exploited weaknesses in Rule 22 that had been apparent—and occasionally exploited—for decades, but his colleagues felt that his postcloture filibustering subverted the will of the Senate. One response was stricter enforcement of Senate rules: on June 10, 1976, senators voted 49–36 to rule one of Allen's procedural motions dilatory and, thus, impermissible after cloture had been invoked.

In early 1977, Majority Leader Robert Byrd (D-WV) proposed a rules change to suppress postcloture filibustering. The Republican minority opposed it, however, and Byrd backed off ("Senate Filibuster Rule" 1981). In September 1977, using Allen's tactics two liberal senators—Howard Metzenbaum (D-OH) and James Abourezk (D-SD)—conducted a postcloture filibuster against a bill to deregulate the price of natural gas. They filed 508 amendments before losing a cloture vote 77–17, and, after the cloture vote, they called up their amendments for roll call votes. Byrd responded with round-the-clock sessions that exhausted the chamber:

> Shortly before sunrise one day last week, the Hon. Ernest F. Hollings, Democrat of South Carolina, appeared on the Senate floor in a bright green jogging suit. "It makes good pajamas," he observed. In the corridors and cloakrooms around him, less comfortably attired colleagues padded about in stocking feet or dozed fitfully on cots provided by the Army and Air Force. "Barbaric," croaked rumpled, unshaven Minority Leader Howard Baker as he surveyed the blanket-littered hallways. "An outrage," seconded

Majority Leader Robert Byrd. Over the ayes, nays and occasional snores of his bleary-eyed colleagues, Senator Robert Dole told of encountering a woman who had come to observe the all-night session. It was the best show in town, she explained: "The zoo was closed." ("Night of the Long Winds" 1977)

Attrition was ineffective, so, on October 3, 1977, Byrd and Vice President Mondale came to the Senate floor determined to end the stalemate. Amid dozens of angrily protesting senators, Byrd called up thirty-three amendments for Mondale to rule dilatory (and, therefore, not deserving consideration); as long as Mondale recognized only Byrd, no one else could call for a vote or register a protest on the Senate record. Afterward, Byrd and Baker appointed informal committees to plug the loopholes in Rule 22 ("A Filibuster Ends" 1977).

When the Ninety-sixth Congress convened in January 1979, in order to streamline Senate business Byrd proposed a hundred-hour cap on postcloture debate and other reforms, such as making motions to take up a bill immune to filibusters and allowing immediate votes on cloture petitions after September 1, that is, when a session was coming to an end (*Congressional Quarterly Almanac* 1979, 594). He paired these proposals with a veiled threat to force them through by majority vote ("Byrd Seeking Changes" 1979, 19). Republicans balked at the streamlining reforms but agreed to vote on a compromise proposal that included the hundred-hour cap and some other minor changes in exchange for Byrd's promise not to utilize majoritarian tactics (*Congressional Quarterly Almanac* 1979, 594). Later, in 1986, the Senate amended Rule 22 to further restrict postcloture debate to thirty hours. As explained by Richard Fenno (1989), this reform was entwined with the decision to allow C-SPAN to televise Senate procedures; some senators feared that the spectacle of a hundred-hour filibuster would damage the reputation of the Senate.

Instead of reducing obstruction, these reforms institutionalized the notion that filibustering was an ordinary element of Senate decisionmaking. The 1975 reform may have lowered the threshold for cloture slightly (or not, depending on participation), but it also stabilized the threshold—thereby reducing the incentive to hold multiple cloture votes—while implicitly marking senators' acceptance of supermajority rule in the Senate. The biennial ritual of debating the wisdom of majority rule ended after 1975 (with a halfhearted revival in 1995), and references to principled voting decreased after 1975. Subsequent revisions codified the notion that obstruction should end after a cloture vote and that postcloture debate should not drag on but did not question the legitimacy of obstruction.

In addition, Congress passed several laws prohibiting Senate obstruction pf specific classes of policy proposals. The most prominent restrictions were the following:[40]

- "fast track" consideration of trade pacts (1974): if Congress grants authority to the president to negotiate trade treaties under this statute, the resulting trade agreement is guaranteed a vote without amendment or filibustering;
- congressional budget resolutions and budget reconciliation legislation (1974);
- the War Powers Act (1973);
- military base closures (1991): presidential proposals to downsize military bases cannot be amended or filibustered;
- regulatory review and veto (1996): efforts to reject a new regulation cannot be filibustered.

One common thread in these statutes is that senators typically have strong policy or institutional incentives to consider these proposals in a timely fashion. That is, failure to consider them would tend to harm the national interest and the collective reputation and influence of Congress. At the same time, senators may have strong political incentives to filibuster on behalf of local interests (budgets, trade, military bases) or on behalf of an allied president (war powers, regulatory review). Absent a statutory prohibition on obstruction, a filibuster might succeed against important legislation even though senators believe ex ante (i.e., before their political stakes are fully revealed) that the bills ought to pass.[41]

These statutory restrictions have two implications for this study. First, there are probably a number of "missing" filibusters. Legislation on trade, budget, and executive branch reductions faced several filibusters prior to the enactment of these statutes, and, but for these laws, we would probably have observed several more filibusters in recent years. By the same token, there may be missing cases of reform deterrence. The conditions that seem to lead to these ex ante constraints—important policy goals, high political stakes—are also the conditions under which we might see a majority use or threaten extreme measures against a stubborn minority.

FILIBUSTERING IN THE CONTEMPORARY SENATE

By 1979, the main procedural features of the contemporary Senate were in place. First, the primary method for managing Senate floor debate is the unanimous consent agreement. Second, filibustering no longer requires individual effort on the Senate floor. Instead, senators signal their intent to filibuster proposals via private letters to their party leaders or messages to party secretaries. By placing a hold on a measure or a nomination, senators can keep it off the Senate floor temporarily. Third, the primary means for heading off a filibuster are compromise and cloture. Compromises may take the form of bipartisan committee proposals or postcommittee bargains that satisfy interested senators. Much obstructive behavior is intended to obtain votes on nongermane issues that provide fodder for the media or the next election cycle. If compromise is unattainable or less rewarding than confrontation, the dominant response to obstruction is attempting cloture.

In the contemporary Senate, cloture has gone from taboo to commonplace. From 1973 to 2006, the Senate voted 646 times on cloture, as shown in figure 8.4. Another 271 cloture petitions were filed but did not come to a vote. The shift in senators' attitude toward cloture is evident in their motives for filing cloture petitions and holding cloture votes. In addition to the obvious desire to force a decisive vote on some measure, cloture votes can be used to signal senators' preferences on some issue, for example, the Senate's 1997 vote to invoke cloture on a bill granting President Clinton special authority to negotiate trade treaties. The Senate could not pass the underlying bill since revenue measures must begin in the House, so senators held the cloture vote to show their support for the proposal (*Congressional Quarterly Almanac* 1997, 2-85–2-88). Second, senators sometimes propose and vote on cloture to impose a germaneness requirement rather than to limit debate. Again, once cloture is invoked on a bill, senators can only call up amendments that pertain to that bill. Cloture can, therefore, be used to avoid direct votes on amendments that are nongermane and politically costly to vote on.

In the contemporary Senate, much of the filibustering that we observe is over the ground rules for floor debate, and it can be difficult to distinguish between filibustering and insisting on a fair opportunity to offer amendments. Cloture votes and accusations of filibustering often follow the breakdown of negotiations between party leaders on how to debate a major bill. The majority party leader may believe that his or her party is ready and willing to pass a bill, so debate and amendments can only waste valuable time and weaken the coalition supporting the bill. Minority party members may insist on offering and voting on dozens of germane amendments and also on holding votes on proposals that are important to the minority party but not germane. Finally, an interesting feature of the sixty-vote Senate is that, while we observe a great deal of partisan wrangling and petty piques, senators rarely exploit the full range of their procedural options. Filibustering senators, for example, typically focus their obstruction on a single stage of the legislative process—the motion to take up a measure, the measure

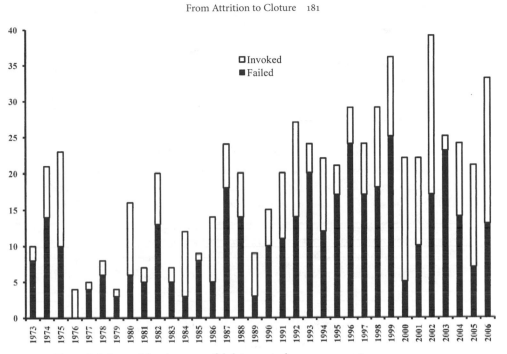

Figure 8.4. Successful and unsuccessful cloture votes by year, 1973–2006.

Source: http://www.senate.gov/pagelayout/reference/cloture_motions/clotureCounts.htm.

itself, motions to go to conference, or a subsequent conference report, but rarely every possible stage. Majority party senators, on the other hand, rarely make use of some procedural opportunities to circumvent obstruction. For example, motions to take up a bill cannot be filibustered if they are proposed during the "morning hour," a portion of the Senate day set aside for routine business. Nonetheless, senators continue to bring their bills up in regular session and endure any obstruction that results.[42] Also, notwithstanding Republicans' flirtation from 2003 to 2005 with the nuclear option (discussed below), senators rarely propose curtailing the right to filibuster by simple majority vote. This suggests that an element of self-constraint and reciprocity persists in the Senate to this day.

Although cloture is the dominant response to obstruction in the modern Senate, wars of attrition still occur on occasion. Some occur when a single senator begins an unannounced filibuster and Senate leaders simply wait out a long speech. Some examples include:

· December 1982: Majority Leader Baker tried to sit out a filibuster against a gas tax increase by four conservative senators ("Filibuster Stalls Key Money Bill" 1982, 1).

- November 1986: New York senators D'Amato and Moynihan successfully stalled a spending bill for twenty-three and a half hours to ensure
  procurement of a plane made in New York ("Top Guns" 1986).
- October 1992: D'Amato stalled a tax bill for fifteen hours to save a
  provision aiding the Smith Corona Company but eventually relented
  ("Urban Aid Tax Bill Veto" 1993, 106).

In these cases of lone or small-group filibustering, it was still possible for
Senate leaders to outlast or outwit senators. Most of these cases arose in the
final days of a session when individual senators had a great deal of leverage
by threatening to keep their colleagues away from their homes or off the
campaign trail.

In addition, there have been occasional efforts to conduct old-fashioned
attrition battles against minority party filibusters. The most spectacular of these occurred in late February 1988. Majority Leader Robert Byrd
scheduled round-the-clock debates on a campaign finance reform bill on
which the Democrats had tried and failed to invoke cloture *seven* times in
1987. Byrd declared that this would be a classic filibuster, with the Democrats willing to jump on any opportunity to vote on the bill. Republicans
responded with quorum breaking, that is, requesting the presence of a
quorum while all Republicans were hiding outside the Senate chamber.
Byrd moved to request the attendance of missing members and then to
arrest missing members. Subsequently, the Senate sergeant at arms and
several police officers found Senator Bob Packwood (R-OR) barricaded in
his office, pushed the door open, and carried Packwood's prone body to
the floor of the Senate. Byrd eventually conceded that such tactics would
not succeed and agreed to a final, hopeless cloture vote ("Search and
Seizure" 1988).[43]

In 2003, Senate Republicans staged an all-night talkathon to draw
attention to Democratic obstruction of judicial nominations (Hurt 2003).
However, this was *not* a genuine attrition effort. Republicans did much of
the speaking and announced their schedule for the "reverse filibuster" in
advance. Most recently, in November 2007, Majority Leader Reid threatened
night sessions on a bill expediting troop withdrawals from Iraq (Raju and
Soraghan 2007) but did not follow through on the threat.

In the modern Senate, threats to engage in old-school attrition attract
attention to minority party obstruction and provide photo opportunities of
aides rolling cots into the Senate. In chapter 6, we noted that the eight most-
covered filibusters of the modern era all occurred before 1970, even though
the number of filibusters has increased since 1970. The key difference, presumably, is the covert nature of modern filibusters. In 1988 and 2003, the
majority party sought to draw attention to the minority party's behavior—to

convert obscure behavior into overt obstruction. In both cases, attrition was ineffective as a legislative tactic but effective as a political gambit.

JUDICIAL NOMINATIONS AND THE GANG OF FOURTEEN, 2003-5

While cloture is the dominant response to obstruction in the modern Senate, from 2003 to 2005 some Republicans threatened drastic reform to obtain "up or down" votes on President Bush's judicial nominations.[44] Because the judicial branch is the primary forum for salient issues like abortion, gay rights, civil rights, and environmental regulation, Republicans and Democrats have jousted over the partisan and ideological composition of the federal judiciary, including appellate court appointments (Scherer 2005), with interest groups allied with each party urging on the fight.

After Republicans regained majority status in 2003, President Bush renominated several judges whose nominations had languished in committee during the Democrat-controlled 107th Congress. For the next two years, the Democrats selectively blocked appellate court nominees whom they considered too "extreme"; ten of thirty-four appellate nominees were defeated after cloture votes revealed that they were supported by the Republican majority but less than three-fifths of the Senate.

Republicans grew frustrated when the Democrats filibustered Miguel Estrada's nomination to the DC Circuit Court of Appeals. On February 26, 2003, Ted Stevens (R-AK) commented that the Republicans could end the debate and approve the nomination right then if he took over as chair and ruled that filibustering nominations was out of order (VandeHei and Babington 2005, A15). The idea gained momentum among Republicans who considered the Democrats' tactics unprecedented (Bolton and Earle 2003). Democrats labeled Stevens's proposal the *nuclear option* since they would retaliate against a majoritarian coup with full-scale obstruction that would bring the Senate to a halt.[45]

It was doubtful that Republicans could muster a bare majority from their own members for a majoritarian strategy (Bolton 2003). Instead, they continued to attempt and lose ordinary cloture votes on Estrada and other judges. Republicans seemed to believe that they could win the war over judges by losing battles. By forcing Democrats to vote on cloture on stalled nominations (and other legislation), they hoped to build a record of Democratic filibustering and then campaign against the obstructionist Democrats in the 2004 elections ("Senate GOP Preps" 2004). The Republicans netted four seats in the 2004 elections.

After the 2004 election, Republicans' interest in suppressing filibusters against judicial nominations increased dramatically since President Bush would probably nominate replacements for one or more Supreme Court justices. To head off a conflict, the new minority leader, Harry Reid, the new leader of the Democrats, negotiated with Frist over the ground rules for judicial nominations (Earle 2005). These negotiations were hampered by uncertainty. It was unclear whether Frist could muster a majority to carry out a nuclear option, and Republican aides later admitted that the Republicans lacked the votes (Hurt 2005; Klein 2006). On the other side: "Some of the party's senators from states Bush carried in the presidential election could be reluctant to support a filibuster for fear of being portrayed as obstructionist—a tactic the GOP used successfully in congressional elections this year and in 2002" ("GOP May Target" 2004, A1).

Opinion polls suggested that a confrontation would be costly for both parties. A March 2005 *Newsweek* poll reported that a 57 percent majority opposed the imposition of majority cloture for judicial nominations while only 32 percent supported it, with a 55 percent–33 percent majority supporting the nuclear option among Republicans. In the same poll, respondents opposed a postreform Democratic shutdown by a margin of 46 percent–40 percent, with a majority of Democrats supporting nuclear retaliation by a 65 percent–29 percent margin.[46] Republican-allied business interests were also fearful that they would suffer in the fallout from a struggle over the rules as their legislative priorities might be dragged into a postreform cycle of retaliation (Bolton 2005c).

Despite ambivalence on both sides, Reid and Frist were constrained by the keen interest of outside actors in the nomination battle. Conservative groups like the Christian Coalition, the American Conservative Union, and Focus on the Family formed umbrella groups like the National Coalition to End Judicial Filibusters to advocate a more conservative judiciary at any cost.[47] Evangelical organizations held a televised "Justice Sunday" rally to urge the Senate to approve conservative judges (Babington 2005, 1), while President Bush had long supported reform in the nomination process (Allen and Goldstein 2002). On the other side, liberal groups like the Sierra Club, the Service Employees International Union, Planned Parenthood, and People for the American Way mobilized to support Democrats' right to filibuster judicial nominations. These outside actors made it difficult to compromise since Frist and Reid were reluctant to disappoint the organizational core of their own parties. Frist, in particular, was contemplating a run for the presidency and needed to maintain his conservative credentials (Bolton 2005b).

On May 13, 2005, Frist announced that he planned to bring the appellate court nominations of Priscilla Owen and Janice Rogers Brown to the Senate floor. Negotiations between Frist and Reid ended three days later with Reid decrying Frist's "all-or-nothing" approach (Hulse 2005), although a few Republican and Democratic moderates continued to meet. The Senate debated Owen's nomination on May 18 and 19; then Republicans filed a cloture petition on May 20. Implicitly, this meant a showdown on May 23.

On May 23, hours before a vote on cloture and, perhaps, a nuclear option, fourteen senators announced a deal to resolve the conflict. According to the deal, all fourteen senators agreed to vote for cloture on three of five nominees facing a filibuster (including Owen and Brown), leaving another two nominees exposed to a filibuster. For all future nominations—including Supreme Court nominations—the agreement stated: "Nominees should only be filibustered under *extraordinary circumstances*, and each signatory must use his or her *own discretion and judgment* in determining whether such circumstances exist" (*NYT*, May 24, 2005 [emphasis added]).

Who were the "Gang of Fourteen"? The Democrats were Ben Nelson (NE), Robert Byrd (WV), Joseph Lieberman (CT), Mark Pryor (AR), Mary Landrieu (LA), Ken Salazar (CO), and Daniel Inouye (HI). The Republicans were John Warner (VA), John McCain (AZ), Lindsey Graham (SC), Susan Collins (ME), Olympia Snowe (ME), Lincoln Chafee (RI), and Mike DeWine (OH). The best predictor of membership in the "Gang" was ideological moderation (Koger 2008); moderates would be highly conflicted in a showdown vote.

What did the agreement mean? *Extraordinary circumstances* is an ambiguous standard, implying that a filibuster is not justified if a majority of the Senate is willing to suppress it. This, in turn, meant that, if all non-Gang Republicans were willing to vote for a nuclear option and all Democrats (plus Jim Jeffords [Ind-VT]) would oppose such an attempt, a filibuster was justified if six of the seven Gang Republicans agreed that it was. However, in deciding whether to suppress a filibuster or not, the members of the Gang of Fourteen also promised to make up their own minds—a major commitment on a topic as politicized as judicial nominations. Afterward, senators and pundits wondered whether the agreement heralded a power shift toward the responsible moderates in the Senate. The Gang of Fourteen reconvened after President Bush nominated John Roberts and Samuel Alito for the Supreme Court and in both cases deemed any filibuster against these nominations unwarranted.

At first glance, this case nicely illustrates the claim that threats of reform can deter minorities from filibustering. We observe a sequence of obstruction, threat, and minority withdrawal that is consistent with deterred filibustering. Notably, all the major players in this fight—senators, staffers, reporters, interest groups—easily accepted the premise that the Republican majority could impose majoritarian reform if it was sufficiently committed and ruthless. At the same time, this episode illustrates the difficulty that majorities face when attempting to bully minorities into acquiescence. For many Republicans, using drastic tactics to impose majority cloture on judicial nominations represented a major break from the comity that underlies day-to-day functioning of the Senate. It also represented a transfer of power from Senate moderates, who provide critical swing votes under the current system (as embodied in the Gang of Fourteen), to the president and the associated interest groups, who select nominees and advocate for them.

On the other side, Reid and the Democrats had a difficult time making a credible threat to "go nuclear" in a postreform Senate. The reason is simple: Democrats were presumably already filibustering in every situation where the benefits of obstruction exceed the costs. Any punitive filibustering on their part would require obstructing in situations where the costs otherwise exceed the benefits. They could have tried to minimize the political repercussions by attributing their filibusters to the Republicans' procedural roughshodding, but individual Democrats would still find themselves voting against cloture on bills that are politically popular or urgently needed. Consequently, Reid exempted several topics from his threat of a legislative shutdown, including appropriations bills and legislation related to "supporting our troops," while other Democrats were reluctant to obstruct bills on highway funding or energy policy (Bolton 2005a). In the end, the compromise spared both parties from trying to follow through on threats that would have been very costly to redeem and embarrassing to recant.[48]

CONCLUSION

The acceptance of a supermajority cloture rule as the primary response to filibustering was a critical event in the history of the Senate. This chapter draws on news accounts and senators' archives to explain how and why Senate filibusters ceased to be all-night wars of attrition and became ordinary exercises in tallying votes. At the beginning of the twentieth century, senators were content to wait it out when their colleagues filibustered, unless the obstruction occurred at the end of a short session when only a few days or hours remained. This general pattern continued *after* the adoption of the first cloture rule in 1917. After a few experiments with the rule, many senators developed a distaste for voting for cloture, so cloture was attempted infrequently and rarely successful. Instead, senators led by George Norris pushed for the adoption of the Twentieth Amendment, which eliminated short sessions.

After the debacle of the 1960 Civil Rights Act debate, senators began to adopt cloture as their primary response to filibusters. The imposition of cloture on the 1962 Comsat bill and the 1964 Civil Rights Act reduced the taboo against voting for cloture, and senators gradually accepted filibustering and voting for cloture as normal behavior. Underlying this switch was the transformation of senators' worlds: the Senate's agenda became crowded with bills large and small, treaties, and nominations as the federal government grew in size and power. Senators also became more active outside the Senate, traveling the country and the globe or returning to their states to campaign. When they were in the Senate, they adopted a more activist style, offering amendments and giving speeches. This made cloture a less costly alternative to remaining in the Senate for days or weeks trying to exhaust their colleagues' stubbornness.

Behind the scenes, Senate party leaders developed a system for holding legislation, including threats to filibuster bills and requests by senators to be included in the negotiations over how a bill will be debated on the Senate floor. Thus, the right to filibuster was *institutionalized* in the Senate's agenda-setting process. Changes in the Senate cloture rule had comparatively little influence on senators' willingness to filibuster, except that the 1975 rule change seemed to bring an end to the perennial debate over cloture reform and legitimize both filibustering and cloture.

The current sixty-vote Senate has been stable despite the ability of a bare majority of the Senate to curtail or revoke the right to filibuster. In a handful of cases, Senate majorities have threatened to reduce the right to obstruct, and (anticipating this strategy) the minority has backed down to avoid provoking lasting reforms. This includes a recent dispute over judicial nominations, in which the Republicans threatened to use the nuclear option of imposing majority cloture for judicial nominations and Democrats threatened to refuse all cooperation in a chamber that runs on mutual consent. This dispute was resolved by an agreement brokered by moderate senators known as the Gang of Fourteen. While these threats of majoritarian reform are theoretically interesting, the high political and institutional costs for imposing majority rule seem to limit the use of threats as a response to obstruction. The right to obstruct, however contingent, is deeply woven into the daily operations of the contemporary Senate.

The Future of the Senate

The flesh rides herd on the spirit. Soon I must lie down and let Morpheus embrace me.

Everett Dirksen, quoted in *Time* **in March 1960**

Filibustering is an inherently fragile practice. It empowers minorities against majorities in legislative settings where majorities typically dominate and in a political culture where majority rule is the default practice. From time to time, it is inevitable that senators and citizens will question the role of filibustering in the lawmaking process. This afterword reviews the classic arguments for and against restricting obstruction, summarizes the implications of the transformation of the Senate into a sixty-vote chamber, and then discusses the effects of obstruction in a polarized era. Finally, I discuss options for reforming Senate filibustering.

As I draft this afterword, the Democratic Party is the majority party in both chambers of Congress, and a Democrat is in the White House. The Democrats are on the verge of controlling sixty Senate seats, but the Republican contingent in the Senate will undoubtedly still work to delay or block the Democratic agenda. The more the Republicans succeed, the more likely it is that some Democrats (in and out of the Senate) will consider restrictions on filibustering as a means of achieving their policy goals. This afterword will, I hope, inform such debates.[1]

FILIBUSTERING: THE DEBATE

In legislative texts, newspaper columns, Internet blogs, and the halls of Congress, the debate over obstruction is often framed as a choice between majority rule and supermajority rule, that is, what portion of a body should be sufficient to make a decision. However, this choice is complicated by the fact that members of Congress are politicians working as the agents of their constituents and their parties. Some argue that filibusters help politicians resolve conflicts among their goals, while others contend that filibustering thwarts meaningful representation by responsible parties. A third strand of the debate posits that obstruction can serve as a measure of preference intensity. This section summarizes these arguments.

Should Majorities Rule?

In our modern democratic culture, the notion that legislative majorities should dominate is seemingly obvious. This intuition is consistent with the nominal equality of each legislator. By assumption, legislative rules consider each member equally intelligent and relevant. When equal legislators disagree with each other, we must assume that the faction with more members possesses a greater sum of knowledge and that greater utility will be gained if the more numerous faction wins.

In a classic summation of the argument for (or against!) majority rule, Kenneth O. May (1952) states four necessary conditions for majority rule to be the best decision process:

1. Majority rule must actually lead to a decision.
2. All voters should be weighted equally.
3. All policy options are weighted equally.
4. A change in majority preferences should yield a change in outcomes.

Subsequent theoretical work suggested that the first condition is problematic if there are two or more dimensions and any amendment is allowed (e.g., McKelvey 1976; Plott 1967; and Schofield 1978). The fourth condition is simply a defining feature of majority rule. The second and third conditions are of special interest for the debate over filibustering.

Equal Weighting of Votes?

Since the days of Athenian democracy, philosophers have argued that majorities may be wrong and, consequently, that simply following majority opinion may lead to bad collective decisions. Majorities may put philosophers and generals to death and then regret their mistakes. Though inegalitarian, this critique of majority sentiment has its echoes in legislative debates. A recurring theme of congressional research is that some legislators are harder working, wiser, and more knowledgeable on a given issue than others (e.g., Fenno 1966; Hall 1996; Krehbiel 1991; Matthews 1960; and White 1955); why should their votes count the same as a shirking backbencher? Formally weighting votes by quality would be controversial and unworkable, but, at least in theory, differences in expertise may justify deviations from the equal weighting of votes.

Second, some voters or legislators have a more intense interest in a question than others. Robert Dahl suggested that a special reason to respect political minorities is that they may have more intense preferences than an opposing majority, with the result that enacting the majority-preferred policy results in a net loss of social utility (1956, 123). Imagine that you are a senator and all the other senators get together and propose to collect the nation's nuclear waste and store it in your state indefinitely. As the recipient, your state has a deeper stake in this issue than any donor state; should your vote be weighted the same as everyone else's? During the 1990s, the senators from Nevada were in this situation and filibustered to emphasize their opposition to the proposal. By permitting intense minorities to have extra influence in such cases, filibustering may actually promote the general welfare.[2]

The notion that political rules should reflect substantial minority interests motivated John C. Calhoun's prescription to "give to each division or interest . . . either a concurrent voice in making and executing laws or a veto on their execution" (1953, 20). Calhoun's proposal was that each substantial political interest (read: the antebellum South) would have a collective veto on national policy while making internal decisions on the basis of majority rule.

Under the right conditions, however, filibustering can accommodate differences in preference intensity by enabling a political minority to credibly signal its intensity. If the costs of waiting out a filibuster are comparable to the costs of filibustering, an indifferent majority will be likely to defer to an intense minority rather than force the issue to a vote. Of course, intense minorities can protect their interests only if they are represented. As we have seen, in the past, Southern legislators frequently obstructed to preserve slavery and racial inequality in the South, while Southern blacks had few intense advocates to defend them.[3]

In the contemporary Senate, individual senators can demonstrate their intensity by using the power to filibuster to advance their personal legislative priorities (Sinclair 1989). In 1995, for example, Jesse Helms (R-NC) was frustrated that his bill reorganizing foreign policy agencies was blocked by a unified Democratic minority. He responded by blocking nominations for ambassador and key treaties. Not to be outdone, Senate Democrats responded by blocking two more of Helms's priorities—a constitutional amendment banning flag desecration and a bill increasing sanctions on Cuba. In another case, during the 109th Congress, Patty Murray (D-WA) and Hilary Clinton (D-NY) placed holds on two nominees for director of the Food and Drug Administration to force a decision on a request to make "Plan B" contraceptives available without a prescription. The FDA had ignored deadlines for making a decision, and Murray and Clinton concluded that the agency would procrastinate indefinitely unless forced to act.

They were eventually successful and released their hold (Kaufman and Stein 2006; Schor 2005).

Equal Weighting of Policies?

Some supporters of the filibuster argue that there should be a bias toward the status quo in the policy process. While current policy may have known imperfections, policy change may have unintended consequences that are far worse. Risk-averse actors may prefer rules that make it more difficult to adopt new policies than to preserve the old. James Madison extols the virtues of policy stability in Federalist No. 62: "A continual change even of good measures is inconsistent with every rule of prudence and every prospect of success. . . . [G]reat injury results from an unstable government. The want of confidence in the public councils damps every useful undertaking, the success and profits of which may depend on a continuance of existing arrangements." Of course, legislators obstruct to *promote* change as well, so it is not clear that filibustering necessarily induces a bias toward status quo policy.

Furthermore, critics of the filibuster would note that the American policy process already has multiple veto points to slow down policy change. The constitutional framework of bicameralism with a presidential veto already biases the legislative process toward the status quo. In addition, the rules and practices of each chamber have often granted veto rights to committees and party leaders (Cox and McCubbins 2005). Given these multiple checks on legislative majorities, it may be excessive to add another brake on the lawmaking process.

Ensuring Representation

Two additional arguments are specific to the protection of *legislative* minorities. First, a legislative minority may actually represent the majority public opinion on an issue, providing a majoritarian rationale for minority obstruction. A minority may drag out a debate in the hope that the general public will become informed and involved on a previously ignored issue. Filibustering can, thus, "expand the game" (Schattschneider 1960) by bringing public opinion to bear on an internal debate.

In the U.S. Senate, a specific version of this argument is that, owing to variation in state size, a majority of the Senate may represent a minority of the nation's population. Reference to the 2000 census estimates used for apportionment indicates that, in fact, senators representing just 17.7 percent of the nation's population can form a majority in the Senate. Consequently, some senators have argued that the most malapportioned legislature in the world should have a supermajority procedure to keep small states from dominating large states.[4]

Second, legislative majorities often seek to maintain tenuous coalitions by limiting minority opportunities to amend, debate, or bring up alternative legislation. In the U.S. House, for example, major legislation is often considered under a "closed" or "semiclosed" rule; that is, either all amendments are forbidden, or the House Rules Committee selects the amendments that the House debates. The House majority party can, thus, protect its proposals from killer amendments and protect its members from casting votes that can be used against them in the next election.

Senators often express disapproval of the House's limited debate and extol the comparatively free deliberation of the Senate. One reason that senators have more latitude to speak and offer amendments is that they can filibuster to extort access to the Senate floor. If deliberation improves legislative output and informs voters of legislators' priorities and legislative minorities use obstruction to preserve deliberation, obstruction helps improve legislation and democratic choice.[5]

Arguments against Obstruction

The basic normative argument against obstruction is that, while it permits a minority to dominate the majority, a system that values every individual and policy alternative equally will give weight to the alternative favored by the most participants (Dahl 1956, 34–62; Federalist No. 22). This is a particularly strong concern when the majority has a special responsibility to act. Responsible party government models of democracy, for example, posit that elections should be clear, well-informed choices between parties and that the victorious party should enact the policies promised during the election. If a legislative minority prevents the majority party from enacting its policy goals, the linkage between elections and policy outcomes is undermined. For this reason, the authoritative argument for responsible parties in American politics states that "the present cloture rule [requiring a two-thirds majority] . . . is a serious obstacle to responsible lawmaking" and endorses simple-majority cloture (APSA Committee on Political Parties 1950, 65). At the least, obstruction can delay the resolution of controversial policy problems. While legislators await consensus that may never develop, citizens and the national interest may suffer.[6]

However, legislators often express doubts about the merits of party government and majority rule. If we define parties broadly to include congressional leaders, presidents, party-loyal donors, and affiliated interest groups, then parties may be able to induce legislators' public support for proposals they privately oppose. In such situations, obstruction by an apparent minority may help ensure that the outcome preferred by a *true* majority of the chamber is achieved. Thus, senators have expressed support for majority rule in principle yet fear it in practice as an invitation to coercion by party leaders and special interests (Koger 2006a, 2007).

FILIBUSTERING IN A POLARIZED ERA

One implication of the switch from attrition to cloture is that filibustering has become a team sport. While there are still occasional solo filibusters, the necessary condition for a sustained filibuster is a coalition of forty-one senators, and party organizations provide a natural basis for coalitions that large. Consequently, modern filibusters typically take the form of a minority party coalition preventing the majority party from making progress on its legislative agenda. If the minority party is vetoing a proposal that the majority party campaigned on, this behavior diminishes the linkage between elections and outcomes that some political scientists consider essential to a healthy democracy (APSA Committee on Political Parties 1950; Wilson 1885).

In the modern age, Senate minority parties often filibuster to ensure a hearing for amendments to majority-proposed bills. The minority party may band together and convince its members to vote against cloture (even if some senators support the underlying bill) to compel the majority party to offer a reasonably open debate. Also, the Senate minority party often strives to force a vote on its "message" issues, especially when it senses that the majority party is trying to score political points (Evans and Oleszek 2001).

The broader context for modern filibustering is a contest for party reputation (Cox and McCubbins 2005; Erikson, Mackuen, and Stimson 2002; Evans and Oleszek 2001; Lebo, McGlynn, and Koger 2007). Both parties compete for an edge in public support, and this competition influences senators' decisions whether to filibuster. Cloture votes can create a record of which party is proposing a bill and which party is preventing it from succeeding. Even if most minority party members oppose a bill or nomination, the Senate minority party may make a collective decision that it does not want to take political responsibility for obstruction. In November 2003, for example, the Democrats refrained from blocking the Medicare Prescription Drug Act (cloture was invoked 70–29) even though there were enough votes against the conference report (54–44, with nine Republican opponents) to filibuster. The Democrats were worried that blocking a major expansion in Medicare would earn them the ire of senior voters, even if done in the name of a more generous proposal (Carey 2003). In a partisan era, therefore, concern for party reputations increases the role of national public opinion as a constraint on obstruction.

Another implication of filibustering in a polarized Senate is that members of the majority party—especially outside the Senate—may urge the adoption of majority closure in the Senate and pressure majority party senators to take the drastic steps necessary to curtail filibustering without the consent of the minority party. The nuclear option debate of 2003–5 is not an isolated example. When a minority party uses an endogenous right to frustrate majority party ambitions, it risks an escalation of conflict. In the long run, it is sensible for the minority party to strategically select its battles by focusing on proposals with weak popular support or on which the majority party is internally divided while avoiding must-pass bills, major nominations, and legislation with a clear electoral mandate.

REFORM OPTIONS

Senators who are considering institutional changes to curtail filibustering should consider all their options and the implications. This section outlines the various steps that could be taken.

Revise the Cloture Threshold

For casual observers, the most obvious reform is to make it easier to invoke cloture by lowering the threshold for cloture. The Lieberman-Harkin proposal of the 104th Congress is a typical example: it retained the cloture rule in its current form but lowered the threshold for cloture by three votes after each failed cloture votes until a bare majority is necessary (see Binder and Smith 1997). If there are one hundred senators, this means that sixty votes are necessary to invoke cloture on the first attempt, fifty-seven on the second, then fifty-four, then fifty-one.[7]

For senators or other interested parties, this approach is a common response to the narrow defeat of a favorite measure. "If only the cloture threshold was lower," one thinks, "that bill would have passed." This logic assumes that the Senate would function the same way under a new cloture rule. However, in chapter 7, we learned that previous attempts to revise the cloture rule have not reduced filibustering in the Senate and may even have increased the number of filibusters since 1975. The same outcome is likely with the Lieberman-Harkin proposal. If a minority faction knows that it can be quashed by a simple majority vote on a given proposal but only if the majority goes through a multistep process, it has the incentive to multiply delays—to filibuster uncontroversial bills as a means of taking hostages, to reject all unanimous consent agreements, and to force roll call votes on everything possible—to regain some of the bargaining leverage eliminated by the new cloture rule.

Impose Complete Majority Rule

If half measures only invite innovation, one alternative is to impose true majority rule: a majority of the Senate can call up whatever bill it prefers, debate it as it chooses, and hold a final vote whenever it pleases a majority of the Senate. The Senate, in this approach, would become a smaller version of the U.S. House, trading deliberation and consensus building for efficiency and majority rule.

Senators have discussed this option for decades and rejected it. Over the last three decades, the U.S. House has illustrated the fragility of minority rights in a majority-rule chamber. The majority party now often denies minority party members the right to offer amendments or bring up new agenda items. In a majority-rule Senate, senators fear that the majority party's political incentives to constrain debate will similarly trump the members' commitment to deliberation and minority participation.

Furthermore, as E. E. Schattschneider puts it, "majority rule is an invitation to party organization" (1942, 39). In earlier work on the years before and after the adoption of the 1917 cloture rule, I find that senators repeatedly rejected majority cloture because they feared that they would become the targets of intense pressure from party leaders, presidents, and interest groups trying to buy enough votes to manufacture a narrow majority (Koger 2006a, 2007). The U.S. House demonstrates this principle often as major legislation (e.g., the 2003 Medicare Prescription Drug Act) is often passed only after majority party leaders have persuaded some of their members to switch their votes.

Finally, it is likely that the adoption of majority rule is irrevocable. Once the majority party of the Senate has a firm grip on the Senate agenda, any attempt to restore the right to obstruct will probably provoke consternation from the general public and from outside actors who prefer the simplicity of a majority-rule chamber.

Expand the Set of Legislation That Is Immune from Obstruction

As discussed in earlier chapters, some proposals cannot be filibustered: budget legislation, trade agreements, etc. One option for reform is to make more proposals immune to obstruction. For any issue, the case for making it immune is that it can be very important to have timely legislation on that issue and that filibustering could prevent expeditious action. Senators might make this case for legislation raising the federal debt limit (too much delay would drive the government into default), reauthorization of farm programs (delay could disrupt crop planting), and spending on national security, including supplemental appropriations for ongoing military operations. On each topic, of course, senators can argue that past filibustering on that issue has been responsible and has led to favorable compromises and that reform is, therefore, unnecessary.

Make Filibustering More Costly

The central narrative of this text is that legislators obstruct more often when it is easy to win by doing so. The straightforward implication is that senators will filibuster *less* if it becomes *more costly* for them to do so. The challenge, however, is to identify realistic options to make filibustering more costly.

One answer is to enhance the *political* costs of filibustering. If senators who filibuster incur serious criticism from the national media, their own constituents, and donors and interest groups, they will filibuster only when they are willing to pay these costs. In particular, if the minority party's reputation and fund-raising tend to suffer when the party votes against cloture, minority party senators will be more selective about filibustering.

The political costs of filibustering have varied over time. They seemed to be high after the ship arming bill and during the 1950s, and, in 2003–4, the Republicans loudly blamed Senate Democrats for delaying their agenda. The Republicans fielded a strong challenge to Senate minority leader Tom Daschle (D-SD) and made his obstruction a main issue in his 2004 reelection campaign, which ended in his defeat ("On Capitol Hill" 2004, WK3).

A majority party could try to incite disdain for the practice of filibustering as an affront to Americans' generic support for majority rule. Alternatively, the majority party could propose legislation that is popular and important and then highlight any minority party efforts to block its agenda, without questioning the broader right to filibuster in the Senate. In the latter case, the majority party's goal is simply to make clear who bears the responsibility for legislative failure; just as a president must take responsibility for his or her vetoes, senators must be accountable to the public for their obstruction.

The constraint on the "political costs" strategy is that it relies on the news media to referee legislative disputes. In the early twentieth century, many reporters seemed to possess the savvy to understand Senate politics and enough faith in their readers to explain the nuances of congressional strategy. Modern reporters seem less likely to play the role of arbiter, particularly since the conflicts often take the form of unpublished threats to filibuster and (on the surface at least) disputes over whether the minority is being provided a fair opportunity to debate and amend a bill.

Second, the majority party in the Senate could try to make filibustering more physically demanding. During the nuclear option debate, several opinion writers suggested this approach as an alternative to a majoritarian strategy (e.g., Morris 2005). A "real" filibuster might be an effective way to force the passage of a single top priority and of focusing national attention on the minority's obstruction, although it would not alleviate everyday obstruction against time agreements and minor bills. Now that the Senate is the biggest potential hurdle for the Democratic agenda, Democrats have urged Majority Leader Harry Reid to force the Republicans to carry out a classic attrition filibuster (Grim 2009).

Yet there is a reason that previous generations of senators abandoned attrition as a strategy: the costs of waiting out a filibuster were greater than the rewards of victory. In order to revive attrition as an option, the majority of the Senate should be prepared to reverse this imbalance. Ideally, this would mean denying obstructionists the right to force quorum calls or procedural votes so that a single "sentinel" from the majority faction could wait and observe while obstructionists hold the floor day and night and into the weekend. Furthermore, senators would have to be willing to initiate votes as opportunities arise rather than when consensus emerges. Lyndon Johnson was willing to take advantage of others' lapses to obtain votes on bills he wanted, and modern senators would have to be willing to do the same. Finally, senators may want to devise a system for starting a vote (say, in the middle of the night) and then, like the House, rolling the vote over until a reasonable hour arrives.

A final tactic that a sincere and determined majority could use to augment its attrition efforts is to insist strictly on decorum in debate and call to order any senator who "transgresses the rules or otherwise . . . in speaking or debate" (Senate Rule 19[4]). This has the effect of forcing a simple majority vote to "bench" a senator for the remainder of a day. If obstructionists are taking shifts holding the floor, calling an obstructionist to order can disrupt the rotation of senators long enough to initiate a roll call vote on an amendment or a bill. Of course, this is a hardball tactic and may incite the minority to greater resistance. Yet it also underscores the forgotten notion that filibustering is *not* normal; it is a calculated defiance of the norms of legislative democracy, and disqualification can be a fitting response to parliamentary blackmail.

All these "back to the future" suggestions, however, are more difficult to implement than they sound. One of the key points of chapter 8 is that filibustering is now thoroughly institutionalized in the daily operations of the Senate. This system gives ample opportunity for discontented senators to retaliate by blocking all legislation and rejecting all unanimous consent agreements. A serious attempt at attrition requires a level of aggression that is difficult for a contemporary senator to comprehend. Grim (2009) conveys Reid's belief that attrition is futile since a single Republican could force a limitless number of quorum calls. Neither Reid nor his advisers contemplate invoking precedents against such behavior or simply ruling legislators out of order for such behavior; they would probably consider such hardball tactics unthinkable.

Above all, senators should take decisions about obstruction seriously. Filibustering remains the defining institution of the Senate because generations of legislators have resisted the occasional effort to impose majority cloture on their chamber. Neither temporary frustration nor political expediency justifies transforming the Senate into a majority-rule body. Instead, senators should take the long view and weigh the benefits of greater efficiency against the value of making policy and setting the agenda through consensus. The U.S. Congress has tolerated filibustering throughout its history despite inconvenience, instability, and delay; senators should take this history seriously as they chart the future of the Senate.

EPILOGUE

Filibustering is endemic to the legislative process. As long as individuals and minority factions have a right to participate, some legislators will be tempted to use those rights to delay and defeat proposals they oppose and promote bills they support. From the beginning, members of Congress could obstruct, and, over time, both chambers have witnessed intense parliamentary stalemates. This behavior has a variety of effects: sometimes it is mere noise and posturing, and other times it kills legislation or extracts concessions while the nation's fate hangs in the balance. Legislators have filibustered to gain a hearing for lost causes and political minorities, and legislators have filibustered to prevent redemption of this nation's promise of civil rights.

While the roots of obstruction run through congressional history, we observe periods of relative dormancy, rising obstruction, supermajority legislating, and, in the U.S. House, institutional crisis. The emergence of a supermajority Senate over the last fifty years has made that Senate the primary hurdle of the legislative process, especially during periods of unified government. The main source of this variation, we have learned, lies in the value that legislators attach to their time. When legislators are willing to remain in the chamber to outlast any filibuster, obstruction is rare. But, when majorities are unwilling to spend their own time or the time of their chamber to win a contest—or they have run out of time to spend—then we observe rising rates of obstruction. While the House's drastic reforms of the 1890s reduced filibustering, the adoption and revision of the Senate cloture rule per se has had little apparent effect on the rate of filibustering. Indeed, the willingness of senators to attempt cloture rather than attrition removed much of the cost of filibustering and led to the institutionalization of the supermajority Senate.

In the contemporary Senate, filibustering is less visible but permeates the daily operations of the chamber. Gone are the candlelight contests and squads of Southern senators. The contemporary Senate, however, still embodies the notion that every legislator should have influence, that minorities should be heard, and that there are bounds to the bonds of party.

Notes

1. Other definitions emphasize intent over form. According to *Merriam-Webster's Collegiate Dictionary* (10th ed., 1998), to filibuster is "to delay legislation, by dilatory motions or other artifices." According to Merriam-Webster Online, it is to employ "extreme dilatory tactics in an attempt to delay or prevent action especially in a legislative assembly." I use *filibustering* interchangeably with the term *obstruction*, and this text is focused on obstruction on the chamber floor, or plenary.

2. By a vote of 35–13, the Senate prevented La Follette from simply requesting quorum counts all night long; in the end, he requested around thirty quorum calls. During the vote on this parliamentary question, the presiding officer also set a precedent by counting nonvoting members toward a quorum. Additional trickery was necessary to end the contest. One of La Follette's allies, Thomas Gore (D-OK), was completely blind. He finished his speech with the expectation that William Stone (D-MO) would carry on the struggle, but Stone had briefly gone to the cloakroom. In a rush, the majority (led by Nelson Aldrich) began the vote to approve the conference report (Burdette 1940). While this trickery shortened the filibuster, the outcome was foreordained: "The filibuster was doomed from the start, because there were not enough [senators] to carry it through" ("Pass Currency Bill" 1908, A1).

3. Cox and McCubbins (2005) note that negative agenda power can be used for bargaining leverage, and they find a significant increase in the ability of House majorities to censor legislation after the suppression of obstruction in the 1890s.

4. There is a much earlier set of books on Congress with very informative discussions of filibustering (e.g., Alexander 1916; Haynes 1938; Kerr 1895; and Luce 1922). They are cited in later chapters, but I focus here on the recent literature on filibustering.

5. For a parallel and more generalized account of veto player politics, see Tsebelis (2002).

6. To be fair, at this point Krehbiel is most interested in pooling data from cloture votes and makes a valid argument that cloture votes per se are not a sound measure of the number of filibusters that occur. That argument, however, seems to reflect his general disinterest in variation in filibustering over the time span used for the empirical analyses.

7. Their text has several other interesting analyses not directly tied to our main question, including a study of which senators were more likely to filibuster during the antebellum era, one of which filibusters were more likely to succeed, and a convincing demonstration that the adoption of the Senate cloture rule was *not* due to the passage of the Seventeen Amendment, which required the direct election of senators.

8. For an application of this idea to the pivotal politics model, see Koger (2004).

CHAPTER 2

1. Thurmond did not make any dilatory motions or request any quorum calls; the entire twenty-four-hour period was filled with talking. Much of his speech consisted of quotes from other texts.

2. Senate rules limit members to two speeches on a single issue during each "legislative day." A legislative day begins with a prayer, reading the *Journal*, messages, etc. and ends when the legislature adjourns. Legislators may stretch a legislative day for weeks of real time by taking recesses every night instead of adjourning.

3. During the nineteenth century, germaneness was also enforced while debating private bills in the "Committee of the Whole House" but not the "Committee of the Whole House on the State of the Union," which discussed public legislation, e.g., appropriations bills (Hinds 1907, 5:136, 133).

4. Other important considerations are whether an obstructionist can ask the clerk to read printed materials—books, newspapers, previous debates—aloud and whether a speaking member can yield to another legislator for a question without losing control of the floor.

5. In order to make a motion, a legislator must be "recognized" by the presiding officer. The rules of both chambers oblige the presiding officer to call on any member who stands and seeks recognition and, if more than one person seeks recognition, to call on the one who does so first. In practice, House speakers gradually developed some discretion in recognition during the 1880s. As described in chapters 3 and 4, Randall's refusal to acknowledge dilatory motions in 1877 is an early example of a speaker asserting such a right, one that was again asserted by Speaker Reed in 1890. Senate presiding officers' discretion has shrunk over time, with the result that, by the 1930s, the Senate's presiding officer is obliged to call on the majority party leader if he or she seeks recognition.

6. *Voting* means "declaring aye, nay, or present." In both chambers, legislators who are likely to disagree (especially if they are from different parties) may "pair off," i.e., agree not to vote unless both of them are in the chamber. Paired votes usually have not counted toward a quorum, but this is debatable.

7. Was this an isolated incident? Only for those unfamiliar with the colorful history of the Rhode Island legislature. In January 1923, the Democratic minority in the Senate began obstructing all major legislation in an effort to force the Republican majority to call for a new constitutional convention. They were aided by the Democratic lieutenant governor presiding over the Senate, Felix Toupin, who refused to recognize any Republican unless he called for a constitutional convention. This conflict reached a peak in June 1924 when the Senate stayed in session for twenty-two hours until the Republican majority simply walked out. Three days later, they returned for a forty-two-hour day-and-night session that began with a mass fistfight over control of the gavel and ended when Republican operatives placed a poison-soaked rag behind Toupin to gas him out of the presiding officer's chair. No one was permanently harmed, but the Republican majority relocated to Massachusetts for six months until Republican victories in the 1924 elections put an end to the struggle (the episode is chronicled in multiple articles in the *New York Times* during the period 1923–24).

8. The House made a series of subsequent amendments to its suspension rule. The suspension rule is now used primarily as an expedited process for considering uncontroversial bills, but, during the nineteenth century, it was also used to set the agenda, to limit obstruction, and to generally bend the rules for specific cases.

9. Note that I use *cloture* to refer to the Rule 22 procedure and *closure* to refer, more generally, to a rule for limiting debate and forcing a decisive vote on a proposal.

10. Rule 22's provisions regarding amendments have evolved. The 1917 rule required amendments to be germane and "presented and read" prior to the cloture vote. In 1976, the rule was amended to require amendments to be submitted in writing (not read) to the *Journal* clerk before the end of the cloture vote. In 1979, this process was revised: first-degree amendments had to be filed by 1 P.M. the day after the petition was filed, and second-degree amendments had to be filed at least one hour before the cloture vote. The 1979 reform also clarified that amendments need not be read aloud by the clerk when called up.

11. For an introduction, see McCarty and Meirowitz (2007, 275–319). Here, I rely on the general insight that "patience is power," but it could be useful to develop a more extensive bargaining model of filibustering.

12. The relevant passage of the Constitution reads: "Each House may determine the Rules of its Proceedings" (art. 1, sec. 5). Obviously, this discretion is constrained by other clauses of the Constitution.

13. Typically, such efforts invoke some higher authority to supersede Senate rules—the U.S. Constitution, "general parliamentary law," the Universal Declaration of Human Rights, etc. Such rhetoric may help sell the effort to the general public, but it is not necessary (or sufficient) to win the point of order.

14. Even if the chair denies this logic, under Senate Rule 20 there is no debate on secondary points of order.

15. Here, the key idea is not citizens' *current* opinions about Senate rules, but their *latent* opinions, i.e., the opinions they could have if the media, losing legislators, and electoral challengers actively criticize the reform effort (see Arnold 1990).

16. This model is based on formal models of obstruction developed with Kathleen Bawn (Bawn and Koger 2005, 2008), a revised version of the pivot model (Koger 2004), and my dissertation (Koger 2002). For a more formal presentation, see Koger (2006b). While this theory shares some features with that presented in Wawro and Schickler (2006), e.g., the ideas that attrition and reform are possible responses to obstruction, it was developed independently.

17. Teams of legislators may find it difficult to make collective decisions and to allocate the costs of joint efforts. The former problem is ameliorated by allowing legislators to base their choice of teams on their preferences. The latter problem is partially resolved by position-taking benefits—if effort is rewarding in itself, there is little difficulty inducing members to contribute. Otherwise, I expect that teams will choose leaders to coordinate members' efforts.

18. As we shall see in later chapters, major changes in closure rules and credible threats of major reform are relatively rare. Attrition and closure are the main candidates for the dominant response to filibustering, so hypotheses 1 and 2 below are framed around this choice.

19. The assumption here is that Con is genuinely opposed to the bill. If Con actually supports a bill but has a strong political incentive to filibuster, then it is *more* likely to filibuster if it will *lose* a closure vote.

20. In practice, standing committees have a central role in screening proposals and drafting legislation. Once a committee makes a proposal to the chamber, the reported bill becomes available for floor consideration, and the process for choosing among these "eligible" bills varies across chambers and over time. Party leaders and members provide oversight, and both chambers permit a chamber majority to override committee gatekeeping.

21. If we relax the assumption that Con is a unified faction, then Pro may have an incentive to compromise to buy off some of the members of the Con team, thereby weakening Con's ability to filibuster.

22. In the modern House, this is often done using special rules proposed by the Rules Committee (Sinclair 1995; Smith 1989). In earlier years, majorities often used the PQ motion to limit amendments.

CHAPTER 3

1. All citations of the Federalist Papers are taken from the Library of Congress online version, available at http://thomas.loc.gov/home/histdox/fedpapers.html.

2. David Mayhew's (2000) analysis of major congressional actions—as noted by historians—further illustrates this point. Drawing on a set of American history texts, Mayhew identified 2,304 actions from the entire breadth of American history, of which only 15 were filibusters.

3. One source of measurement error is small changes in the rules of the House and Senate over time that influenced the *type* of motion used to obstruct. For example, in 1836, the House restricted debate on points of order after the previous question was moved, so obstructionists may have shifted to raising more points of order or alternative dilatory motions.

4. Nor am I concerned that, by not measuring filibustering by speaking, the results are biased against the Senate, which had fewer constraints on speaking than did the House. The Senate's lax debate rules—no time limit, no germaneness requirement—were the product of relatively abundant floor time, which also diminished the prospects for filibusters. On the other hand, there is an unknown and possibly sizable amount of unmeasured filibustering activity in the nineteenth-century House. There are a number of votes that are not recorded in the *House Journal* (and, thus, not measured here) because they occurred in the Committee of the Whole or because the minority broke a quorum on an unrecorded teller vote. While collecting data for this chapter, I found such cases in the House on July 6, 1832; June 9, 1836; July 29, 1850; September 25, 1850; and April 28, 1892.

5. I identified these votes by searching for the key words *adjourn, recess,* and *executive* in the roll call descriptions accompanying ICPSR 0004, the congressional roll call voting records available from the Inter-University Consortium for Political and Social Research (available at http://www.icpsr.umich.edu). I do not include motions to table bills for fear that, when it is used, this motion may be intended as a test vote.

6. Even if some of the members absent for a given vote were deterred from voting by the "opportunity costs" of showing up for work, their shirking facilitates dilatory behavior by their remaining colleagues. For some all-night filibusters, it appears from the record of debates that a portion of the filibustering members are, in fact, home in bed while others are present in the chamber and refusing to vote. Both are counted as nonvoters because, although their methods differ, they contribute to quorum breaking.

7. Party affiliations are based on coding developed by the historian Kenneth Martis (1989). "Independent Democrat" and "Independent Republican" members were recoded "Democrat" and "Republican," respectively. The Thirty-fourth House (1855–57) coding is based on the final vote for speaker (for an analysis of this contest, see Jenkins and Nokken [2000]). Majority and minority parties were identified using information on opening day membership from the House clerk and Senate Web sites: clerkweb.house.gov and www.senate.gov.

8. I tried two other methods of identifying DQs. First, I picked votes on which less than 50 percent of at least one party (but potentially both) voted and the difference between the parties was statistically significant at the .001 level. Second, I coded a vote as a DQ if one party's voting rate was less than half the other party's and the difference was statistically significant at the .001 level. All three measures produced virtually identical estimates of the number of DQs

during this period. I use the "majority voting vs. majority nonvoting" measure since it mimics the conventional definition of a *party vote*.

9. For example, Alexander (1916) claims that the Democrats obstructed the first special rule by refusing to vote on the night of February 26–27, 1883. My method successfully identified this incident of obstruction. On the other hand, DQs by a cross-party coalition during a 1893 filibuster to preserve government purchasing of silver were undercounted.

10. Specifically, the House voted against forming a committee to recommend a punishment for Adams.

11. This raises the possibility that senators may be trying to defeat a proposal, not with filibusters, but with "killer motions"—proposing alternative bills so that a motion to postpone unites the proponents of one bill and the opponents of another. This strategy helped defeat the 1891 elections ("force") bill (Koger 2002) and a 1918 majority cloture proposal (Koger 2006a).

12. Robinson (1930, 184–86) suggests that Weaver was attempting to force consideration of a bill to organize the Oklahoma Territory.

13. These items were mentioned in the 1888 Republican Party platform.

14. This rule codified precedents set during an 1882 contested election case (see chapter 4) and an 1883 tariff battle: a report from the Rules Committee receives immediate consideration, and dilatory motions are limited while the House considers the report.

15. Reed convinced the Republicans that they would gain politically by forcing Democrats to choose between their pro-obstruction posturing and their need to produce legislative outcomes (Schickler 2001).

16. The rule varied slightly from Reed's original version in that, rather than count himself, the speaker appointed a member from each side of a vote to count nonvoting members.

CHAPTER 4

1. For this final step, I ignored single dilatory motions at the beginning or the end of a day unless they were possibly part of a multiday pattern of obstruction.

2. For incidents from 1789 to 1807 in the House of Representatives, see Luce (1922, 284–85).

3. The House had previously rejected this argument twice. On December 15, 1807, House members voted 14–103 against an effort to shut off post-PQ debate. On December 1, 1808, the House approved, 101–18, a ruling that debate *is* permitted after the PQ is adopted.

4. Typically this historical detail is used to support the broader claim that filibustering was possible but rare in the early Senate. Relative to the House and the Gilded Age Senate, this is correct.

5. The bill increased the draw (or raising portion) of the bridge, authorized modifications in the bridge design, and paid the owners of the bridge $10,000 on completion of the bridge.

6. This section is based largely on Smith (1980).

7. The period 1789–1831 is discussed above.

8. Ten of these are classified as miscellaneous; others are issue linked, e.g., rules changes related to accepting slavery petitions are classified as civil liberties.

9. The Committee on Territories was composed of five Democrats, three Republicans, and one American from Tennessee, which afforded a 6–3 proslavery majority. On four votes to refer the bill to a special committee, the six members identified as proslavery voted solidly to send the bill to the Committee on Territories, while the three antislavery members voted solidly against reference to the Committee on Territories.

10. The cross-party antislavery majority held against the Democratic proslavery members; the message was referred to a special investigatory committee appointed by the Democratic speaker, James Orr, which was also stacked with proslavery members.

11. Obviously, this predates the 1939 executive reorganization bill discussed by Binder and Smith (1997). In both texts, the earliest known case are presented; further research may unearth an even earlier statutory restriction on filibustering.

12. Challenges must be made by a member of the House *and* a senator. In 2000, several challenges to the electoral votes from Florida failed because no senator cosponsored the challenge. In 2004, Senator Boxer (D-CA) joined in a challenge to the electoral votes from Ohio that was rejected by both chambers.

13. Earlier, Hayes vetoed an army funding bill with a more explicit ban. The House sustained his veto (Burdette 1940, 36).

14. Readjusters were a faction in Virginia politics that sought to reduce state debt.

15. Green (2007) and Jenkins (2007) argue that these election cases were part of a broader Republican strategy to enforce voting laws through election challenges.

16. On election cases as party questions, see Alexander (1916, 323), Jenkins (2004), and Polsby (1968).

17. This filibuster is ably chronicled by Wawro and Schickler (2006, 76–87), so I limit my discussion of it.

CHAPTER 5

1. For each session, I arranged the votes from earliest to last, then assigned a percentile ranking so the first vote was a a 1, the last vote was a 100, and all other votes were in between. Then for each era, chamber, and session type, I calculated the mean attendance rate for each percentile, yielding a series from 1 (earliest) to 100 (latest). The last step was to smooth the results using a polynomial trend line of order 4.

2. To calculate these scores, I first identified every vote that pitted most of one party against most of the other party; these are known as *party votes*. Party unity scores for a session are the mean of party unity across party votes.

3. The model also predicts an increase in filibustering as Pro increasingly reverts to closure. This is more relevant to the twentieth-century Senate, in which we often observe some signs of filibustering before the majority attempts cloture or can at least distinguish between Senate cloture and ordinary agenda-setting motions. The closure techniques adopted by the House in the 1890s, e.g., increased use of special rules and ignoring dilatory motions, generally limit filibustering ex ante, so there is little observable evidence of filibustering. For decades after the 1890s reforms, however, newspaper articles occasionally refer to filibustering in the U.S. House.

4. An alternative approach is some sort of event count regression, which is appropriate for integer data clustered near zero. Both Tobit and negative binomial regression models yield similar results in this case; Tobit had the additional advantage of being easily combined with instrumental variable analysis.

5. I use STATA 9.1's *ivtobit* procedure.

6. Table 5.1 below displays the results for all 270 sessions, including special and Senate-only sessions.

7. I estimated the same equation with a dummy variable for the special session of the Forty-seventh Senate (1881), which is a significant outlier. While this new variable was significant, all other estimates were essentially unchanged.

8. I also estimated models in which short sessions were included as an exogenous predictor of obstruction, with the intuition that short sessions are not just shorter than long sessions but also have a fixed end date that may have invited filibustering. There are individual cases of this strategic logic during the historic Congress, and short session filibustering becomes prevalent in the twentieth-century Senate. However, the *short* coefficient was not close to statistical significance in any version of the analysis—all sessions, long and short sessions, or lagged sessions—while all other estimates were essentially unchanged.

CHAPTER 6

1. The *Congressional Quarterly Almanac* provides more detailed summaries but was not available online as this book was being written.

2. The *NYT* has traditionally presented itself as a serious news source, while *Time* was jaunty and irreverent in its early years. In the early decades of the twentieth century, many considered *Time* a more conservative news source than the *NYT*.

3. In the statistical analyses that follow, any measurement error is folded into the error term. I assume that the propensity for error is randomly distributed through time and across cases.

4. Some of these incidental references were borderline, e.g., articles noting that senators could (i.e., have the power to) filibuster a specific bill in the Senate or even stating that a filibuster "might" materialize against a given bill.

5. Two research assistants, Charles Gregory and Tessa Zolnikov, did preliminary coding of most of the *NYT* articles. To ensure consistency, however, I personally coded each article and use my own coding for this work.

6. By definition, an *active filibuster* delays a target bill, and all other bills must wait for floor consideration. For coding purposes, *delay* means that an article mentions the delay as being consequential.

7. There were two motions to adjourn, five quorum calls, and five motions to rise out of the Committee of the Whole.

8. Calendar Wednesday is a process on Wednesday of each week allowing bills reported out of committee to come to the House. This rule was developed to circumvent the majority party leadership's control over the floor agenda and is now rarely used.

9. Identification is based on coding as of August 2007.

10. A by-product of the Battle of the Reeds is the decision in *Reed v. County Commissioners*, 277 U.S. 376, 48 S.Ct. 531 (1928). The Supreme Court decided that the Reed committee continued to exist after March 3, 1929: "The status of the special select committee is a continuing one." Later senators would interpret this as constitutional evidence that the Senate is a standing body with permanent rules, implying that any reform to Rule 22 must be adopted in accordance with existing rules.

11. For example, the first point on the line "1901–9" sums up filibuster mentions in April 1902, April 1904, April 1906, and April 1908.

12. Specifically, veterans could take out loans for up to 50 percent of bonuses they were due in 1945.

13. This effort was echoed in 1985, when profarmer senators blocked the nomination of Edwin Meese for attorney general until the Senate scheduled a bill providing farmers with $2 billion in loans. The bill passed but died after a Reagan veto ("Congress Seeks Package" 1985, 21).

14. Specifically, a bill is killed if it did not advance past the stage when the filibustering occurs.

15. Table 6.4 is limited to proposals that explicitly deal with civil rights. Race was a subtext of a number of other proposals, e.g., cloture reform, the admission of Alaska and Hawaii as states, and judicial nominations. The exception is the 1949 cloture reform effort, which was so closely identified with the fate of civil rights legislation that journalists referred to it as a "civil rights filibuster."

16. The Powell amendment prohibited the distribution of federal education funds to school districts with segregated schools. Several researchers have studied these amendments as examples of "killer amendments," i.e., amendments intended to reduce overall support for the bill so that it fails (e.g., Denzau, Riker, and Shepsle 1985; Gilmour 2001; and Krehbiel and Rivers 1990). Several news articles suggest that, in addition to complicating outcomes in the House, these amendments invited filibusters in the Senate.

17. For an example of how legislators might obstruct to promote the interests of a disadvantaged group, see Dion's (1997) account of Charles Stewart Parnell's advocacy for Ireland in the British House of Commons.

18. According to this same article, Southerners feared that, if the conference report was blocked by a filibuster, the conference committee would meet and remove some of the weakening amendments added by the Senate.

19. Another possibility is that Southerners feared that conservative Republicans, led by Vice President Nixon, would begin to desert them on critical cloture votes (see Caro 2002, 863–65; and Evans and Novak 1966, 125–26).

20. One measure of this emphasis is the number of words in the sentences devoted to race, voting, and civil rights in the various platforms: 790 and 980 in the 1960 and 1964 Democratic platforms, respectively, compared to 1,259 and 334 in the 1960 and 1964 Republican platforms.

21. It is not clear how sincere Southern senators were in their opposition to the bill. Some, like Richard Russell, were genuine supporters of the racial status quo (Caro 2002; Mann 1996) and wanted to defeat the bill. Others may have held more moderate views on civil rights and begun to calculate their strategies in a postsegregation South (Mann 1996, 401). Even these senators, however, had a significant political stake in fighting the civil rights bill (Valeo 1999, 161–62).

22. Two other interesting veins are public vs. private control of essential industries (banking, energy) and (since 1970) subsidized access to the court system (i.e., the Legal Services Corporation) and litigation reform.

23. Soft money was donations to political party organizations that could be used for purposes other than campaigning. *Campaigning*, however, was so narrowly construed that a party could use soft money for television advertisements praising its candidates or criticizing the candidates of the opposing party as long as it avoided words and phrases like *reelect*, *vote for*, etc. There was no limit on the size of soft money donations, which led to accusations that special interests had undue influence on some issues.

24. Roll call data are from ICPSR 0004. I identified final-passage votes from the codebooks.

25. This is an unexplained phenomena that may be worthy of further research.

26. The trend lines are the predicted values of an ordinary least squares regression.

CHAPTER 7

1. For example, Binder, Lawrence, and Smith (2002) use the number of federal employees to measure Senate time constraints.

2. In this era, the number of days with a vote does not seem to be endogenous. I estimated an instrumental variables Tobit regression using presidential requests as an instrument, and

the results of a Wald test of exogeneity strongly supported the null expectation: $\chi^2 = 0.00$, Prob $> \chi^2 = 0.9672$. Variables for session type do predict the number of voting days, but (as shown later in this chapter) session type also has an independent relation to the number of filibusters.

3. In 1986, the Senate allowed C-SPAN to broadcast the Senate and revised Rule 22 to include a thirty-hour limit on postcloture debate (see Fenno 1989). Mixon, Gibson, and Upadhyaya (2003) suggest that televising Senate proceedings invited grandstanding, including filibusters carried out for public consumption. They analyze the Beth (1994) data and find that the 1986 reforms *increased* obstruction, but they do not control for variation in the value of time. In a variation on the model presented below, one with a separate variable for the 1986 reform (available on request), I find that the 1986 reform had a minimal effect once the 1975 revision is considered.

4. In Wawro and Schickler's (2006) account, the endogeneity of Senate rules is melded with the notion that the Senate used to operate on the basis of informal norms; implicit in the notion of informal rules is the threat that they may be made formal. Thus, a legislator may refrain from obstruction that provokes the majority to codify its expectations.

5. Four special sessions were omitted from the regression analysis because no votes were held during those sessions.

6. The recent nuclear option debate, discussed in chapter 8 below, illustrates this idea. A key question in the debate was whether Democrats were violating a Senate norm by filibustering judicial nominations on the Senate floor. Democrats and outside experts could reasonably point to previous judicial filibusters, e.g., that of Abe Fortas in 1968. Nonetheless, such filibusters had not happened recently, e.g., when Ginsburg and Breyer were confirmed in 1993 and 1994, respectively, so, to the Republicans, the Democrats' behavior *seemed* new.

7. Specifically, a partial autocorrelation plot of deviations from the mean number of filibusters revealed a correlation for one time period. My thanks to Patrick Brandt for his advice on this test.

8. This is implemented by the STATA command <arpois>.

9. In preparation for this section, I explored various configurations of session types and historical periods that are not shown but quite similar. Given a single time series and continuous variables that trend over time, institutional parameters should be used and interpreted with care. I have collapsed the periods 1975–85 and 1986–present since they have similar effects, and I have omitted variables for post-1933 sessions (first vs. second) for the same reason.

10. If we omit Tuesday–Thursday vote percentage and repeat the analysis with a time trend variable, the trend variable is statistically significant, but the overall fit of the model is reduced.

CHAPTER 8

1. However, in chapter 1, I note a pair of precedents set in 1908 during La Follette's filibuster against the Aldrich banking bill that Binder and Smith (1997) list as a major restriction on obstruction.

2. This case is drawn from Bawn and Koger (2008).

3. ICPSR 0004, 63rd Senate, variables 528–30. For the Democratic dissidents' varied motives, see *Congressional Record* 52, pt. 4 (February 16, 1915): 3843–45; and Link (1956, 153).

4. Before the Democrats gave up, Ollie James (D-KY) proposed a majoritarian strategy to force a vote on the shipping bill by moving the previous question and overriding the chair's ruling that the Senate rules include no such motion (*Congressional Record* 52, pt. 4 [February 13, 1915]: 3738). Democrats considered James's plan but lacked the votes to win the appeal (*Washington Post*, February 17, 1915, A2; *Washington Post*, February 18, 1915, A5).

5. The text describes the main contest. The Senate subsequently passed a watered-down version of the bill and requested a conference with the House on the condition that the conference not report until February 27. The *NYT* described this as "tantamount to dropping the Ship Purchase Bill" (February 19, 1915, A1). The conference report was easily killed by a low-intensity filibuster in the last days of the Sixty-third Congress.

6. Specifically, the start date is the first time an article mentions an ongoing filibuster or, if the filibuster is merely threatened, the date of the first threat. Four cases are excluded because the first mention occurs after the Congress concludes.

7. The debate was not continuous. Several other bills were considered during this span.

8. The specific targets of the petition were five irreconcilable opponents of the treaty: La Follette, Gronna (R-ND), Norris (R-NE), France (R-MD), and Reed (D-MO).

9. Harding made the first address on November 21, 1922.

10. In a unidimensional model, we might say that these senators are close to the cut point of a unidimensional policy space and that the cloture penalty shifts some legislators from the procloture side of the cut point to the anticloture side.

11. A *prisoner's dilemma* is a situation in which players have a choice between *cooperating* (which is socially optimal but achieved only if enough players cooperate) and *defecting* (i.e., not cooperating, which is individually optimal because one either takes advantage of others' cooperation or, at least, avoids being a sucker). The term derives from a police interrogation strategy of separating criminals and offering them leniency if they confess, particularly if the other criminal(s) do not confess. For an introduction, see Dixit and Nalebuff (1993).

12. The farm bloc's success was temporary; the bill died when Coolidge vetoed it.

13. Additionally, Senator Thomas (D-OK) threatened to block any unanimous consent request while the cloture petition was pending and to continue his blockade if the vote succeeded. This would severely impede a chamber that relies on these agreements for its day-to-day functions (Burdette 1940, 175).

14. The precedent was supported by a 41–24 vote (Republicans 39–1, Democrats 2–22) on November 29, 1922.

15. In fact, from 1917 to 1933, one cloture vote (the first) occurred in a special early session, three during long sessions, and seven during short sessions—five during the short session of the Sixty-ninth Congress.

16. The relevant portions of the Twentieth Amendment read:

Sec. 1: The terms of the President and Vice President shall end at noon on the 20th day of January, and the terms of Senators and Representatives at noon on the 3d day of January, of the years in which such terms would have ended if this article had not been ratified; and the terms of their successors shall then begin.

Sec. 2: The Congress shall assemble at least once in every year, and such meeting shall begin at noon on the 3d day of January, unless they shall by law appoint a different day.

17. A second consequence of eliminating the postelection short session is that filibustering members would share in one of the main costs of obstruction: time spent obstructing legislation or waiting out a filibuster would be less time to campaign at home before the election. Norris also claimed that the amendment would reduce the influence of lame-duck legislators, avoiding controversies like the ship subsidy bill in 1923 (Goodman and Nokken 2004).

18. Long is also one of the few senators to have his own theme song: "Every Man a King."

19. The shift toward germane speeches as the dominant form of filibustering had unintended consequences for the collective understanding of filibustering. Newspaper articles were increasingly likely to define *filibustering* in terms of speaking and omit any reference to dilatory tactics. This redefinition helped the House's tradition of filibustering fade from collective memory. Eventually, scholars and reporters would claim that, since unlimited speaking had long been forbidden in the House, filibustering must be impossible there and has been since the previous question rule was adopted. This fallacy, however, was a consequence of a narrowing of the definition of *filibustering* to refer exclusively to speaking.

20. The notion of a club of Senate elites is typically associated with the dominance of conservative Southern Democrats and Republicans. These are correlated but distinct events. Several of the senators who worked to restrain Long were New Deal Democrats, and, while the conservative coalition began forming in the mid-1930s, conservatives did not dominate the Senate committee system until 1947 (Gould 2005; Zelizer 2004).

21. Indeed, as the Seventy-third Congress drew to a close, majority party leaders refused to announce their party's agenda publicly for fear that they would be signaling to zealous senators which bills would make the best hostages ("Tariff Bill Voted by Senate" 1934, 1).

22. Bilbo narrowly won the requisite majority in the party primary over four opponents after a campaign in which he ran as the most ardent foe of civil rights in the field ("Bilbo Vote" 1946, 1). After the primary, he admitted that he was a member of the Ku Klux Klan ("K.K.K." 1946).

23. Another failed solo effort occurred in 1950. At first, Nevada's George Malone (R) successfully protected his state's gambling industry by filibustering a bill banning the interstate transportation of slot machines. However, three months later, he came down with laryngitis, and the proponents of the bill passed it while Malone was unable to speak ("Slot Machine Curb" 1950, 36).

24. The Mansfield Archive is the Mike Mansfield Archive, Maureen and Mike Mansfield Library, University of Montana. Citations from the archive follow the pattern series number, box number, and folder number.

25. The DPC Minutes for the period 1953–60 were provided by the Senate Historian's office on CD-ROM.

26. Johnson's trickery increased distrust and monitoring costs. Currently, each party posts a sentinel on the floor, but, during Johnson's reign, each party *faction* was compelled to post a guard on the Senate floor (Valeo 1999, 38).

27. This was clearly Mansfield's personal point of view. Mansfield often edited draft speeches prepared by his staffers to stress the futility and negative publicity of wars of attrition. See also Rich (1974, A2).

28. There is a practical reason for Senate leaders to respect the prerogatives of every senator: one senator deprived of his or her prerogatives can ensnarl the chamber by filibustering or blocking unanimous consent requests. Wayne Morse did so in 1965 when Russell Long—Huey's son—tried to deny him the right to offer amendments to a bill ("Senate Defeats Latin Loan Curbs" 1965, 7).

29. One effect of this rules debate was that Southerners were deterred from filibustering the reauthorization of the Civil Rights Commission, which came up in August 1961. They feared that blocking this relatively minor bill might fuel the drive for a stronger cloture rule, so they relented ("Rights Unit's Life" 1961, 57).

30. Was this a stroke of strategic genius by liberals hoping to transform the politics of cloture? It seems not since the obstructionists were shocked by their defeat and carried on a four-day postcloture filibuster in retaliation for this violation of the Senate's commitment to free speech ("Washington" 1962, 144).

31. This move can be traced in Valeo to Mansfield, "Comment on the Ken Teasdale Memorandum on Civil Rights," November 19, 1963, Valeo to Mansfield, "Civil Rights Procedure in Relation to the Tax Bill," February 13, 1964, and "Minutes of Meeting with Senator Russell," February 19, 1964, Mansfield Archive, XXII, 28, 6.

32. Also, in September 1964, there were twenty-one switchers on a proposal to delay the Supreme Court–mandated congressional redistricting. Cloture failed 30–63, but the tabling motion also lost 38–49.

33. Filibuster threats are often expressed in the polite terminology of the Senate; senators claim that they will "speak at length and offer many amendments," "exercise the prerogatives of unlimited debate," etc.

34. At the beginning of the 106th Congress, party leaders Trent Lott (R-MS) and Tom Daschle (D-SD) circulated a letter telling members that, in order to place a hold, they must also notify the bill sponsor and the committee of jurisdiction ("New Rule" 1999). Senators Wyden (D-OR) and Grassley (R-IA) continue to push for full publicity.

35. Randall Ripley (1969, 227), however, refers to the ability of senators to delay legislation by communicating concerns or requests to a party leader.

36. The LRC also objected to passing bills by unanimous consent if they were simply too important for quick passage, e.g., appropriations bills (Harry McPherson to Edmund Muskie [D-ME], February 16, 1961, Mansfield Archive, XXII, 93, 14).

37. Specifically, in 1953, Lyndon Johnson sent a letter to all Democratic senators stating: "Should a Senator wish to object to a bill scheduled to come up on a day when he will not be in the Senate, his staff can contact [the DPC counsel,] Mr. [Gerald] Siegel. He will arrange for the objection to be registered in the name of such Senator, by [LRC members] Senators Smathers or Gore" (DPC Minutes, February 24, 1953).

38. As discussed in n. 6, chapter 2 above, *pairing* occurs when two legislators refrain from voting if one of them is absent.

39. That is, the number of aye, nay, paired, and absent votes for each roll call, aggregated by year.

40. For a more complete list, see Binder and Smith (1997, 188–94) and any *Senate Manual*.

41. This is conjecture, of course, and, thus, an opportunity for further research.

42. About 23 percent of all cloture petitions filed from 1973 to 2006 were intended to force a vote on a motion to proceed (see http://www.senate.gov/reference/reference_index_subjects/Cloture_vrd.htm).

43. Daschle threatened a repeat of Byrd's tactics to push through the conference report for a 2002 campaign reform bill. Instead, the Republican opposition folded quietly after a 68–32 cloture vote ("Quick Debate" 2002, 19).

44. This section is based on Koger (2008).

45. The Republicans refer to their threatened gambit as the *constitutional option*, ignoring a general rule of political rhetoric: the label with fewer syllables wins.

46. Accessed 4/12/2005 at http://www.pollingreport.com/congress.htm. $N = 1,012$; the margin of error is +/– 3 percent. Internal Republican polls reportedly echoed these results (Bolton 2005d).

47. Outside groups also pressured senators to toe the line. After Senate Republican whip Mitch McConnell (R-KY) expressed reservations about "going nuclear," he was criticized by the conservative radio host Rush Limbaugh, and the Family Research Council threatened to run television ads in Kentucky urging McConnell to change his position (Bolton 2005c). On the broader network of links between interest groups and formal party organizations, see Cohen et al. (2008), Koger, Masket, and Noel (2009), Masket (2009), and Sinclair (2006).

48. For a formal discussion of the credibility of the Gang of Fourteen agreement, see also Rohde and Shepsle (2007).

AFTERWORD

1. Readers should note, however, that this afterword is not meant to support one party, one set of politicians, over the other. Since I started this project, there have been a Republican majority in the Senate and a Democratic president, a Republican Senate and a Republican president, a Democratic Senate and a Republican president, and now a Democratic president and Democratic Senate. In the years to come, I expect similar variation in party fortunes. The claims in this afterword are institutional in nature, regardless of which party is in power.

2. Not that I endorse Nevada's position on nuclear waste policy. I simply suggest that Nevada has a greater stake in this debate than does Hawaii, Alaska, or Maine.

3. This does not mean that the filibuster is an inherently conservative practice, however. We have seen that filibustering can help expand the legislative agenda as well as block proposals. In the English House of Commons, e.g., the filibuster was utilized during the late nineteenth century to *promote* the interests of a historically disadvantaged group: the Irish (Dion 1997).

4. The opposite argument has been used *against* the filibuster: senators representing less than a sixth of the nation's population can block legislation favored by senators representing the rest of the country.

5. The 106th Senate (1999–2000) illustrates this point. The Democratic minority filibustered to obtain votes on legislation to restrict firearms sales, hire teachers, restrict campaign donations, and regulate managed health care. None of these proposals became law, but voters in the 2000 election were better able to contrast Republican and Democratic priorities on the basis of concrete legislative actions.

6. Some respond that majorities can be transitory; additional debate or the passage of time may transform citizen and elite preferences. Thus, today's minority may serve the interest of the true deliberative majority by obstructing hasty legislation (Lippmann 1982, 217–19).

7. Other proposals include majority cloture on bills that have been debated for two weeks or requiring 60 percent of voting senators to invoke cloture.

References

Adams, John Quincy. 1969. *Memoirs of John Quincy Adams, Comprising Portions of His Diary from 1795 to 1848.* Edited by Charles Francis Adams. 12 vols. Reprint, Freeport, NY: Books for Libraries.

"Adopt Reservation, 46–33." 1919. *New York Times*, November 14, 1.

"Agreement in Senate." 1933. *New York Times*, January 17, 1.

Ainsworth, Scott, and Marcus Flathman. 1995. "Unanimous Consent Agreements as Leadership Tools." *Legislative Studies Quarterly* 20:177–95.

Alexander, De Alva Stanwood. 1916. *History and Procedure of the House of Representatives.* Boston: Riverside.

Allen, Mike, and Amy Goldstein. 2002. "Bush Has Plan to Speed Judicial Confirmations." *Washington Post*, October 31.

Alter, Alison B., and Leslie Moscow McGranahan. 2000. "Reexamining the Filibuster and Proposal Powers in the Senate." *Legislative Studies Quarterly* 25:259–84.

American Political Science Association (APSA) Committee on Political Parties. 1950. "Toward a More Responsible Two-Party System." *American Political Science Review* 44, no. 3, pt. 2, suppl.

Arnold, R. Douglas. 1990. *The Logic of Congressional Action.* New Haven, CT: Yale University Press.

"The Art of Filibustering." 1915. *New York Times*, January 31, C2.

Babington, Charles. 2005. "Frist Urges End to Nominee Filibusters." *Washington Post*, April 25, 1.

"Bank Bill." 1927. *Time*, February 28.

"Bar on Filibusters Planned in Senate by Amending Rules." 1935. *New York Times*, August 29, 1.

"Battle of the Bonus." 1931. *Time*, March 2.

Bawn, Kathleen, and Gregory Koger. 2005. "The Dynamics of Filibustering in the Senate." Paper presented at the annual meeting of the Midwest Political Science Association, Chicago.

———. 2008. "Effort, Intensity and Position Taking: Reconsidering Obstruction in the Pre-Cloture Senate." *Journal of Theoretical Politics* 20:67–92.

Beeman, Richard R. 1968. "Unlimited Debate in the Senate: The First Phase." *Political Science Quarterly* 83:419–34.

Bell, Lauren Cohen, and L. Marvin Overby. 2007. "Extended Debate over Time: Patterns and Trends in the History of Filibusters in the U.S. Senate." Paper presented at the annual meeting of the Midwest Political Science Association, Chicago.

Beth, Richard S. 1994. "Filibusters in the Senate, 1789–1993." Washington, DC: Congressional Research Service.

———. 1995. "What We Don't Know about Filibusters." Paper presented at the annual meeting of the Western Political Science Association, Portland, OR.

"Big Michigander." 1939. *Time*, October 2.

"Bilbo Is Held Off." 1947. *New York Times*, January 4, 1.

"Bilbo Vote Tops Opponents by 4,102." 1946. *New York Times*, July 4, 1.

Binder, Sarah A. 1997. *Minority Rights, Majority Rule*. Cambridge: Cambridge University Press.

———. 2003. *Stalemate: Causes and Consequences of Legislative Gridlock*. Washington, DC: Brookings Institution Press.

Binder, Sarah A., Eric D. Lawrence, and Steven S. Smith. 2002. "Tracking the Filibuster, 1917 to 1996." *American Politics Research* 30:406–22.

Binder, Sarah A., Anthony J. Madonna, and Steven S. Smith. 2007. "Going Nuclear, Senate Style." *Perspectives on Politics* 5:729–40.

Binder, Sarah A., and Steven S. Smith. 1997. *Politics or Principle? Filibustering in the U.S. Senate*. Washington, DC: Brookings Institution Press.

Bolton, Alexander. 2003. "GOP Splits over Tough Tactics on Bush Judges." *The Hill*, May 14. Available at http://thehill.com.

———. 2005a. "Nelson: Let's Make a Deal." *The Hill*, April 13. Available at http://thehill.com.

———. 2005b. "On Judges, Conservatives and Liberals Agree: No Deal." *The Hill*, April 27. Available at http://thehill.com.

———. 2005c. "Santorum: Frist Will Go Nuclear." *The Hill*, April 7. Available at http://thehill.com.

———. 2005d. "Santorum Reads Nuke Polls, Applies the Brakes." *The Hill*, April 21. Available at http://thehill.com.

Bolton, Alexander, and Geoff Earle. 2003. "Hatch Group May Go 'Nuclear' on Judges." *The Hill*, May 7. Available at http://thehill.com.

"Borah to Tour against League." 1919. *New York Times*, February 21, 1.

Brady, David W., and Craig Volden. 2006. *Revolving Gridlock: Politics and Policy from Jimmy Carter to George W. Bush*. 2nd ed. Boulder, CO: Westview.

Burdette, Franklin L. 1940. *Filibustering in the Senate*. Princeton, NJ: Princeton University Press.

"Butler Confirmed by Senate, 61 to 8." 1922. *New York Times*, December 22, 11.

"Byrd Seeking Changes in Rules to Speed Up Business in the Senate." 1979. *New York Times*, January 14, 19.

Calhoun, John C. 1953. *A Disquisition on Government*. Indianapolis: Bobbs-Merrill.

Campbell, Andrea, Gary Cox, and Mathew McCubbins. 2002. "Agenda Power in the U.S. Senate, 1877–1986." In *Party, Process, and Political Change in Congress, Volume 1: New Perspectives on the History of Congress*, ed. David W. Brady and Mathew D. McCubbins, 146–65. Stanford, CA: Stanford University Press.

Carey, Mary Agnes. 2003. "GOP Wins Battle, Not War." *Congressional Quarterly Weekly*, November 29, 2956–63.

Carmines, Edward G., and James A. Stimson. 1989. *Issue Evolution: Race and the Transformation of American Politics*. Princeton, NJ: Princeton University Press.

Caro, Robert A. 2002. *Master of the Senate*. New York: Vintage.

"Chalmers and His Tale." 1882. *New York Times*, May 26, 4.

Chiou, Fang-Yi, and Lawrence S. Rothenberg. 2003. "When Pivotal Politics Meets Partisan Politics." *American Journal of Political Science* 47:503–22.

———. 2006. "Preferences, Parties, and Legislative Productivity." *American Politics Research* 34:705–31.

"Civil Rights Attorneys' Fees, 1976." 1977. *Congress and the Nation* 4:607–8.

Clausen, Aage. 1973. *How Congressmen Decide: A Policy Focus*. New York: St. Martin's.

Clinton, Joshua D., and John S. Lapinski. 2006. "Measuring Legislative Accomplishment, 1877–1994." *American Journal of Political Science* 50:232–49.

Cohen, Marty, David Karol, Hans Noel, and John Zaller. 2008. *The Party Decides: Presidential Nominations Before and After Reform*. Chicago: University of Chicago Press.

"Compromise Closure Rule Adopted by Senate, 63 to 23; Filibuster Battle Is Ended." 1949. *New York Times*, March 18, 1.

"Conferees Clash on Air Bill Power over Contractors." 1939. *New York Times*, March 10, 1.

"Congress Delays Its Adjournment until Mid-Week." 1961. *New York Times*, September 24.

"Congress Ends; Big Bills Killed by a Filibuster." 1919. *New York Times*, March 5, 1.

"Congress Seeks Package to Aid Farmer; Meese Filibuster Goes On." 1985. *New York Times*, February 21, 21.

"Congress Will Hear Veto of Cash Bonus Read Today." 1935. *New York Times*, May 22, 1.

Cooper, Joseph. 1962. *The Previous Question: Its Standing as a Precedent for Cloture in the United States Senate*. Washington, DC: U.S. Government Printing Office.

Cooper, Joseph, and Cheryl D. Young. 1989. "Bill Introduction in the Nineteenth Century: A Study of Institutional Change." *Legislative Studies Quarterly* 14, no. 1:67–105.

Cox, Gary W., and Mathew D. McCubbins. 1993. *Legislative Leviathan: Party Government in the House*. Berkeley and Los Angeles: University of California Press.

———. 2005. *Setting the Agenda: Responsible Party Government in the U.S. House of Representatives*. Cambridge: Cambridge University Press.

Dahl, Robert A. 1956. *Preface to Democratic Theory*. Chicago: University of Chicago Press.

Davidson, Roger H. 1985. "Senate Leaders: Janitors for an Untidy Chamber?" In *Congress Reconsidered* (3rd ed.), ed. Lawrence C. Dodd and Bruce I. Oppenheimer, 225–51. Washington, DC: Congressional Quarterly Press.

"Dawn over Capitol Hill." 1950. *Time*, October 2.

"The Deadlock Continues." 1878. *New York Times*, May 16, 1.

"Dead-Lock in Senate Remains Unbroken." 1903. *New York Times*, February 22, 1.

"Demand Ouster of Bilbo." 1946. *New York Times*, August 22, 17.

"Democrats Refuse to Alter Ship Bill." 1915. *New York Times*, January 30, 13.

"Democrats Split, Senate Hopes Rise for Atom Bill Test." 1954. *New York Times*, July 26, 1.

Denzau, Arthur, William Riker, and Kenneth Shepsle. 1985. "Farquharson and Fenno: Sophisticated Voting Homestyle." *American Political Science Review* 79:1117–33.

"Desertions Deal Blow to Ship Bill; Fresh Plans Made." 1915. *New York Times*, February 11, 1.

"Did and Didn't." 1925. *Time*, March 16.

Dion, Douglas. 1997. *Turning the Legislative Thumbscrew: Minority Rights and Procedural Change in Legislative Politics*. Ann Arbor: University of Michigan Press.

Dixit, Avinash K., and Barry J. Nalebuff. 1993. *Thinking Strategically: The Competitive Edge in Business, Politics, and Everyday Life*. New York: Norton.

"Drive to Curb Filibusters Is Defeated in Senate Test." 1961. *New York Times*, September 20.

Earle, Geoff. 2005. "Frist-Reid Talks Touch on 'Nuclear Option,' Other Issues." *The Hill*, February 17. Available at http://thehill.com.

Erikson, Robert S., Michael Mackuen, and James A. Stimson. 2002. *The Macro Polity*. Cambridge: Cambridge University Press.

Evans, C. Lawrence, and Daniel Lipinski. 2005. "Obstruction and Leadership in the U.S. Senate." *Congress Reconsidered* (8th ed.), ed. Lawrence Dodd and Bruce I. Oppenheimer. Washington, DC: Congressional Quarterly Press.

Evans, C. Lawrence, and Walter Oleszek. 2001. "The Procedural Context of Senate Deliberation." In *The Contentious Senate: Partisanship, Ideology, and the Myth of Cool Judgment*, ed. Colton C. Campbell and Nicol C. Rae, 107–27. New York: Rowman & Littlefield.

Evans, Rowland, and Robert Novak. 1966. *Lyndon B. Johnson: The Exercise of Power*. New York: New American Library.

"Everybody's Getting Fat." 1962. *Time*, May 18.

"Farm Debt Bill Sent to President." 1934. *New York Times*, June 19, 2.

Faulkner, Harold U. 1929. "The Development of the American System." *Annals of the American Academy of Political and Social Science* 141:11–17.

Fenno, Richard. 1966. *Power of the Purse*. Boston: Little, Brown.

Fenno, Richard F., Jr. 1989. "The Senate through the Looking Glass." *Legislative Studies Quarterly* 14:313–48.

"Fifty Years of Crusading for the Negro." 1940. *New York Times*, December 22, 81.

"51 Senators Sign Cloture Demands on Peace Treaty." 1919. *New York Times*, November 13, 1.

"A Fight for a Post Office." 1881. *New York Times*, October 27, 1.

"Fight $10,660,000 for Boulder Dam." 1930. *New York Times*, June 24, 5.

"Filibuster!" 1942. *Time*, November 23.

"Filibuster by Long Delays Relief Bill." 1935. *New York Times*, March 9, 9.

"A Filibuster Ends, but Not the Gas War." 1977. *Time*, October 17.

"Filibuster for Extra Session." 1917. *New York Times*, March 1, 1.

"Filibuster Killed by Words of Praise." 1948. *New York Times*, June 20, 35.

"Filibuster Menaces Ship Subsidy Bill." 1922. *New York Times*, December 1, 2.

"Filibuster Plan Outlined." 1947. *New York Times*, January 3, 2.

"Filibuster Stalls Key Money Bill on Senate Floor." 1982. *New York Times*, December 19, 1.

"A Filibuster That Kept Banker's Hours." 1946. *New York Times*, February 14, 23.

"Filibuster Threat on Lynching Bill Hangs over Senate." 1935. *New York Times*, April 22, 1.

"Filibuster Threat Renewed." 1941. *New York Times*, February 25, 10.

Fisk, Catherine, and Erwin Chemerinsky. 1997. "The Filibuster." *Stanford Law Review* 49:181–254.

Foley, Michael. 1980. *The New Senate: Liberal Influence on a Conservative Institution, 1959–1972*. New Haven, CT: Yale University Press.

Follett, Mary Parker. 1974. *The Speaker of the House of Representatives*. Reprint, New York: Burt Franklin.

"For Homeland Security Bill, a Brakeman." 2002. *New York Times*, July 13, 17.

"Friendly Filibuster." 1962. *Time*, April 6.

"A Frustrated Dole Temporarily Halts Minimum Wage Talks." 1996. *New York Times*, May 15, 19.

Frymer, Paul. 1999. *Uneasy Alliances: Race and Party Competition in America*. Princeton, NJ: Princeton University Press.

Gailmard, Sean, and Jeffery A. Jenkins. 2007. "Negative Agenda Control in the Senate and House: Fingerprints of Majority Party Power." *Journal of Politics* 69:689–700.

Garraty, John A. 1953. *Henry Cabot Lodge*. New York: Knopf.

Gilmour, John B. 2001. "The Powell Amendment Voting Cycle: An Obituary." *Legislative Studies Quarterly* 26:249–62.

Glantz, Oscar. 1960. "The Negro Voter in Northern Industrial Cities." *Western Political Quarterly* 13:999–1010.

Goodman, Craig, and Timothy P. Nokken. 2004. "Lame-Duck Legislators and Consideration of the Ship Subsidy Bill of 1922." *American Politics Research* 32:465–89.

"GOP May Target Use of Filibuster." 2004. *Washington Post*, December 13, A1.

Gould, Lewis L. 2005. *The Most Exclusive Club: A History of the Modern United States Senate.* New York: Basic.

Green, Matthew N. 2007. "Race, Party, and Contested Elections to the U.S. House of Representatives." *Polity* 39:155–78.

Grim, Ryan. 2009. "The Myth of the Filibuster: Dems Can't Make Republicans Talk All Night." *Huffington Post*, February 23. Available at http://www.huffingtonpost.com.

"Half the Session Gone." 1923. *New York Times*, January 16, 20.

Hall, Richard. 1996. *Participation in Congress.* New Haven, CT: Yale University Press.

Hall, Richard L., and Alan V. Deardorff. 2006. "Lobbying as Legislative Subsidy." *American Political Science Review* 100, no. 1:69–84.

"Harding Abandons Ship Subsidy Bill." 1923. *New York Times*, February 28, 7.

Harvey, James C. 1973. *Black Civil Rights during the Johnson Administration.* Jackson: University and College Press of Mississippi

Haynes, George H. 1938. *The Senate of the United States: Its History and Practice.* Boston: Houghton Mifflin.

"Head Winds." 1962. *Time*, August 10.

Heaton, Herbert. 1941. "Non-Importation, 1806–1812." *Journal of Economic History* 1:178–98.

Hinds, Asher C. 1907. *Precedents of the House of Representatives of the United States.* 5 vols. Washington, DC: U.S. Government Printing Office.

"Homeland Security Bill Gains, If Only a Bit." 2002. *New York Times*, September 13, 13.

Hoogenboom, Ari. 1995. *Rutherford B. Hayes: Warrior and President.* Lawrence: University Press of Kansas.

"House Votes TV Debates After 27 Hour Filibuster." 1968. *New York Times*, October 10, 1.

"Huey for 15 Hours." 1935. *New York Times*, June 16, E1.

Hulse, Carl. 2005. "Senate Leaders Break Off Talks on Judicial Nominees." *New York Times*, May 17.

"Humphrey Asks Speed on Rights." 1964. *New York Times*, April 18, 17.

Hurt, Charles. 2003. "GOP Claims Win in Judges Talkathon." *Washington Times*, November 23.

———. 2005. "Support Falters for the 'Nuclear Option.'" *Washington Times*, March 23.

"Impasse on Wage Issue Stalls Effort to Lower Gasoline Tax." 1996. *New York Times*, May 8, B9.

Inter-University Consortium for Political and Social Research (ICPSR) and Congressional Quarterly (CQ). 1998. *United States Congressional Roll Call Voting Records, 1789–1996 (ICPSR 0004).* Ann Arbor, MI: ICPSR.

Irving, Florence B. 1957. "The Future of the Negro Voter in the South." *Journal of Negro Education* 26:390–99.

Jefferson, Thomas. 1801/1993. *A Manual of Parliamentary Practice.* Washington, DC: U.S. Government Printing Office.

Jenkins, Jeffery A. 2004. "Partisanship and Contested Election Cases in the House of Representatives, 1789–2002." *Studies in American Political Development* 18:113–35.

———. 2007. "The First 'Southern Strategy': The Republican Party and Contested-Election Cases in the Late Nineteenth-Century House." In *Party, Process, and Policy Political*

Change in Congress, Volume 2: Further New Perspectives on the History of Congress, ed. David W. Brady and Mathew D. McCubbins, 78–90. Stanford, CA: Stanford University Press.

Jenkins, Jeffrey A., and Timothy P. Nokken. 2000. "The Institutional Origins of the Republican Party: A Spatial Voting Analysis of the House Speakership Election of 1855–56." *Legislative Studies Quarterly* 25:101–30.

Kaufman, Marc, and Rob Stein. 2006. "FDA Allows OTC Sales of Plan B." *Washington Post,* August 24.

Kerr, Clara Hannah. 1895. *The Origin and Development of the United States Senate.* Ithaca, NY: Andrus & Church.

"K.K.K." 1946. *Time,* August 19.

Klein, Joe. 2006. "Prognosis Looks Grim, Doc." *Time,* April 1.

Koger, Gregory. 2002. "Obstruction in the House and Senate: A Comparative Analysis of Institutional Choice." Ph.D. diss., University of California, Los Angeles.

———. 2003. "Position-Taking and Cosponsorship in the U.S. House." *Legislative Studies Quarterly* 28:225–46.

———. 2004. "Pivots for Sale: Transaction Costs, Endogenous Rules, and Obstruction in the Senate." Paper presented at the annual meeting of the American Political Science Association, Chicago.

———. 2006a. "Cloture Reform and Party Government in the Senate, 1918–1925." *Journal of Politics* 68, no. 3:708–19.

———. 2006b. "Going to the Mattresses: Filibustering in the U.S. House and Senate, 1789–1901." Paper presented at the annual meeting of the Midwest Political Science Association, Chicago.

———. 2007. "Filibuster Reform in the Senate, 1913–1917." In *Party, Process, and Policy Political Change in Congress, Volume 2: Further New Perspectives on the History of Congress,* ed. David W. Brady and Mathew D. McCubbins, 205–25. Stanford, CA: Stanford University Press.

———. 2008. "Filibustering and Majority Rule in the Senate: The Contest over Judicial Nominations, 2003–2005." In *Why Not Parties? Party Effects in the United States Senate,* ed. Nathan W. Monroe, Jason R. Roberts, and David W. Rohde, 159–77. Chicago: University of Chicago Press.

Koger, Gregory, Seth Masket, and Hans Noel. 2009. "Partisan Webs: Information Exchange and Party Networks." *British Journal of Political Science* 39:633–53.

Krehbiel, Keith. 1991. *Information and Legislative Organization.* Ann Arbor: University of Michigan Press.

———. 1998. *Pivotal Politics: A Theory of U.S. Lawmaking.* Chicago: University of Chicago Press.

Krehbiel, Keith, and Adam Meirowitz. 2002. "Minority Rights and Majority Power: Theoretical Consequences of the Motion to Recommit." *Legislative Studies Quarterly* 27:191–218.

Krehbiel, Keith, and Douglas Rivers. 1990. "Sophisticated Voting in Congress: A Reconsideration." *Journal of Politics* 52:548–78.

Krock, Arthur. 1935a. "Long's Defeat in Filibuster Checks His Senate 'Mastery.'" *New York Times,* June 14, 22.

———. 1935b. "Senate Finds Itself Blocked by Long's Tactics." *New York Times,* March 12, 20.

———. 1937. "Legislative and Political Phases of Court Fight." *New York Times,* July 8, 22.

Kucinich, Jackie. 2007. "House Members Call Temporary Truce on Procedural Battle." *The Hill,* May 16. Available at http://thehill.com.

"The Last, Hoarse Gasp." 1957. *Time*, September 9.

Lebo, Matthew, Adam McGlynn, and Gregory Koger. 2007. "Strategic Party Government: Party Influence in Congress, 1789–2000." *American Journal of Political Science* 51, no. 3:464–81.

"Legislative Record of the 70th Congress." 1929. *Editorial Research Report*, March 4. Available at http://library.cqpress.com/cqresearcher.

"Legislative Summary, 69th Congress, 3rd Session." 1927. *Editorial Research Report*, March 31. Available at http://library.cqpress.com/cqresearcher.

Link, Arthur S. 1956. *Wilson: The New Freedom*. Princeton, NJ: Princeton University Press.

Lippmann, Walter. 1982. *The Essential Lippmann*. Cambridge, MA: Harvard University Press.

Lodge, Henry Cabot. 1893. "Obstruction in the Senate." *North American Review* 157, no. 444:523–29.

"Log Jam Broken." 1954. *Time*, August 9.

"Long's Filibuster Lasts 15½ Hours." 1935. *New York Times*, June 14, 2.

Luce, Robert. 1922. *Legislative Procedure*. Boston: Riverside.

Ludlum, Robert P. 1941. "The Antislavery 'Gag-Rule': History and Argument." *Journal of Negro History* 26:203–43.

"Lynch Bill Fought." 1937. *New York Times*, November 17, 1.

"Lynching Bill Foes Plan to Filibuster." 1935. *New York Times*, April 20, 1.

Madison, James. 1908. *The Journal of the Debates in the Convention Which Framed the Constitution of the United States May–September, 1787*. Edited by Gaillard Hunt. Vol. 2. New York: Putnam's.

"The Majority Rules." 1947. *Time*, June 30.

Mann, Robert. 1996. *The Walls of Jericho: Lyndon Johnson, Hubert Humphrey, Richard Russell, and the Struggle for Civil Rights*. New York: Harcourt Brace.

Martis, Kenneth C. 1989. *The Historical Atlas of Political Parties in the United States Congress, 1789–1989*. New York: Macmillan.

Masket, Seth E. 2009. *No Middle Ground: How Informal Party Organizations Control Nominations and Polarize Legislatures*. Ann Arbor: University of Michigan Press.

Matthews, Donald. 1960. *U.S. Senators and Their World*. Chapel Hill: University of North Carolina Press.

May, Kenneth O. 1952. "A Set of Necessary and Sufficient Conditions for Simple Majority Decisions." *Econometrica* 20:680–84.

Mayhew, David. 1974. *Congress: The Electoral Connection*. New Haven, CT: Yale University Press.

———. 1991. *Divided We Govern: Party Control, Lawmaking, and Investigations, 1946–1990*. New Haven, CT: Yale University Press.

———. 2000. *America's Congress: Actions in the Public Sphere, James Madison through Newt Gingrich*. New Haven, CT: Yale University Press.

———. 2003. "Supermajority Rule in the Senate." *PS: Political Science and Politics* 36:31–36.

McCarty, Nolan, and Adam Meirowitz. 2007. *Political Game Theory: An Introduction*. New York: Cambridge University Press.

McCarty, Nolan, Keith T. Poole, and Howard Rosenthal. 2006. *Polarized America: The Dance of Ideology and Unequal Riches*. Boston: MIT Press.

McKelvey, Richard D. 1976. "Intransitivities in Multi-Dimensional Voting Models and Some Implications for Agenda Control." *Journal of Economic Theory* 12:472–82.

McKinley, William. 1890. "What Congress Has Done." *North American Review*, no. 408:513–18.

McPherson, Harry. 1985. Oral History Interview with Michael L. Gillette. September 19. Lyndon Baines Johnson Library, Austin, TX. Available online at http://www.lbjlib.utexas.edu.

"Message Viewed as Election Key." 1964. *New York Times*, January 9, 1.

Mill, John Stuart. 1861/1991. *Considerations on Representative Government*. Amherst, NY: Prometheus.

"Missing Papers Found in Huey Long's Pocket." 1934. *New York Times*, June 19.

Mixon, Franklin G., Jr., M. Troy Gibson, and Kamal P. Upadhyaya. 2003. "Has Legislative Television Changed Legislative Behavior? C-SPAN2 and the Frequency of Senate Filibustering." *Public Choice* 115:139–62.

Morris, Dick. 2005. "A Better Option on Judges: Bring on a Real Filibuster." *The Hill*, April 27. Available at http://thehill.com.

Morris, Roy, Jr. 2003. *Fraud of the Century: Rutherford B. Hayes, Samuel Tilden, and the Stolen Election of 1876*. New York: Simon & Schuster.

"Morton Rips Up Petition by Morse on Filibuster." 1960. *New York Times*, March 4, 1.

"Move to Fix Date for Vote on Court." 1926. *New York Times*, January 20, 4.

"Mr. Randall in 1877." 1883. *Harper's Weekly*, July 7.

"New Court Bill Faces Filibustering Barrage." 1937. *New York Times*, July 4, 35.

"New Filibuster Holds the Senate." 1927. *New York Times*, March 3, 1.

"New Rule Ends Senate's Secret Holds." 1999. *Roll Call*, March 5.

"New Ship Clauses to Push Arms Bill." 1941. *New York Times*, October 18, 12.

Nichols, Jeannette Paddock. 1935. "The Politics and Personalities of Silver Repeal in the United States Senate." *American Historical Review* 41:26–53.

"Night of the Long Winds." 1977. *Time*, October 10.

"No Drifting." 1938. *Time*, September 18.

"No Longer a 'Problem' but a Revolution." 1963. *New York Times*, June 16, 148.

Nokken, Timothy P., and Brian R. Sala. 2002. "Institutional Evolution and the Rise of the Tuesday-Thursday Club in the House of Representatives." In *Party, Process, and Political Change in Congress, Volume 1: New Perspectives on the History of Congress*, ed. David W. Brady and Mathew D. McCubbins, 270–86. Stanford, CA: Stanford University Press.

Norris, George W. 1926. "Reform of the Senate Rules: In Answer to Vice President Dawes." *Saturday Evening Post*, February 13, 27ff.

"Notes from Washington." 1881. *New York Times*, November 1, 5.

O'Connor, Patrick. 2007. "In Minority, GOP Delights in Sending Bills Back." *Politico*, April 18. Available at http://www.politico.com (accessed July 25, 2007).

"Offshore Bill Foes Set Back in Senate on Own Proposals." 1953. *New York Times*, April 28, 1.

"Offshore Oil Vote Is Set for Tuesday to Break Debate." 1953. *New York Times*, April 29, 1.

"Ohioan Arrives to Cheers, Begins Activities at Once Despite of Lack of Sleep." 1948. *New York Times*, June 21, 1.

"Old Twins." 1929. *Time*, June 10.

"On Capitol Hill, the Majority Doesn't Always Rule." 2004. *New York Times*, November 7, WK3.

Oppenheimer, Bruce I. 1985. "Changing Time Constraints on Congress: Historical Perspectives on the Use of Cloture." In *Congress Reconsidered* (3rd ed.), ed. Lawrence C. Dodd and Bruce I. Oppenheimer, 393–413. Washington, DC: CQ Press.

"Pass Currency Bill by Aldrich Strategy." 1908. *New York Times*, May 31, A1.

Peskin, Allan. 1973. "Was There a Compromise of 1877?" *Journal of American History* 60, no. 1:63–75.

"Pitiable and Contemptible!" 1933. *Time*, January 30.

Plott, Charles R. 1967. "A Notion of Equilibrium and Its Possibility under Majority Rule." *American Economic Review* 57:787–806.

Polsby, Nelson. 1968. "The Institutionalization of the U.S. House of Representatives." *American Political Science Review* 62:144–68.

Poole, Keith T., and Howard Rosenthal. 1997. *Congress: A Political-Economic History of Roll Call Voting.* New York: Oxford University Press.

"President Speeds Court Bill Vote." 1937. *New York Times*, June 16, 16.

"Prince of the Peckerwoods." 1946. *Time*, August 1.

"Progress on Marshall." 1962. *New York Times*, September 9, 190.

"Proposition to Limit Debate in Senate." 1903. *New York Times*, March 12, 5.

"Quick Debate Is Expected for Campaign Finance Bill." 2002. *New York Times*, March 19, 19.

Raju, Manu. 2009. "Dems Need Franken More Than Ever." *Politico,* March 6, 2009. Available at http://www.politico.com.

Raju, Manu, and Mike Soraghan. 2007. "Senate Dem Leaders Float Plan for Forced Filibuster." *The Hill*, November 14. Available at http://thehill.com.

"Record of the 75th Congress." 1937. *Editorial Research Report*, August 22. Available at http://library.cqpress.com/cqresearcher.

"Record of the 75th Congress." 1938. *Editorial Research Report*, June 16. Available at http://library.cqpress.com/cqresearcher.

Remini, Robert V. 2006. *The House: The History of the House of Representatives.* New York: Smithsonian Books.

"Repeal Vote Today Set in the Senate; Filibuster Broken." 1933. *New York Times*, February 16, 1.

Rich, Spencer. 1974. "Allen a Master of New-Style Filibuster." *Washington Post*, July 1, A2.

"Rights Unit's Life May Be Extended." 1961. *New York Times*, July 30, 57.

Riker, William H. 1955. "The Senate and American Federalism." *American Political Science Review* 49:452–69.

Ripley, Randall B. 1969. *Power in the Senate.* New York: St. Martin's.

Ritchie, Donald A., ed. 1998. *Minutes of the U.S. Senate Democratic Conference.* Washington, DC: U.S. Government Printing Office.

Roberts, Jason. 2005. "Minority Rights and Majority Power: Conditional Party Government and the Motion to Recommit in the House, 1909–2000." *Legislative Studies Quarterly* 30:219–34.

Robinson, William A. 1930. *Thomas B. Reed: Parliamentarian.* New York: Dodd, Mead.

Rohde, David W. 1991. *Parties and Leaders in the Postreform House.* Chicago: University of Chicago Press.

Rohde, David W., and Kenneth A. Shepsle. 2007. "Advising and Consenting in the 60-Vote Senate: Strategic Appointments to the Supreme Court." *Journal of Politics* 69:664–77.

Rothman, David J. 1966. *Politics and Power: The United States Senate, 1869–1901.* New York: Atheneum.

Rubinstein, Ariel. 1982. "Perfect Equilibrium in a Bargaining Model." *Econometrica* 50:97–109.

"Russell Assails Nixon on Rights." 1957. *New York Times*, August 31, 1.

Ryley, Thomas. 1975. *A Little Group of Willful Men.* Port Washington, NY: Kennikat.

"Sabath Continues Battle for FEPC." 1945. *New York Times*, July 2, 1.

"A Satisfactory 'Compromise.'" 1947. *New York Times*, January 6, 22.

"Saturday Night & After." 1935. *Time*, September 2.

Schattschneider, E. E. 1942. *Party Government.* New York: Holt, Rinehart & Winston.

———. 1960. *The Semisovereign People: A Realist's View of Democracy in America*. Fort Worth, TX: Harcourt Brace Jovanovich.

Schatz, Joseph J. 2009. "Senate Scales Back Its Stimulus." *Congressional Quarterly Weekly Report*, February 9, 306–8.

Scherer, Nancy. 2005. *Scoring Points: Politicians, Activists, and the Lower Federal Court Appointment Process*. Stanford, CA: Stanford University Press.

Schickler, Eric. 2001. *Disjointed Pluralism: Institutional Innovation and the Development of the U.S. Congress*. Princeton, NJ: Princeton University Press.

Schofield, Norman. 1978. "Instability of Simple Dynamic Games." *Review of Economic Studies* 45:575–94.

Schor, Elana. 2005. "Crawford Nomination Stalls in Senate over Plan B Delay." *The Hill*, June 15. Available at http://thehill.com.

Schwartz, J., C. Spix, G. Touloumi, L. Bacharova, T. Barumamdzadeh, A. le Tertre, T. Piekarksi, A. Ponce de Leon, A. Ponka, G. Rossi, M. Saez, and J. P. Schouten. 1996. "Methodological Issues in Studies of Air Pollution and Daily Counts of Deaths or Hospital Admissions." *Journal of Epidemiology and Community Health* 50, no. 2, suppl. 1:S3–S11.

"Search and Seizure on Capitol Hill." 1988. *Time*, March 7.

"See Long Beaten in Closure Vote." 1933. *New York Times*, January 20, 3.

"Senate Calls Off 24-Hour Sessions in Move for Vote." 1960. *New York Times*, March 9, 1.

"Senate Defeats Latin Loan Curbs." 1965. *New York Times*, February 25, 7.

"Senate Democrats Threaten Balanced-Budget Measure." 1995. *New York Times*, January 28, 8.

"Senate Filibuster Rule, 1977." 1981. *Congress and the Nation* 5:1007.

"Senate Filibuster Stalls Rail Relief Bill." 1975. *New York Times*, February 22.

"Senate GOP Preps to Confront 'Obstruction.'" 2004. *Congress Daily*, April 1.

"Senate Poll Points to Defeat for Dawes." 1925. *New York Times*, May 31, 1925, XX1.

"Senate Prepares for Poll-Tax Fight." 1944. *New York Times*, May 8, 21.

"Senate Tax Bill Faces Filibuster on Dirksen Plan." 1962. *New York Times*, September 4, 1.

"Senate to Vote Tomorrow on Ending Right Debate." 1966. *New York Times*, September 13, 1.

"Senate Unit Backs Easier Gag Rule." 1953. *New York Times*, April 23, 20.

"The Senate's Work Ended." 1881. *New York Times*, October 30, 1.

"Senators Open Partisan Debate on Antifilibuster Rule." 1977. *New York Times*, May 10, 13.

"Senators Pressed on Two Measures." 1940. *New York Times*, November 21, 17.

"Silence in the Senate." 1962. *Time*, August 24.

Sinclair, Barbara. 1989. *The Transformation of the U.S. Senate*. Baltimore: Johns Hopkins University Press.

———. 1995. *Legislators, Leaders and Lawmaking*. Baltimore: Johns Hopkins University Press.

———. 2002. "The 60-Vote Senate." In *U.S. Senate Exceptionalism*, ed. Bruce I. Oppenheimer, 241–61. Columbus: Ohio State University Press.

———. 2006. *Party Wars: Polarization and the Politics of National Policy Making*. Norman: University of Oklahoma Press.

"Slot Machine Curb Passed by Senate." 1950. *New York Times*, December 20, 36.

Smith, Elbert B. 1980. *Francis Preston Blair*. New York: Free Press.

Smith, Steven S. 1989. *Call to Order: Floor Politics in the House and Senate*. Washington, DC: Brookings Institution.

Smith, Steven S., and Marcus Flathman. 1989. "Managing the Senate Floor: Complex Unanimous Consent Agreements since the 1950s." *Legislative Studies Quarterly* 14:349–73.

"Southerners Balk." 1947. *New York Times*, January 3, 1.

"Southerners Win in Poll Tax Fight; Credit Curbs Again." 1949. *New York Times*, August 5, 1.

"Statehood for Alaska and Hawaii, 1947–1959." 1965. *Congress and the Nation* 1:1497–1503.

"Statehood Lines Break." 1903. *New York Times*, February 11, 8.

Stimson, James A. 2004. *Tides of Consent: How Public Opinion Shapes American Politics*. New York: Cambridge University Press.

"Strife Marks Closing Hours of Congress." 1903. *New York Times*, March 4, 2.

Swift, Elaine K., Robert G. Brookshire, David T. Canon, Evelyn C. Fink, John R. Hibbing, Brian D. Humes, Michael J. Malbin, and Kenneth C. Martis. 2000. *Database of Congressional Historical Statistics*. Ann Arbor, MI: Inter-University Consortium for Political and Social Research.

"Taft Maps Move for Offshore Gag." 1953. *New York Times*, April 21, 20.

"Taft Surrenders." 1947. *New York Times*, July 26, 1.

"Tariff Bill Voted by Senate, 57 to 33; Adjournment Dims." 1934. *New York Times*, June 5, 1.

"That Man." 1947. *Time*, January 13.

Theriault, Sean M. 2008. *Party Polarization in Congress*. Cambridge: Cambridge University Press.

"Today: 'The Poll Tax Peril.'" 1944. *Time*, May 22.

"Top Guns, Handguns and Raw Pork." 1986. *Time*, November 10.

"Top Republicans of Senate Decide to Oppose Bilbo." 1947. *New York Times*, January 1, 1.

"Towards Adjournment." 1933. *Time*, June 19.

"Treaty Ratified." 1930. *Time*, July 28.

"Truman Asks 5 Must Bills of Congress." 1950. *New York Times*, November 28.

Tsebelis, George. 2002. *Veto Players: How Political Institutions Work*. Princeton, NJ: Princeton University Press.

"12 Hours, 8 Minutes." 1950. *Time*, June 19.

"Urban Aid Tax Bill Veto, 1992." 1993. *Congress and the Nation* 8:106.

Valelly, Richard M. 2004. *The Two Reconstructions: The Struggle for Black Enfranchisement*. Chicago: University of Chicago Press.

Valeo, Francis R. 1999. *Mike Mansfield, Majority Leader: A Different Kind of Senate, 1961–1976*. New York: M. E. Sharpe.

VandeHei, Jim, and Charles Babington. 2005. "From Senator's 2003 Outburst, GOP Hatched 'Nuclear Option.'" *Washington Post*, May 19, A15.

Von Holst, Herman. 1893. "Shall the Senate Rule the Republic?" *Forum* 16:263–71.

"Vote or Talk." 1926. *New York Times*, January 23, 14.

"War Tax in Snarl; Move for Closure." 1917. *New York Times*, August 28, 3.

"Washington." 1962. *New York Times*, August 19, 144.

Wawro, Gregory J. 2005. "Peculiar Institutions: Slavery, Sectionalism, and Minority Obstruction in the Antebellum Senate." *Legislative Studies Quarterly* 30:163–91.

Wawro, Gregory J., and Eric Schickler. 2004. "Where's the Pivot: Obstruction and Lawmaking in the Pre-Cloture Senate." *American Journal of Political Science* 48:758–74.

———. 2006. *Filibuster: Obstruction and Lawmaking in the U.S. Senate*. Princeton, NJ: Princeton University Press.

———. 2007. "Cloture Reform Reconsidered." In *Party, Process, and Policy Political Change in Congress, Volume 2: Further New Perspectives on the History of Congress*, ed. David W. Brady and Mathew D. McCubbins, 226–48. Stanford, CA: Stanford University Press.

Welch, Richard E. 1965. "Federal Elections Bill of 1890: Postscripts and Preludes." *Journal of American History* 52:511–26.

Wellborn, Fred. 1928. "The Influence of the Silver Republican Senators, 1889–1891." *Mississippi Valley Historical Review* 14:462–80.

Whalen, Charles, and Barbra Whalen. 1985. *The Longest Debate: A Legislative History of the 1964 Civil Rights Act.* Cabin John, MD: Seven Locks.

White, William. 1955. *Citadel: The Story of the U.S. Senate.* Boston: Houghton Mifflin.

"Will Veto Bonus Bill by Next Thursday." 1931. *New York Times*, February 21.

Wilson, Woodrow. 1885. *Congressional Government.* Boston: Houghton Mifflin.

"Wilson Warns Foes of Food Bill of Nation's Blame." 1917. *New York Times*, June 19, 1.

Wolfinger, Raymond E. 1971. "Filibusters: Majority Rule, Presidential Leadership, and Senate Norms." In *Readings on Congress*, ed. Raymond Wolfinger, 286–305. Englewood Cliffs, NJ: Prentice-Hall.

Woodward, C. Vann. 1951. *Reunion and Reaction: The Compromise of 1877 and the End of Reconstruction.* Boston: Little, Brown.

Yackee, Susan Webb. 2003. "Punctuating the Congressional Agenda: Strategic Scheduling by House and Senate Leaders." *Political Research Quarterly* 56:139–49.

Zelizer, Julian. 2004. *On Capitol Hill.* Cambridge: Cambridge University Press.

Index